Health Food Devotions

Health Food Devotions

Kenneth E. Hagin

Unless otherwise indicated, all Scripture quotations in this volume are from the *King James Version* of the Bible.

Second Printing 2005

ISBN 0-89276-532-1

In the U.S. write:
Kenneth Hagin Ministries
P.O. Box 50126
Tulsa, OK 74150-0126
1-888-28-FAITH
www.rhema.org

In Canada write:
Kenneth Hagin Ministries
Box 335, Station D,
Etobicoke, Ontario
Canada, M9A 4X3

Introduction

In twelve years of pastoral work, I never buried even one church member. During that time, I held only five or six funerals. Those were for relatives of people who attended our church, or for people who used to be members but had moved away. I realize, of course, that if Jesus tarries His coming, believers will live their life out on this earth and go home to be with the Lord. But we don't have to leave early; we don't have to die of sickness and disease.

In this book, I want to teach you just what I taught those whom I pastored. If it worked for them, it will work for you.

Many times, people expect to be healed when hands are laid upon them, and so they receive healing. But they don't realize that they must do something in order *to keep* their healing. They must feed on the Word of God themselves if they want their healing to last.

Someone may receive healing through the faith of another, or by the operation of the gifts of the Spirit, or by the corporate faith of a group of believers. But that individual will not be able to keep his healing unless he builds a faith of his own.

The Bible teaches us that we have an enemy — the devil — arrayed against us, and he's going to do his best to rob and cheat us out of our healing. John 10:10 says, *"The thief cometh not, but for to steal, and to kill, and to destroy. . . ."* But when you're equipped with the Word of God, you can resist the devil. The purpose of this book is to equip you through a variety of messages with God's Word concerning healing.

It takes time to teach people the Word of God and build faith in them. In the natural, when you go to a doctor and he says, "Take this medicine without fail three times a day," you take the medicine. When he tells you to keep taking that medicine until it's all gone, you do it. You don't give a second thought to following a doctor's orders. It's very normal and natural to you.

Well, just as it takes time for natural medicine to take effect, it also takes time for *God's* medicine to take effect. This book makes available to you a daily dose of God's medicine — His Word. If you will give the Word of God the same opportunity that you give the natural medicine a doctor prescribes, I guarantee that you will be healed.

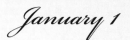

*My son, attend to my words; incline thine ear unto
my sayings.
Let them not depart from thine eyes; keep them in
the midst of thine heart.
For they are life unto those that find them, and
health to all their flesh.*

— PROVERBS 4:20-22

God's Word Is Medicine

According to *The New Strong's Exhaustive Concordance of the Bible*, the Hebrew word in verse 22 translated "health" actually means *medicine*. In other words, this scripture actually says, ". . . they (God's words) are life unto those that find them and *medicine* unto all their flesh."

Notice that this passage of Scripture begins, *"My son, attend to my words. . . ."* What does it mean to attend to God's words? It means to put His words first. Then we are told to incline our ears unto His words, or to listen to them. Finally, we are told to keep His words in the midst of our heart. So there are three things we are told to do with the Word of God: (1) Attend to it or put it first; (2) listen to it; and (3) keep it in the midst of our heart.

Why are we told to do this? Verse 22 says, *"For they [God's words] are life unto those that find them, and health [medicine] to all their flesh."* I believe that! God's words are medicine. Does God have medicine? Yes! What is it? It's His Word! His Word is medicine to all your flesh. That means it's good for stomach troubles, blood diseases, and for all your flesh — liver, kidneys, heart, eyes, ears, nose, mouth, and so forth!

Confession:

I attend to God's Word. I put it first in my life. I listen to it. I keep it in the midst of my heart. God's Word is medicine to all my flesh!

January 2

Who his own self bare our sins in his own body on the tree, that we, being dead to sins, should live unto righteousness: by whose stripes ye were healed.

— 1 PETER 2:24

Accept Christ as Your Healer

While pastoring a Full Gospel church in north central Texas, I visited a dear woman and her husband in their home in the country. They had several children and many acres of farmland. They were wonderful people. Sister Foster had a Methodist background.

She said to me, "You know, Brother Hagin, my grandmother lived with us right in this very house. I remember the time someone came to town, rented a store building, and had a meeting there. Grandma was ninety-three years old then. My husband and I went to the meeting, and I came back and told Grandma about it. She said, 'Sounds like old-fashioned Methodism to me.' She encouraged us to go back.

"We went back, and the man announced that he was going to have a healing service. He was going to lay hands on the sick and anoint them with oil according to James 5:14. He said that the Lord still heals the sick today as He did in days gone by. I thought to myself, *I'll tell Grandma about that and she won't want us to go back.* I didn't want to go back, anyway.

"The next day, I told Grandma about it. She said, 'You must go hear him. Forty years ago in our Methodist church, a man came along preaching healing. He had everyone come down front and accept Christ as their Healer, just as we accepted Him as our Savior. I went down there and accepted Christ as my Healer. Do you remember me ever being sick in the last forty years?'

"I said, 'No. I just always thought you had a strong constitution.'

"She said, 'No. I accepted Christ as my Healer, and I haven't been sick in forty years. In fact, I'll have you know that I'm going to live and die without having sickness or disease in my body. You both go back and hear that.'" They listened to Grandma. They went back and got filled with the Holy Ghost.

Confession:

Just as I accepted Jesus as my Savior for life, I accept Him as my Healer for life. I no longer have to live with sickness and disease. I can enjoy a long life

— PSALM 91:16

Live Long on the Earth

At ninety-four years of age, Sister Foster's grandmother insisted on making up her own bed and sweeping her own floor. She also washed the breakfast dishes while Sister Foster cleaned up the rest of the house. They had a big house with lots of kids, about eight children all together. At ninety-four, she was washing the dishes and cleaning up the kitchen! She was still very alert!

Each morning at about 10:00 a.m., they would be done with the cleaning, so they would go into the sewing room. Sister Foster would darn socks and patch overalls, while Grandma would read the Bible to her.

But one day at the breakfast table, Grandma said, "I'm going home today."

Mr. Foster, who wasn't saved then, said, "Well, *this* is your home." They thought she was getting old and senile.

After the kitchen was cleaned, Grandma went into the sewing room with her Bible. Sister Foster sewed some of the boys' overalls while Grandma read to her. Grandma read the twenty-first and twenty-second chapters of Revelation. She read about Heaven. Then she said, "I told you I was going home today. There's Jesus. Whoo! Glory! I'm going; good-bye." And she left her body and went home to be with Jesus at the age of ninety-four.

Confession:

God has promised me long life. I choose to live long on the earth, to go home when I am full of years and satisfied.

January 4

Jesus said unto him, If thou canst believe, all things are possible to him that believeth.

— MARK 9:23

You Must Believe

I remember that while preaching in a large Full Gospel church in Oklahoma in 1950, I saw a young woman in the services. I didn't know whether or not she was a member of the church, but I saw that she was on crutches. She could swing her body along between crutches by putting enough weight on her feet to move the crutches along. It would take her about ten minutes to go twenty or twenty-five feet.

Well, I noticed that she didn't get in any of the healing lines, although she was in the services. One night, she stopped me as I went out the side door after the service. She had positioned herself there because she knew that I would go out that door.

She said, "Brother Hagin, who's going to have faith for my healing — me or you?"

I said, "Most of the time, people are healed by a mutual faith — in other words, a combination of both yours and mine. I'm going to have enough faith to pray for it, and you must have enough faith to receive it."

"Well," she said, "if I'm supposed to believe anything, just forget it!" And she didn't come back to hear me preach anymore. I was there two weeks after we spoke, and she never attended another one of my services.

Confession:

All things are possible to those who believe. And I believe God's Word. I'm a believer, not a doubter.

— ROMANS 10:17

Faith Comes by Hearing

Two years later, I went back to that same church in Oklahoma and noticed that the young woman who had refused to believe anything was there. Again, the meeting ran four weeks. I noticed her sitting there with her Bible and a notebook; she was taking notes as I taught in both the day and night services.

For two solid weeks, this young woman sat there, listened, and took notes. On Friday night of the second week, she positioned herself on the front pew. One of the ushers put his hands under her arms, lifted her to her feet, and helped her up onto her crutches. She was the first person in the healing line that night.

She said, "I've come for my healing. Just put your hands on me and I'll be healed." She lifted her hands and began to praise God. One crutch fell one way, and one fell the other way. And she walked off completely well!

You see, she listened to the Word of God and got the Word in her. Faith comes by hearing the Word.

Confession:

God's Word always works! If the Word of God worked for that woman in Oklahoma, the Word of God will work for me!

January 6

For it is God which worketh in you both to will and to do of his good pleasure.

— PHILIPPIANS 2:13

Why People Fail To Receive Healing

The number one reason people fail to receive their healing is that they do not believe that it's God's will for them to be healed. Many say, "Well, maybe God has some purpose in this." No, He doesn't!

God's will is for you and me to be in health. So I stay in health because I know that's what His will is. According to Philippians 2:13, God is working in me, both to will and to do of His own good pleasure. He is working in me every day to will and to do of His own good pleasure.

You need to settle the question about God's will concerning healing for you. How are you going to settle it? How are you going to find out what God's will is? Go to the will of God, the New Testament, and find out.

At the reading of a will, someone reads the last will and testament of the deceased. A testament is a will, and the New Testament is the will of God. It is His plan, His purpose, and it is a testament of all that He wants you to have.

It is God's will not only to heal you, but also to heal everyone else who is sick, because healing is in God's redemptive plan. Settle that in your mind and heart. Then you don't have to ask any questions. And you don't have to wonder. You know!

Confession:

God wants me well. It is the will of God that I be healthy, that I live the full length of my life down here on earth without sickness, infirmity, pain, or disease. That is the will of God! I accept His will today.

That it might be fulfilled which was spoken by Esaias the prophet, saying, Himself [Jesus] took our infirmities, and bare our sicknesses.

— MATTHEW 8:17

Jesus Bore Your Sicknesses

Jesus took our infirmities and bore our sicknesses. Since He bore them, why should we bear them?

Isaiah 53:4 says, *"Surely he hath borne our GRIEFS, and carried our SORROWS: yet we did esteem him stricken, smitten of God, and afflicted."* In the Hebrew, the words "griefs" and "sorrows" mean *sicknesses* and *pains.* So Jesus bore our sicknesses and carried our pains. That's the same thing as saying, *". . . Himself took our infirmities, and bare our sicknesses"* (Matt. 8:17).

Another reference in the New Testament is First Peter 2:24: "Who his own self bare our sins in his own body on the tree, that we, being dead to sins, should live unto righteousness: by whose stripes ye were healed." The Bible says, "In the mouth of two or three witnesses let every word be established" (Matt. 18:16). I've given you three references right here.

So settle it in your mind and heart once and for all that God wants you healed just as much as He wants you saved. God has provided for you to be healed physically, just as much as He has provided for you to be born again — to receive the remission of sins and become a new creature in Christ Jesus.

Confession:

It is written in Matthew 8:17 that Himself, Jesus, took my infirmities and bare my sicknesses. What He bore, I need not bear! Because He bore my infirmities, because He bore my sicknesses, I'm healed! I'm free!

For ever, O Lord, thy word is settled in heaven.
— PSALM 119:89

God's Word Never Changes

I was preaching at a convention in St. Louis on one occasion. After the service was over, a gentleman stopped me in the lobby of the hotel to speak with me.

He said, "I want you to meet my wife and three children. Last year when you were in Syracuse, New York, teaching on faith, we came to hear you. We're from Boston, Massachusetts, and it was the first Full Gospel meeting we had ever been to. At that time, my boy was thirteen and a half years old, and doctors couldn't figure out what was wrong with him. They encouraged me to take him to some specialists in New York City, so I did."

The gentleman continued, "The specialists said that he had an incurable disease and there was nothing they could do for him. In fact, the doctors said that they only knew of three people on the North American continent who had ever had this disease. They told us that he would be dead by the time he turned fifteen. But somebody told us about God's healing power, and we went to the convention in Syracuse seeking help."

At the meeting in Syracuse, I taught the people to let their heart agree with the Word they speak out of their mouth. God's Word doesn't change, and since He said, "Jesus took your infirmities and bare your sicknesses" (Matt. 8:17), you can settle on that!

Confession:

According to the Word of God, I am healed. I believe it in my heart, and I say it with my mouth.

'It's Mine'

The father of the boy from Massachusetts continued to share his story with me: "Now there was some medication available that my boy could take that would help keep him going a little better. So he was taking this medication. After we left the service in Syracuse, the time came for him to take his medication, but he said to me, 'No, I don't need it. I'm healed.'"

The father said, "Son, you'll begin suffering if you don't take it. You'll begin to hurt."

The son responded, "No, I won't begin to hurt. I'm healed."

"Well, how do you know you are?" the father asked.

The son said, "Didn't you hear Brother Hagin preach that Jesus took my infirmities and bore my sicknesses? I stood right there and confessed it with my mouth. So I know it's mine!"

That boy never had another symptom. They took him back to be examined, and doctors couldn't find anything wrong! In fact, the doctors wanted to keep him so that they could examine him for a few days. They kept him for five days, and when the father went to pick his son up, the doctors said, "We want to talk to you. We've run every test we can run, and we can't find a trace of the disease. It's all gone. It has disappeared. What happened?"

Confession:

The Word of God says that Jesus took my infirmities and bore my sicknesses. Therefore, according to the Word, I am healed!

And he [Jesus] said unto her, Daughter, be of good comfort: thy faith hath made thee whole; go in peace.

— LUKE 8:48

Your Faith Can Make You Whole

Many years ago, I read an article in a secular magazine. The article was written by a group of doctors from the University of Minnesota. They had a grant for several thousand dollars from the government to study alternative healing methods.

In the article, the doctors said, in effect, "We went back and examined all the old American Indian remedies. And we found that some of them that we had said wouldn't work did work. After running them through our laboratory, we found out why they worked. We even tried old wives' remedies. We didn't turn any of them down. We're in the healing business."

They continued, "We also found out that divine healing works. We have records of people who were in the last stages of cancer, and were going to die. But after a man of God came in, anointed them with oil, and laid hands on them, these people got up and left the hospital completely well, sometimes within two or three days. We couldn't find a trace of the disease in their bodies! We know divine healing works, but we can't put it through the laboratory like we did the other remedies. If we knew how it worked, we would share that healing with people also."

When I read that, I thought, *My Lord, I believe I'll write to them and tell them how it works. I know how it works; it works by faith. Jesus said to the woman with the issue of blood, "Daughter, thy faith has made thee whole."*

Confession:

If the woman in Luke 8:48 could be made whole by her faith, then my faith can make me whole.

Agree With God

Let your heart agree with the following as you speak the words out of your mouth:

Heavenly Father, I thank You today, because You are my Father. Because I have been born again, I am Your very own child, and You are my very own Father. Thank You, Father, for Your great plan of redemption which you planned and then sent the Lord Jesus Christ to consummate.

Thank You, Father, that the plan of redemption not only provided for the remission of sins and the New Birth, but provided for healing for my physical body. For it is written in Matthew 8:17 that Himself, Jesus, took my infirmities and bare my sicknesses. What He bore, I need not bear. Because He bore my infirmities, because He bore my sicknesses, I'm healed; I'm free. I no longer have sickness. I no longer have disease. Jesus bore sickness and disease for me.

It is also written in First Peter 2:24, "By whose stripes ye were healed." If we were healed, I was healed. I am now healed by His stripes. I am healed now; I am well now. I believe that in my heart, and because I believe that in my heart, I say it with my mouth. By His stripes, I am healed. Hallelujah!

January 12

Surely he [Jesus] hath borne our griefs [sicknesses], and carried our sorrows [pains]: yet we did esteem him stricken, smitten of God, and afflicted.
But he was wounded for our transgressions, he was bruised for our iniquities: the chastisement of our peace was upon him; and with his stripes we are healed.

— ISAIAH 53:4,5

Healing Is in God's Redemptive Plan

It is the will of God for you to be healed. It is God's will that you be in health. The biggest thing that hinders people is that they question God's will. They think, *Maybe God has some great purpose in this illness or disease.* But let the Word of God settle the issue for you. It is God's will to heal you because healing is provided for you in His redemptive plan. These verses in Isaiah have to do with God's redemptive plan.

Isaiah chapter 53 gives us a picture of the coming Messiah. This passage of Scripture not only tells us that He bore our sins, but that He bore our sicknesses and carried our pains. He was wounded for our transgressions or iniquities. Then we read in verse 5 that with His stripes, we are healed. Isaiah is not talking about being healed of sins, because you don't get healed of sins. A sinner's spirit doesn't get *healed*; his spirit gets *born again*, and he becomes a new creature in Christ (2 Cor. 5:17).

Notice the words "sicknesses," "pains," and "healed" in Isaiah 53:4 and 5. When Isaiah said, "With His stripes, we're healed," he was talking about being healed from the sicknesses and the pains of our bodies. Yes, Jesus bore our sins, but, thank God, He also bore our sicknesses and diseases.

Confession: ✗

Because Jesus bore my sicknesses and diseases, I don't have to bear them. With His stripes, I am healed.

Then Peter opened his mouth, and said, Of a truth I perceive that God is no respecter of persons.

— ACTS 10:34

God Is No Respecter of Persons

There are many methods of healing. For example, you can be healed by prayer (James 5:14,15), and you can also be healed by the laying on of hands (Mark 16:18). These are just two Bible methods of receiving healing.

But you can also be healed by believing Isaiah 53:4 and 5, Matthew 8:17, and First Peter 2:24 without anyone praying for you — just by acting on these verses yourself. In fact, that's really the best way, because after you are healed, you can then go out and tell someone how you were healed, and they can receive their healing the same way you did. Healing belongs to every one of us.

Some people say, "Well, that just means spiritual healing; the Scripture isn't talking about physical healing." I shared First Peter 2:24 with a woman in Oklahoma who was crippled. The doctors in Oklahoma City had said, "She'll never walk another step the longest day she lives." And she had been in a wheelchair for four years.

Now I wasn't operating in the gifts of the Spirit at the time I gave her that verse. I just gave her First Peter 2:24 and got her to act upon it. And as God is my witness, hundreds of people saw her leap and walk and jump! First Peter 2:24 will also work for you, just as it did for that woman. God is no respecter of persons.

Confession: ✗

According to the Word of God, I'm healed. It is written in First Peter 2:24, "By whose stripes, ye were healed." If we were, then I am. I am healed!

Now faith is the substance of things hoped for, the evidence of things not seen.

— HEBREWS 11:1

Doubt Is an Enemy of Faith

Now what did I say to that woman to get her to act on the Word? You see, initially she was crying out, "Oh, please, Jesus! Please heal me! Oh, Jesus, let me walk! I'm so helpless, and I can't do anything for myself. I've been sitting around these four years. Please heal me!" The longer she went on, the further she got into unbelief and doubt.

So I said to her, "Wait a minute, sister. I can help you." You see, she was on the wrong road. The road she was on didn't lead to healing. Faith doesn't *cry*; faith *shouts*! She was not on the road of faith; she was on the road of unbelief and doubt. Faith doesn't beg God to do something; faith declares it's done. I had to get her turned around and headed in the right direction.

I said to her, "Did you know that you're healed?"

She said, "Oh, am I?"

"Yes," I said, "you are." I could tell by the expression on her face that she thought, *If I'm healed, how come I'm still sitting here and haven't walked.*

Confession:

I side in with the Word, not with my body. I don't side in with my neighbor or my friends. I side in with God, and He said I'm already healed!

You *Were* Healed

Before this woman got the revelation of First Peter 2:24, and received healing, I said to her, "I'll just get the Bible and prove to you that you're healed." I opened it to First Peter 2:24, laid it on her lap as she sat in that wheelchair, and said, "Read First Peter 2:24 aloud for me." And she did.

Then I said, "Notice the last clause of that verse. What does it say?"

She said, "By whose stripes, ye were healed." I said, "Now is 'were' past tense, future tense, or present tense?" She looked at me, startled, and said, "Why, it's past tense. If we *were* healed, then *I was.*" I said, "That's it exactly! Just lift up both of your hands and begin to praise God because according to First Peter 2:24, you are healed. You're not *going* to be; by whose stripes, you *were* healed. In the mind of God, you were healed when the stripes were laid on Jesus. You're already healed."

She lifted up her hands and began to praise God. She said, "Lord, I'm so glad that I'm healed. You know how tired I got sitting around all of those four years. I'm so glad I'm not helpless anymore. I'm so glad that my knees and legs are healed."

Then I turned to her and said, "Rise and walk in the Name of Jesus." She instantly leaped to her feet!

Confession:

I am healed. I am well. I can do the things that I couldn't do before. I'm so glad I'm healed!

Who his own self [Jesus] *bare our sins in his own body on the tree, that we, being dead to sins, should live unto righteousness: by whose stripes ye were healed.*

— 1 PETER 2:24

The Best Way To Be Healed

In this scripture, Peter is looking back to the sacrifice of Christ. He's looking back to the time before Jesus went to the Cross, after stripes were laid upon His back. And Peter said, *". . . by whose stripes ye were healed."* He didn't say, "You're *going to be* healed." He said, "You *were* healed." This means that in the mind of God, your healing was accomplished back then.

There are a number of scriptural methods by which healing can be obtained. But the best one is when we simply know for ourselves — when we know what has been secured for us and what belongs to us. Then we can thank God our Father for our perfect healing and perfect deliverance. And if Satan endeavors to put sickness or disease upon us, we can simply laugh at him because we know what the Word of God says.

Matthew 8:17 says, *". . . Himself took our infirmities, and bare our sicknesses."* You're not *going to be* healed. In the mind of God, you *were* healed when those stripes were laid on Jesus. In the mind of Jesus, we're *already* healed. We're not *going to be* healed; we *were* healed.

Confession:

I was healed over two thousand years ago when the stripes were laid on Jesus' back. I'm not trying to get healed. I'm already healed.

Walk by Faith

In 1971, I was preaching at the First Assembly of God Church in Pasadena, Texas. I had known the pastor of that church, Rev. R.V. Kemp, and his wife for a number of years. His wife had been operated on twice for cancer at a well-known cancer hospital in Houston, Texas. When the cancer came back a third time, the doctors said that it had spread to every gland in her body, and gave her three months to live.

Brother Kemp brought his wife to one of the services. When my wife and I saw her, we almost wept; she looked like the picture of death.

She came forward, and I laid hands on her. The power of God fell on her and she said, "This is it. This is it. I know according to the Word of God I'm healed."

Yet she still had all the symptoms. She was still helpless. Her husband had to get her out of bed and dress her. He had to prepare her meals, then pick her up in his arms, and sit her down in a chair at the table.

Confession:

I know according to the Word of God that I'm healed. I choose to walk by faith in God's Word, rather than by sight.

January 18

We having the same spirit of faith, according as it is written, I believed, and therefore have I spoken; we also believe, and therefore speak.

— 2 CORINTHIANS 4:13

Speak in Faith

Every time Brother Kemp and his wife would start to pray over their food, she would burst out laughing. She would say, "I'm healed. The Word says I'm healed." On the tenth day after I laid hands on her, every single symptom disappeared.

Afterward, she said, "I knew according to the Word of God that I was healed when you laid hands on me; the power of God came on me. Yet I had all the symptoms I ever had."

You see, this woman could have reasoned, *Well, if I'm healed, why am I still sitting here?* She could have reasoned herself right out of her healing. But she began to praise God.

She began to say, "Oh, I'm so glad I'm well. I'm so glad I can walk. I'm so glad I'm not bound to this chair anymore." She was speaking in faith because she believed what First Peter 2:24 says.

Confession:

It is written in First Peter 2:24 that by His stripes, ye were healed. If we were, then I am; I am healed. I am well. I am in good health. I can do things that I couldn't do before. I'm so glad I'm healed.

*For he that eateth and drinketh unworthily, eateth
and drinketh damnation to himself, not discerning
the Lord's body.
For this cause many are weak and sickly among you,
and many sleep.*

— 1 CORINTHIANS 11:29,30

Rightly Discern the Lord's Body

Paul is inferring that there shouldn't be any physically weak or sickly among the Church of Jesus Christ. There shouldn't be any who die prematurely. He indicates that many people are weak and sickly because they aren't rightly discerning the body. This observation has a twofold application.

First, Paul is talking about the Lord's Supper. The broken bread represents Jesus' broken body that was broken for your physical sustenance. You can partake of that broken body just as a routine ceremony, and it won't mean a thing in the world to you; it will just be a ritual. Or when you hold that piece of broken bread in your hand, you can say, "Thank God, the body of Jesus was broken for my physical sustenance. His blood was shed for the remission of my sins. I'm eating the bread as a sign, as evidence, that I'm partaking of His broken body and, therefore, I'm healed. With His stripes, I am healed. I no longer have sickness or disease." When you do this, you are discerning the Lord's body.

There is another spiritual aspect to this scripture, which is that the Body of Christ is one. The spiritual Body in the earth today is one, and you must walk in love toward your fellow Christians. If you don't discern the Body of Christ and walk in love toward your fellow Christians, you'll open the door to sickness and disease.

Confession:

I will walk in love toward all Christians. I'll honor and reverence all Christians. I may not always agree with all Christians, but I'll not be disagreeable.

January 20

For if we would judge ourselves, we should not be judged.

— 1 CORINTHIANS 11:31

Judge Yourself That You Be Not Judged

Years ago, God told me to talk to one of the most outstanding healing evangelists of that time in America. In his ministry, I saw some of the greatest healings I have ever seen — blind eyes opened and deaf-mute people healed instantly!

God said to me, "You go tell that man that if he doesn't judge himself, he won't live much longer. First, tell him to walk in love toward his fellow man, particularly his fellow ministers. Second, tell him to judge himself on money. And, third, tell him to judge himself on diet."

Well, he didn't judge himself. Within three years time, he was dead. Was it the will of God? No. Yet there were many healings and miracles under this man's ministry. Brother Oral Roberts said to me, "I believe that man was the greatest man of faith. He had more faith than anyone I've ever seen."

I said, "I guarantee that's true. He was a man of faith; he would dare the devil." But the problem was, he started daring God. You can get by with daring the devil, but when you start daring God, you're in trouble. But it didn't have to be that way. It wasn't the highest purpose of God for him to die early.

If you'll judge yourself, you'll not be judged. If you've sinned and done wrong, just say, "That's wrong. I've sinned." If you've missed it, admit you did and ask God for forgiveness. If you'll judge yourself, you won't be judged, and you can walk on in health.

Confession:

I will judge myself. I will turn from wrong ways and will follow God's ways. Then I will walk in health and healing.

20

O give thanks unto the Lord, for he is good: for his mercy endureth for ever.

— PSALM 107:1

God's Goodness and Mercy

When we think about the goodness and mercy of God, we instinctively think about His goodness and mercy in remitting our sins as sinners and forgiving our sins as Christians. But God's goodness and mercy go further than that; it's stated a number of times in the four Gospels as those who were sick cried out to Jesus, "Have mercy on us" (Mark 10:47).

Again and again, Jesus had compassion on people and healed them (Matt. 14:14; 20:34; Mark 1:41). Now the New Testament was originally written in Greek. And in the Greek, the word "compassion" is translated *mercy*. So literally, the original Scriptures read, "He had *mercy* on them and healed them." That's what Jesus did. People cried out for mercy, and He had mercy on them and healed them.

I want you to think about God's goodness in healing — about His healing mercy. Acts 10:38 says, *"How God anointed Jesus of Nazareth with the Holy Ghost and with power: who went about doing good, and healing all that were oppressed of the devil; for God was with him."* What was the good that Jesus went about doing? He was healing all that were oppressed.

Think about the fact that God is good, not only to save, but to heal. He's merciful, not only to forgive, but to heal. He wants to heal you just as readily as He wants to forgive your sins.

Confession:

For the Lord is good, and His mercy endureth forever. He wants to heal me just as readily as He wants to forgive my sins.

January 22

Jesus said unto him, If thou canst believe, all things are possible to him that believeth.

— MARK 9:23

It's Easy To Receive Healing

When I was preaching down in Texas in the early 1950s, a woman was brought to my service in a wheelchair. In 1950, the polio vaccine had not been invented yet, so polio was rampant. Not only did this woman have polio and was paralyzed, her six-year-old daughter also had polio and could not walk. In the meeting, the little girl was healed. She jumped down off her mother's lap and ran up and down the aisles of the church.

But the mother was still in the wheelchair. However, when I laid hands on her, the mother received the Holy Ghost and spoke with other tongues. I kept saying to her, "You can receive healing just as easily as you received the baptism of the Holy Ghost and spoke in other tongues. You can receive healing just as easily as your daughter did."

She said, "Brother Hagin, I wish I could believe that." You see, she was saved and filled with the Holy Ghost, but she just couldn't believe receiving healing was that easy. So she stayed in her chair.

Confession:

It is the will of God that I be well. It is the will of God that I walk in good health. God's will for me is healing and health, both spiritually and physically. I will walk in the will of God, and I expect to walk in health, for that is the will of God for me.

— MATTHEW 9:29

According to Your Faith

Sixteen years later, the woman who had polio and was paralyzed wrote me a letter, which read, "Brother Hagin, I just wanted you to know that I'm out of my wheelchair."

It took her many years to get out. No, it didn't take *God* that long; it took *her* that long. She couldn't believe that God wanted to heal her and that she could be healed as quickly as her daughter had been healed.

She continued to say, "A woman came to my house because I couldn't do any housework. I couldn't even use my hand to put a tape in the tape player, so she helped me. Every day, this woman came to my house, put a tape in the player, and I kept listening to tapes from your services. Over the course of several years, I received my healing. I'm out of my wheelchair, and I'm doing all my housework. It's so wonderful to get up in the morning and fix my husband's breakfast before he leaves for work."

Now why did she receive her healing gradually? Because she took hold of the truth gradually. Was that the highest will of God? No, it wasn't God's best, but it sure did beat spending the rest of her life in a wheelchair.

She could have been healed like her daughter was in that first meeting. But she just couldn't believe that she could receive healing that easily.

Confession:

I believe I receive healing from the top of my head to the soles of my feet. It is easy to receive healing.

For ever, O Lord, thy word is settled in heaven.
— PSALM 119:89

Sickness Is Not From God

I like to say, "Himself took *my* infirmities (as though I were the only person in the world) and Himself bare *my* sicknesses." That means it's the will of God to heal me and for me to have what Jesus purchased for me. God wants me well.

Don't let your head think any other way. Because people have been religiously brainwashed instead of New Testament-taught, they think, *Well, maybe God has some purpose in this sickness.* God doesn't have any purpose in it, because God didn't put that sickness on you to begin with. Sickness and disease are not of God — they do not come from God — nor do they come from Heaven, because there isn't any sickness there.

When you get it settled once and for all that it is God's will to heal you, you have won at least fifty percent of the battle. Settle on the fact that God wants you well, and that it is not the will of God for you to be sick. Settle it, not based on what I say, but based on what the Word of God says. When you get the Word of God inside you, then neither the devil nor anyone else can move you from it.

Why did Jesus take our infirmities and bare our sicknesses? So that we could be free from sickness and disease.

Confession:

God wants me well. Healing is the will of God because healing is in God's redemptive plan. Health and healing belong to me.

Every good gift and every perfect gift is from above, and cometh down from the Father of lights, with whom is no variableness, neither shadow of turning.

— JAMES 1:17

Where Does Sickness Come From?

Sickness comes from Satan. It doesn't come from God. Sometimes, if you find out where something comes from, you won't be so quick to accept it or acknowledge it. Not only that, but I remember that my mother taught me as a little boy that it was wrong to have something that belonged to someone else.

I remember once when I was eight years old, and wanted to go up the street to play with my cousin. It was just a couple of blocks, and my cousin lived next door to a man who had some prize peach trees in his backyard. People would come from several counties to see his peach trees.

Well, my cousin and I climbed up a ladder to get on top of a tool shed, which was built right up against his fence. Some of the limbs on one of the peach trees were hanging over the fence. They weren't touching the shed, but when we got up on the shed, the peaches were right there.

Now I didn't dare pick a peach because Momma told me to leave these peach trees alone. But my cousin picked one. He ate half of it and then offered the other half to me. I thought, *I didn't get it; my cousin did. Maybe it would be all right to eat it.* I shouldn't have done it, but I reasoned it all out and decided to eat half the peach even though it didn't belong to me.

Confession:

Sickness doesn't come from God. Sickness and disease belong to the devil. Therefore, I do not accept sickness and disease in my body.

Every good gift and every perfect gift is from above, and cometh down from the Father of lights, with whom is no variableness, neither shadow of turning.

— JAMES 1:17

Don't Accept What Comes From the Devil

Well, naturally, after eating that nice juicy peach, I had peach juice on my hands. After a while, I went home but never thought to wash my hands.

Momma said, "Young man, did you get into Mr. _____'s peaches?"

"No," I said, "I didn't. _____ did." And I called my cousin's name.

She said, "You go knock on that man's door and tell him you've come to pay for that peach you ate."

So I got my nickel and cried all the way to Mr. _____'s house, hoping that he wouldn't be there. I knocked on the door and didn't hear anything for a while, so I knocked again. I was about to turn around and go home when I heard footsteps coming from the back of the house.

When the man opened the door, I said, "Sir, we picked one of your peaches and ate it. I'm sorry. Here's a nickel; I want to pay you for it."

He said, "Son, any time any of you boys want some peaches, you come knock on the door and ask me, and I'll give you one." Then I felt worse than ever, because I could have had a peach without all that trouble.

You see, Momma taught me that it's wrong to have something that belongs to someone else. The same thing is true spiritually. It's wrong for Christians to take something that belongs to the devil. It's wrong for Christians to accept something that belongs to him.

Confession:

I accept only what comes from God. Every good gift comes from God, including health and healing.

*How God anointed Jesus of Nazareth with the Holy
Ghost and with power: who went about doing good,
and healing all that were oppressed of the devil; for
God was with him.*

January 27

— ACTS 10:38

Jesus Healed Them All

What did Jesus do with this anointing of the Holy Ghost and power? He went about doing good and healing all who were oppressed of the devil. First, this scripture tells us that every person was healed. The words "every" and "all" are interchangeable.

Second, we learn that sickness is oppression of the devil. Satan is the oppressor, but Jesus is the Deliverer. Satan is the oppressor, but Jesus is the Healer. We know from this scripture that God wants us well. He doesn't want His Church to be under the oppression of the devil.

Acts 10:38 tells us the source of sickness. Even if we didn't have any more scriptures to rely upon, this text tells us that sickness comes from Satan and that Satan is the author of sickness.

Dr. John Alexander Dowie said, "Sickness is the foul offspring of its father Satan and its mother sin." That's where it came from. And since the time that Adam committed high treason in the Garden of Eden, a stream of sickness and suffering has flowed down into the human family. But throughout the Old Testament and the New Testament, God made provision to stay that plague.

I'm glad I found out that sickness and disease are from the devil. I'm not going to have anything that belongs to the devil. I'm not going to have sickness and disease!

Confession:

Satan is the author of sickness and disease. I know that now. So I'm not afraid of sickness and disease, and I will not have sickness and disease. If Jesus tarries His coming, I'll die without sickness and disease.

And ought not this woman, being a daughter of Abraham, whom Satan hath bound, lo, these eighteen years, be loosed from this bond on the sabbath day?

— LUKE 13:16

Sickness Is Bondage

Jesus went into the synagogue on the Sabbath, and a woman came in whose body was bowed together. She couldn't lift herself up. She must have been bound with something like arthritis, because she couldn't stand up straight.

Who bowed this woman together? Was it the will of God that her body be bowed together so that she couldn't stand up straight like other humans? Did God put that on her? No!

Jesus said to this woman, "*Woman, thou art loosed from thine infirmity*" (Luke 13:12). Then He touched her, she was healed, and immediately she straightened up.

The rulers of the synagogue became angry because Jesus had healed the woman on the Sabbath. (You know, some people think more of a day than they do of the Lord.) Notice that Jesus then said that *Satan* had bound this woman for eighteen years (Luke 13:16). When you're sick, you're under bondage. It's not a blessing; it's not freedom.

I remember when I was paralyzed and bedfast for sixteen months. I know what it means to be bound and in bondage. You want to get up and move, but you can't; you're helpless. Sickness is bondage.

Confession:

It is not the will of God that I be sick. It is the will of God that I be free from every bondage, free from every sickness and disease.

And ye shall know the truth, and the truth shall make you free.

— JOHN 8:32

The Truth Shall Make You Free

Jesus is the truth, and Satan is the oppressor. Sickness comes from Satan — who is the author of it — not God. You see, the more truth you get into you, the more free you'll be. You'll know the truth, and the truth will make you free.

Confession:

It is God's will that I be well. It is God's will that I be healed. That's God's plan and purpose. For it is written, "Himself took my infirmities and bare my sicknesses." What He bore, I need not bare. It is God's will that I walk in health. It is His will that I not be oppressed by the devil. Sickness is satanic oppression, for sickness comes from the devil. Satan is the author of sickness. It is not the will of God that any of His children be under the dominion of Satan. It is not the will of God that I as His child be under the dominion of Satan — under the dominion of sickness and disease. For Jesus took my infirmities and bare my sicknesses. And because He bore them, I'm free! I'm healed! Jesus is the Healer; Satan is the oppressor.

> For it is God which worketh in you both to will and to do of his good pleasure.
>
> — PHILIPPIANS 2:13

God Works From the Inside Out

Healing begins in your spirit. Even physical healing for your body begins in your spirit. God doesn't start on the outside and work to the inside. No, He starts on the inside and works to the outside.

So don't look on the outside for physical healing. Look on the inside because that's where He'll begin working. And if you will look on the inside — if you will yield to that something on the inside of you and not pay so much attention to your outward symptoms — you'll eventually look around for those symptoms and find that they're gone.

Once when death had come to fasten its final throes upon me, I started laughing in my spirit. It bubbled up and started rolling out of my mouth. I was laughing in the face of death.

The devil said, "What are you laughing at?"

I said, "I'm laughing at you. Because, you see, you're going to have to leave. I'm not dying now. God's not through with me. I want you to know that." And the devil left.

The Lord always begins working on the inside. You can know things on the inside that you don't see on the outside. You can know things in your spirit that your head can't comprehend. But because you know it in your spirit and believe it, you begin to say it. And because you say it, it will surely come to pass.

Confession:

It is God who is at work within me, both to will and to do of His good pleasure. It is His will that I walk in health and be well. And He is working in my spirit, soul, and body.

And these signs shall follow them that believe; . . . they shall lay hands on the sick, and they shall recover.

— MARK 16:17,18

'They Shall Recover'

In 1953, I was ministering at the Oakcliff Assembly of God Church in Dallas, when a young woman was brought to the service in an ambulance. She had been bedfast two years due to an automobile accident that broke her neck and her back. After being in the hospital for two years and at home for almost a year, she regained the use of her arms. But from her shoulders down, she was unable to move.

When I knelt by her stretcher and laid hands on her, I had the impression that it would not be an instant healing. When I laid my hands on her feet, I felt a "warmth" go into her. She didn't have any feeling in her feet. But her legs began to tingle and she said, "I feel that warmth coming out of your hands and up my legs."

I said to her, "That's the healing power of God going into you. Move your feet." Well, she moved both feet.

Then I said, "Pull up one leg at a time." She pulled her left leg up, but she couldn't move her right one. Then I said, "Now, sister, when I walked down here, I knew that this wouldn't be an instant healing. Just keep the switch of faith turned on, and you'll walk."

Some time later, I saw the woman again. She said, "Brother Hagin, I had feeling in my left leg, but my right leg wouldn't work for a while. Gradually, it started to work, and now I'm walking everywhere!"

Confession:

Thank You, Father, for Your healing power. Thank You that Your healing power is actively at work in my body to effect a healing and a cure.

February 1

For an angel went down at a certain season into the pool, and troubled the water: whosoever then first after the troubling of the water stepped in was made whole of whatsoever disease he had.

— JOHN 5:4

God's Sovereignty

God in His own right of divine sovereignty saw fit to send an angel down to trouble the waters. I don't know how often He did it, but he apparently didn't send the angel on any kind of a set schedule. If He had, there wouldn't have been any need for the sick people to be out there every day. They could have just gone on a certain day when they knew the angel would show up. But they were there all the time because the angel might come at any time.

When an angel came down from Heaven and troubled the waters of this pool, the first person in got healed. No one else got healed until next time around. Why did God do it that way? The Scripture doesn't say why, but if God wanted to do it that way, He certainly could!

Sometimes God moves this way as a sign. He initiates healings to attract attention to Himself and to His Word. The Bible said that there was a great multitude of sick folk waiting on five porches there, but only one person at a time was healed. However, under the New Covenant, God's Word will work for everyone!

Confession:

I'm so glad I don't have to wait for a sovereign move of God. I can believe what the Bible says. And according to First Peter 2:24, I am healed.

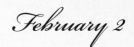
You Can Initiate Healing

God wants you to be well. Some people say, "If God wants me well, why doesn't He heal me?" Well, according to the Bible, God wants everyone saved. Then why aren't all saved? Because they have something to do with it. God has provided salvation for all, but they have a part to play in receiving it.

In the same way, when it comes to healing, we often want to leave it all up to God. Well, although God may initiate healings on His own some of the time, that's not the main way that God heals.

This is where a lot of people miss it: They know God initiates some things on His own, because they've seen Him do it, so they're waiting for Him to initiate something for them. Unfortunately, they might die while they're waiting.

But you can initiate healing yourself. You don't have to wait for God to initiate it; you can claim what belongs to you based on His Word.

Isaiah 53:4 says, *"Surely he hath borne our griefs, and carried our sorrows. . . ."* The original Hebrew says, "Surely He hath borne our *sicknesses* and carried our *pains*, yet we did esteem Him stricken, smitten of God and afflicted." Verse 5 says, *"But he was wounded for our transgressions, he was bruised for our iniquities: the chastisement of our peace was upon him; and with his stripes we are healed."*

Confession:

I know what belongs to me. I claim what belongs to me based on the Word of God. Health and healing belong to me. Thank You, Father, for health and healing.

February 3

And he [Jesus] *could there do no mighty work, save that he laid his hands upon a few sick folk, and healed them.*

— MARK 6:5

The Ministry of Jesus

Many people are healed by a mutual faith — by their faith and the faith of whoever is ministering to them. Most people are healed by knowing and receiving for themselves what the Word of God says. You see, that's the way the majority of people were healed under the ministry of Jesus.

Some people say, "Oh, if only I could have been there when Jesus was on the earth, I would have been healed because everybody always got healed under His ministry, regardless of their faith." A person who says that has never read the Bible very closely. Mark 6:5 in the Greek reads that Jesus *could* do no mighty work except lay His hands on a few sick people with minor ailments. Those are the only ones who got healed under the ministry of Jesus in His hometown of Nazareth.

Well, why didn't others get healed? Let's look at the next verse. *"And he marveled because of their unbelief. And he went round about the villages, teaching"* (Mark 6:6). The reason they failed to get healed was because of their unbelief. So what did Jesus do? He went about their cities and villages teaching in their synagogues. He began to teach, because faith comes by hearing, and hearing the Word of God (Rom. 10:17).

Confession:

I can be healed by simply knowing and receiving what the Word of God says — that healing belongs to me. I receive healing based on the Word of God.

And he [Jesus] said unto her, Daughter, thy faith hath made thee whole; go in peace, and be whole of thy plague.

— MARK 5:34

Individual Cases of Healing

I encourage you to go through the four Gospels carefully and underline with a red pencil all the individual cases of healing. Or better yet, you could write them all down on a sheet of paper. Some examples are the woman with the issue of blood, Jairus' daughter, the centurion who came on behalf of his servant, and the two blind men who followed Jesus. You'll find that there are nineteen specific cases of healing mentioned.

You might think that there are a lot more, but Matthew, Mark, and Luke often recorded the same incident. For instance, Matthew, Mark, and Luke all recorded the healing of the woman with the issue of blood, but it was only one incident. They were all talking about the same thing.

After reading through the Gospels and writing down each incident of healing, you'll find that twelve out of the nineteen incidents speak of the faith of the individual. For instance, in Mark 5:34, Jesus said to the woman with the issue of blood, "Thy faith has made thee whole. Go in peace and be whole of thy plague." Whose faith made her whole? It was *her* faith.

Confession:

Since the people Jesus ministered to on the earth used their faith to receive healing, then I can use my faith to receive healing. And faith comes by hearing the Word of God. I attend to God's Word, and keep it before my eyes and my ears.

As soon as Jesus heard the word that was spoken, he saith unto the ruler of the synagogue, Be not afraid, only believe.

— MARK 5:36

Fear Not

In Matthew chapter 5, when Jesus crossed over the Sea of Galilee, He met Jairus, a ruler of the synagogue. Jairus said, "My little daughter lies at home sick; she's at the point of death. Come and lay Thy hand on her that she may be healed" (Mark 5:23). Jairus believed that when Jesus laid His hands on the girl, she would be healed. So Jesus went with him to his house.

While they were on their way, someone from Jairus' house came to him and said, "Trouble the Master no longer. Your little daughter is already dead" (Mark 5:35).

In the face of such a tragedy, Jesus spoke the simplest, yet most profound statement to Jairus. Jesus said, "Fear not. Only believe" (v. 36). Jesus was a faith preacher! He was encouraging Jairus to believe, even under adverse circumstances. He was encouraging Jairus to have faith, to believe.

God never comes with a message of fear. You can read all through the Old Testament and the New Testament, and every time God sent an angel or a messenger from Heaven for anyone, the first thing the angel said was, "Don't be afraid." Well, what are you going to do if you're not going to fear? Only believe!

Confession:

I will not fear. I will only believe.

Only Believe

The following are two psalms the Holy Spirit gave me:

Fear and doubt —

The two tormenting twins of Satan that have come down here to buffet you
about.

Fear and doubt —

Weapons of the enemy to unsettle your faith and cause you trouble and
worry and sickness too.

Fear and doubt come not from Heaven above, but from Satan below.

Fear and doubt are not of God, as you well know.

But faith and love come from the Lord above.

Faith and love —

Walk in love and live by faith. Shout above the turmoil. Shout above the
doubt.

Shout above the fear. It is done! It is mine!

What God has promised, He's able to perform down here.

Fear not; only believe. *Only believe.*

Two little words — so simple and easy to receive.

"Only believe" is not enough for some who think they know.

Intellectuality said, "We must do something. Yea, arise and work and strive
and seek."

But "Only believe" are the words that fell from the lips of the Master for you
to receive.

So receive His Words and only believe, and find rest unto your spirit and
soul and body too.

Only believe, for He every symptom will relieve.

Only believe, for He is your Healer, your Provider, and Friend.

Yea, only believe, for the Great Physician is at work within.

Confession:

*I resist fear and doubt. I will not waver in my faith, but will stand strong. I
will believe and not doubt, for what God has promised, He is able also to
perform.*

For it is God which worketh in you both to will and to do of his good pleasure.

— PHILIPPIANS 2:13

God Is Working in You

I remember the story of a man who had a malignant growth on the side of his face. It looked like a big purple eggplant, and had grown almost as big as his head. The doctors wouldn't touch it. They had done preliminary examinations, but said that he'd live longer if they left it alone.

The man had been in all kinds of healing meetings, because he believed in divine healing. Healing evangelists had laid hands on him; the pastor had anointed him with oil and prayed; many people had prayed. Then one day the pastor said to me, "I noticed that the growth, though it was still there, began to shrivel. I could see that it was shriveling. The whole church could see it. Within a three-or four-month period, we saw that thing get smaller and smaller. Finally, the man came to church one day, and there wasn't a thing in the world wrong with his face. Every bit of that tumor was gone, and all the skin on his face looked like new baby skin!"

The pastor asked him what happened. He told the pastor that he had been reading his Bible and came to Philippians 2:13. Every morning when he looked in the mirror, he would put his hand on that growth and say, "God's working in that. Philippians 2:13 says that it's God that's at work within me, and He's not only working in my spirit — He's also working in my body." He kept saying that for days and weeks. And after about three months, he saw that the growth was beginning to shrivel, and, eventually, it all just disappeared. Now God didn't single that fellow out to bless him. The man saw the Word, read the Word, and began to believe the Word for himself. And he received what the Word said.

Confession:

God is working in me both to will and to do of His good pleasure. It's the will of God that I be healed and made whole. That's the good pleasure of God.

For let not that man [the man who wavers] *think that he shall receive any thing of the Lord.*

February 8

— JAMES 1:7

According to Your Faith

In Matthew chapter 9, two blind men were following Jesus as he left Jairus' house. They were crying and saying, "Thou son of David, have mercy on us!" Then Jesus asked the blind men a question.

He said, "Do you believe that I am able to do this?"

They said, "Yes, Lord." Did Jesus touch their eyes and say, "According to the faith of your church, so be it done unto you"? No, He didn't say that! Did He say, "According to My faith, the faith of the Son of God, so be it, because I sort of took a liking to you two blind fellows"? No! Did He say, "According to the faith of Kenneth Hagin, so be it done unto you"? No, of course He didn't. Jesus said, "According to *your* faith, so be it done unto you" (Matt. 9:29).

You see, Jesus asked them a question: "Do you believe that I am able to do this?" Then Jesus uttered the great law of faith that determines in every one of our lives the extent and measure of our blessing: "According to your faith, so be it done unto you." And the Bible says that the two blind men's eyes were opened (Matt. 9:30).

What opened their eyes? Their faith. And you can have faith just like the two blind men. Romans 10:17 says, *"So then faith cometh by hearing, and hearing by the word of God."*

Confession:

Faith is coming into my heart, into my spirit, into my inner man. Faith is coming because I'm hearing the Word of God.

If ye abide in me [Jesus], and my words abide in you, ye shall ask what ye will, and it shall be done unto you.

— JOHN 15:7

Get the Word in You

In twelve years of pastoral work, my wife and I did not bury even one church member. We even had eighty-year-old church members who were healed of cancer, lived out their lives, and died in their nineties without sickness or disease. We taught them that was the will of God for them.

Now many of those people didn't receive their healing right away. They had to be taught how to receive. You see, God occasionally does initiate some things on His own. But I can only think of two people during those twelve years of pastoral work who were healed because God initiated their healing. We had to teach the majority of them and get the Word into them.

As their pastor, I would say to them, "You give me the same opportunity and the same chance that you give the doctor, and you'll be healed every time. It won't cost you a dime." You see, folks go to the doctor, and if the doctor says, "Come back Thursday," they'll go back Thursday. Then if he says, "Come back Monday," they'll go back Monday. If he says, "Come back Wednesday," they'll go back Wednesday. If he says, "Come back Friday," they'll go back Friday.

Sometimes people keep going for months and don't think a thing in the world about it. Yet when they come to church, they want to be healed the first time around. If I tell them to come back, they get mad about it. But it takes time to get the Word of God into a person — to get him in position to receive his healing.

Confession:

God's Word always works, and His Word abides in me. I put my faith in His Word, and I ask what I will, and it shall be done unto me.

*Bless the Lord, O my soul, and forget not all his
benefits:
Who forgiveth all thine iniquities; who healeth all thy
diseases.*

February 10

— PSALM 103:2,3

Jesus Is Your Healer

I remember reading the testimony of Dr. A.B. Simpson, founder of the Christian Missionary Alliance. He was a Presbyterian minister and pastor, and in his mid-forties, he developed a serious heart condition. The best specialist of that day said nothing could be done for him.

Dr. Simpson knew nothing at all about the subject of healing. He had never examined the Bible on that subject, even though he was a minister of the Gospel and a graduate of a seminary. Now many in his own Presbyterian church congregation had testified of being healed. And he knew they were healed, because he knew something about their conditions.

So he decided to take a leave of absence from his church and go back to his farm, where every single day, he spent ten to twelve hours examining the Scriptures on the subject of healing. He would take his Bible and a notebook and get away from the house. He would sit in the sunshine under a tree, out in the fresh air. He would lean back against the tree with his Bible and note-book and make notes.

After two weeks of doing that, he became convinced that divine healing belonged to him. So without being any better, with all of his heart symptoms, he wrote down the following: Having studied the Word of God and having come to see that healing for the physical body is ours today just as much as the remission and forgiveness of sins, I now accept Jesus as my Healer.

Confession:

I am a believer, not a doubter. God's Word belongs to me. I accept that Word and acknowledge that God's Word is truth. I will not forget all His benefits. He is my Healer, and according to the Word of God, I'm healed. I receive that healing today.

Bless the Lord, O my soul, and forget not all his benefits:

Who forgiveth all thine iniquities; who healeth all thy diseases.

— PSALM 103:2,3

Believe the Truth

Some time later, Dr. A.B. Simpson was invited to speak at a luncheon. He preached from Matthew 8:17: "Himself [Jesus] took our infirmities and bare our sicknesses." He told the people at the luncheon that he had heard it preached all his life that "Himself took our *sins*," but during his intensive two-week study of the Bible, he had come to see that "Himself also took our *infirmities* and bare our sicknesses."

Then he said, "I'm in my mid-forties, but I want you to know that Himself took my diseases and my heart condition. Therefore, I don't have them anymore." When he said that, he still felt weak. He knew his heart was still not beating right.

His head said, "You've played the fool. You got up and told these folks that you're healed and that Jesus took your infirmities. But you've still got them."

But on the inside of him (that's where you have to believe God — on the inside of you), he said, "Devil, according to Matthew 8:17, I'm healed, because Himself took my infirmities and bore my sicknesses." Then his strength came to him and his heart rhythm straightened out. He started to feel good.

By believing the truth found in the Word of God, Dr. A.B. Simpson was completely healed!

Confession:

In the face of symptoms, in the face of pain, in the face of that which is a lie, I speak the truth because the Word is truth. By Jesus' stripes, I am healed.

Don't Reject God's Word

I've had church folks say to me, "Well, Brother Hagin, if Jesus took our infirmities and bare our sicknesses, why are so many Christians still sick?"

It's because they don't *know* what Jesus did. You see, healing doesn't just fall on you because Jesus took your infirmities and bare your sicknesses. The same is true regarding salvation. Jesus died and bore the sins of the worst sinner today just as much as He did your sins and mine. Well, if He did, why isn't that sinner saved? Either because he hasn't heard about God's gift of salvation and what Jesus did for him, or he did hear and rejected it.

Let me give you an example. Years ago, two ministers of the Gospel I knew were facing death. One was in his forties, and the other was in his fifties. I shared with both ministers the same truths about God's healing power that I've shared with you. One of them rejected that truth and died. The other one said, "Yes, I see that. It's all in the Word," and he was raised up from a deathbed.

Someone said to me, "Well, that was just the will of God. God took one of them and spared the other." No, it doesn't work like that. The same truth was presented to both of them. One of them rejected it, and the other accepted it. Now that doesn't mean that because one of them rejected that part of the Word (healing) that he died and went to hell. Of course, he didn't. It just means he was robbed of the blessings that God intended He should have down here on earth.

Confession:

I want everything that belongs to me in Christ. I don't want to settle for second-best or third-best or fourth-best. If the Bible says it's mine, I'm going to have it. And healing is mine.

February 13

Casting down imaginations [reasonings], and every high thing that exalteth itself against the knowledge of God, and bringing into captivity every thought to the obedience of Christ.

— 2 CORINTHIANS 10:5

Casting Down Reasonings

Many people's minds have never been renewed with the Word of God. They may be saved, filled with the Holy Ghost, and members of a Full Gospel church, but their minds still need to be renewed with the Word of God.

Second Corinthians 10:4 and 5 says, *"For the weapons of our warfare are not carnal, but mighty through God to the pulling down of strong holds; Casting down imaginations, and every high thing that exalteth itself against the knowledge of God, and bringing into captivity every thought to the obedience of Christ."*

Many people are in a battle between their head and their heart. This is spiritual warfare, and these verses say that our weapons are not carnal, or natural. They're not guns, swords, or even fists. But our weapons are mighty through God to the pulling down of strongholds (2 Cor. 10:4). Paul is referring to "casting down imaginations." Imaginations can also be translated *reasonings*, which involve people's minds.

As long as Satan can hold you in the arena of reason, he'll defeat you in every battle. But if you hold Satan in the arena of faith, you'll defeat him in every battle. How do you do that? The Scripture says to "cast down imaginations (reasonings)."

Confession:

I cast down imaginations and reasonings. I bring every thought captive to the obedience of Jesus Christ. If the thought doesn't line up with the Word of God, I reject it. I believe and think on only what God's Word says.

44

For the weapons of our warfare are not carnal, but mighty through God to the pulling down of strong holds;

Casting down imaginations [reasonings], *and every high thing that exalteth itself against the knowledge of God, and bringing into captivity every thought to the obedience of Christ.*

February 14

— 2 CORINTHIANS 10:4,5

Take Your Thoughts Captive

When you're believing God for healing, reason will tell you that it can't happen — that you can't be healed. But you have to cast down reasonings. I didn't say it was easy. (If you're looking for something easy, you'd better just quit now.)

Now what does Paul mean when he says, "Casting down every high thing that exalts itself against the knowledge of God"? He's talking about any kind of knowledge that exalts itself against the knowledge of God and His Word. He's talking about human knowledge here. Some people call it "sense knowledge." If it's in opposition to what God's Word reveals, then cast it down, or throw it away!

Paul also tells us to bring every thought into captivity. Some people have said to me, "Brother Hagin, I'm bothered with all these thoughts. Will you pray and cast that out of me?" I'm not going to do that. The Bible doesn't say to do that. It says for *you* to bring every thought into captivity. The Bible doesn't tell you to do something you can't do.

I like to put it this way: Christ is the Word. John 1:1 says, *"In the beginning was the Word, and the Word was with God, and the Word was God."* Then in John 1:14, we read, *"The Word was made flesh and dwelt among us."* Christ is called the Word of God. So I like to read Second Corinthians 10:5 like this: "Bringing every thought into captivity to the obedience of the Word of God."

Confession:

I bring every thought captive to the obedience of the Word of God. I am a believer, not a doubter. I do have faith. My faith is in God's Holy Word. My faith is in God, the Father, and in the Lord Jesus Christ.

My son, attend to my words; incline thine ear unto my sayings.
Let them not depart from thine eyes; keep them in the midst of thine heart.
For they are life unto those that find them, and health to all their flesh.

— PROVERBS 4:20-22

The Importance of God's Word

Knowing the written Word of God for yourself is very important. I've had people attend my meetings who were there every single service, but they didn't bring their Bibles. Now I didn't tell them, but I knew that if I could get them to bring their Bible one time so they could see for themselves what God says, they would receive their healing.

I remember one fellow in particular. He had been in twenty-one services, yet still failed to receive his healing. I said to him, "Bring your Bible."

He responded, "Well, the only time I take my Bible to church with me is on Sunday morning."

I said, "Bring it with you." I knew he wouldn't accept what I was saying if I just told him, because he thought certain scriptures read a certain way. And they didn't read the way he thought.

One night he brought his Bible and followed me in reading the scriptures. Before I finished my lesson, he jumped up and said, "I just can't wait. I'll receive right now." And he received his healing!

Someone might say, "What if you couldn't have gotten him to bring his Bible?" He wouldn't have received. The Bible is God's Holy Book. The Bible is God speaking to us. Do you want God to speak to you? The Bible is God speaking to you.

Confession:

The Bible is God speaking to me. I attend to God's Word by reading and studying my Bible. I keep His Word before my eyes, and I incline my ears unto it.

That it might be fulfilled which was spoken by Esaias the prophet, saying, Himself took our infirmities, and bare our sicknesses.

— MATTHEW 8:17

How Do You *Know* Jesus Took Your Infirmities?

God wants you to know that Jesus took your infirmities and bare your sicknesses. Some people say, "But I didn't see Him do it." Even those who were there when Jesus died didn't see Him take our diseases and sicknesses. They saw Jesus physically die, but they couldn't see what happened to Him spiritually.

Natural human knowledge can't comprehend what Jesus did. That kind of knowledge is beyond natural human truth. You could never prove from natural human truth that your diseases and sicknesses were laid on Jesus. Because you can't see it with your eyes, you have no comprehension of it from the natural standpoint.

So how do you *know* that He took your infirmities? Even though it doesn't look like He took them because you still have symptoms in your body, it is revealed to you in the Holy Word of God. That's how you know it; you believe God's Word.

That revelation knowledge is the knowledge that you are to walk by, not natural human knowledge. The revelation of the truth that Jesus took your infirmities is the truth that a Christian is to live by.

Confession:

For it is written, Himself, Jesus, took my infirmities and bare my sicknesses. What He bore, I need not bear. Because He bore them, I'm free from sickness and disease. I know that this is true because I believe the Word.

47

February 17

Say What the Bible Says

When you know what the Word of God says, and someone asks, "How do you feel?" you can say, "I'm well, thank you." Even if you are experiencing some symptoms, you're not lying. You're stating that you're well because the Bible says that Jesus took your infirmities and bare your sicknesses. And what He bore, you need not bear.

You see, since Jesus bore your infirmities, you don't have to have them anymore. But as long as you confess them — as long as you say, "I have them" — you will have them.

That's the reason people go through the process of trying to get rid of sickness and disease over and over again. They are prayed for, they have hands laid on them, they are anointed with oil, but they keep holding on to what they have. They don't turn the sickness loose.

If you will believe that Jesus took your infirmities and bare your sicknesses while the symptoms are still there — while all physical evidence says it isn't so — it won't be long before you'll reap a harvest of healing.

Confession:

I'm not moved by what I see or how I feel. I'm moved only by what I believe, and I believe that He, Jesus, took my infirmities and bare my sicknesses.

*For we are labourers together with God: ye are
God's husbandry, ye are God's building.*

— 1 CORINTHIANS 3:9

February 18

You Are God's Garden

When Paul wrote to the Church at Corinth, he said, *". . . ye are God's husbandry. . . ."* Now that's a little bit blind to us today, but another translation says, "Ye are God's garden." You are God's garden.

Picture in your mind a garden. Have you ever seen anyone plant a garden one day and the next day go out and reap something from it? No, of course not.

In First Corinthians 3:6, Paul said, *"I have planted* [talking about the seed of the Gospel], *Apollos watered; but God gave the increase."* Well, what did he plant? What was his seed? The Word of God was his seed.

Paul planted the seed of the Word into people's hearts. Then Apollos came along preaching to them and watered the Word that had already been preached to them, or planted, by Paul. And God gave the increase, or caused the seed to bear fruit.

Psalm 107:20 says, *"He sent his word, and healed them. . . ."* How do you plant the Word in your heart? When you receive the Word — when you accept and confess it — it gets into your spirit, into your heart.

Confession:

It is God's will that I be well. God wants me well. He doesn't want me sick. I let that truth be planted into my heart, and I water it so that it will yield an increase of healing in my life.

49

Sanctify them through thy truth: thy word is truth.
— JOHN 17:17

Accept God's Word as Truth

God laid on Jesus the cause of our sicknesses, our pains, and our diseases, and Jesus bore them. Since God wanted Jesus to bear them, does He want you and me to bear them also? No! The reason Jesus bore our sicknesses and infirmities was so that we wouldn't have to.

But, instead of accepting God's Word just the way it reads and saying, "Yes! That's what the Word says," we are prone to say, "Yes, but. . . ." Well, I can't find a "yes, but . . ." in that scripture anywhere. Why not just accept what it says?

A person said to me once, "But, Brother Hagin, that's not the way I interpret that verse."

I replied, "I'm not interpreting it. It plainly says, 'Himself took our infirmities and bare our sicknesses.' I'm not interpreting it; I'm quoting it."

The person said, "Yes, but I don't interpret that to mean what you say it means."

I said, "I didn't say it means anything."

I added, "What if I said to you, 'My wife and I went to town yesterday, and she bought a new purse'? How would you interpret that? Would you think she bought an automobile? Or would you just plainly understand that we went to town and she bought a purse? Wouldn't you just take me at my word?" Why not take God's Word for what it says?

Confession:

I believe that Jesus took my infirmities and bore my sicknesses. I believe that because He bore them, I'm free. I accept what God's Word says as truth, and because I accept it and believe it, I say it with my mouth.

Every good gift and every perfect gift is from above, and cometh down from the Father of lights, with whom is no variableness, neither shadow of turning.

— JAMES 1:17

Is God Using Sickness To Teach You Something?

Some would say, "If Jesus took my infirmities and bore my sicknesses, then why am I still sick?" Because you don't believe it yet! Now you might mentally agree and say, "Yeah, that's right." But you don't really believe it in your heart, because if you believed it in your heart, you would agree with God and say out of your mouth, "He took my infirmities and bore my sicknesses, so I don't have them anymore."

A person who believes that Jesus took his infirmities and sicknesses will hold fast to his confession even when he's still hurting. He knows that Jesus bore his sicknesses. And those symptoms will disappear if he'll hold fast to that confession.

Many people think that God wants them sick. But when I ask them why in the world He would want them sick, they don't have an answer; they don't know. I've been ministering healing for more than sixty-five years, and I've often had people say to me, "Maybe God is trying to teach me something."

When I ask them, "How long have you been sick?" they might respond, "Twenty-five years."

Then when I ask, "Have you learned anything?," they say, "Well, no."

My reply to them is, "If God has been trying to teach you something for twenty-five years, He's either not a very good teacher, or you're a poor student."

Dear Lord, it would be funny if it weren't so pathetic.

Confession:

God is good, and it is God's will for me to be well. That's His highest and perfect will for me, because His Word is His will, and it is revealed to me in His Word that He wants me well.

February 21
        Every good gift and every perfect gift is from above,
        and cometh down from the Father of lights, with
        whom is no variableness, neither shadow of turning.

— JAMES 1:17

A Well Wife Is Better Than a Sick Wife

I knew a woman years ago who became desperately sick. She couldn't do her housework, she couldn't get up and cook breakfast for her unsaved husband, or do much of anything, for that matter. One night she said to me, "Brother Hagin, you may have wondered why I haven't been in the healing line."

I said, "I sure have."

"Well," she said, "you know I've suffered. I've been sick for nineteen years. I've finally decided that the Lord made me sick so my husband would get saved."

I said, "Dear Lord! Your husband would come closer to getting saved with a well wife than he would with a sick wife. That's not God. You're letting the devil rob you of your healing and cheat you out of your husband's salvation. For goodness' sake, don't tell him that God made you sick so he would get saved! What kind of impression would that leave on him concerning God? He would think that God stole his wife from him. No! It's the devil that's making you sick."

When she said, "Well, maybe I'm wrong about it," I said, "You sure are. You're definitely wrong about it."

But, thank God, this woman began studying the subject and got healed. When her husband found out that God had healed her, he was so grateful, he got saved!

Confession:

Every good gift and every perfect gift comes from God. Because health and healing come from God, I receive my health and healing.

Every good gift and every perfect gift is from above, and cometh down from the Father of lights, with whom is no variableness, neither shadow of turning.
— JAMES 1:17

Sickness Doesn't Make You More Spiritual

Sickness and disease don't make people more spiritual. They don't bring out the best in people — in fact, they usually bring out the worst in them! Sick people can get cantankerous and hard to get along with.

A friend of mine once said, "Maybe God wants me sick," as if to imply it was for some spiritual reason. I replied, "Well, you keep believing that and stay sick. I'll keep believing God wants me well and stay well." And so I *have* stayed well for sixty-five years, and he has been sick all those years. I like my way better.

Now if you want to believe that God wants you sick, go ahead and stay sick. But don't ask me to pray for you. I've had people in a healing line say to me, "Brother Hagin, I believe the Lord just wants me sick." And I've thought, *Well, if He wants you sick, why are you here trying to get healed? If He wants you sick, then it would be a sin for you to try to get well.*

People in the hospital have also said to me, "I don't believe that it's God's will to heal me." Well, if it's not God's will to heal them, why are they in the hospital trying to get well? According to their line of reasoning, if they ever did get well, they would be out of the will of God! No, the truth is that God wants people well.

Confession:

It is God's will that I be well. It is God's will that I be healed. X

*While it is said, To day if ye will hear his voice,
harden not your hearts, as in the provocation.*

— HEBREWS 3:15

Don't Shut the Door on God

Over the years, I've had frustrated saints say to me: "I knew So-and-so twenty years ago. They used to come here to church, but they haven't been to church for years, while I've been faithful and have been here every Sunday. Yet they came to the altar the other night and got healed, and I've been seeking healing for almost a quarter of a century. Why won't the Lord heal me?"

I say to them, "The Lord has already done all He's ever going to do about healing you. The Bible says, 'Himself took your infirmities and bare your sicknesses' [Matt. 8:17]. God laid your sickness and disease on Jesus nearly two thousand years ago, so He's already purchased healing for you. It's yours. God has your healing already packaged up in a nice package with your name on it. He's just waiting for you to come and claim your possession."

They respond, "Yes, Brother Hagin, I know all that, but now let me tell you what I believe about it. I just believe that if it's God's will, He will heal me in His own good time and in His own way."

I say, "He won't, because you've shut the door on Him. You've closed the door in His face."

So how do you keep the door open? Have an open mind and heart and be receptive to the Word. Don't substitute what you think or even what you believe about the situation. Instead, determine what the Word of God says about the situation, and believe that.

Confession:

I will not shut the door on God. I believe what His Word says. Healing already belongs to me, because Jesus purchased it for me nearly two thousand years ago.

And from the days of John the Baptist until now the kingdom of heaven suffereth violence, and the violent take it by force.

February 24

— MATTHEW 11:12

Have the Tenacity of a Bulldog!

Sometimes in the area of healing, particularly when chronic illness is involved, you have to do what the Scripture says: You have to take it by force! Sometimes you just have to get violent about it, and have the tenacity of a bulldog — grab hold of God and His Word and don't ever turn loose!

I'll tell you what I literally did on one occasion. Some time after I was healed as a teenager, all of my heart symptoms came back, and the devil kept bringing to my mind everything that the doctors had said. The devil said, "Now you've got all these symptoms and you're going to die, just like the doctors said. There isn't anything that medical science can do. They've already told you that, so there's no use to look to medical science. You're going to die."

I said, "Mr. Devil, the Bible said, 'Himself took my infirmities and bare my sicknesses.' I don't care what the symptoms are. I don't care how I feel, or what I look like. According to the Word of God, I believe that I am healed."

Then I put my Bible down on the floor and stood on it. I said, "God, to illustrate a spiritual fact, I'm standing on the Word of God." I talked to the devil, then I talked to God. I had barely finished my conversation when every symptom disappeared. Sometimes you just have to get desperate about the situation and say, "That's it. I'm standing on the Word of God, no matter what."

Confession:

I am standing on the Word of God. I don't care what the symptoms are, or how I feel. I believe according to the Word of God that I'm healed.

... *for I am the Lord that healeth thee.*

— EXODUS 15:26

For I am the Lord, I change not. . . .

— MALACHI 3:6

God Is Still in the Healing Business

The Lord said to Israel, "I am the Lord that healeth thee." God was Israel's healer, so God provided physical healing under the Old Covenant. But some people don't believe that the Lord heals today under the New Covenant.

Now the children of Israel were never *sons* of God; they were only *servants* of God. Since God did not want His servants sick — since He had made provision for them to be well and live their full life out down here on earth without sickness or disease — why would He want something less for His sons? Wouldn't it be strange for God to want His servants to be well, but His sons to be sick?

Under the New Covenant, we are God's sons. In the New Testament, Peter says, *"How God anointed Jesus of Nazareth with the Holy Ghost and with power: who went about doing good, and healing all that were oppressed of the devil . . ."* (Acts 10:38). This revelation from the Apostle Peter tells us that those Jesus healed were oppressed of the devil. So Jesus is the healer, and Satan is the oppressor. This text tells us that Satan is the author of sickness and disease.

In the Old Testament, there is no dispute that God was the healer and Satan was the one who made people sick. Yet many people today say that God is not in the healing business anymore. No! God is still in the same business that He has always been in, and the devil is in the same business that he has always been in. God is doing the same works that He has always done, and the devil is doing the same works that he has always done. They have not changed.

Confession:

God does not change. Since He provided healing for His servants under the Old Covenant, He also provides healing for me, His child, today.

And ought not this woman, being a daughter of
Abraham, whom Satan hath bound, lo, these
eighteen years, be loosed from this bond on the
sabbath day?

— LUKE 13:16

You Ought To Be Loosed!

The woman in this account was bowed together and could not lift her-self up. Jesus said, "You ought to be loosed." Jesus is saying the same thing today. If you're bound with sickness, if you're bound with disease, you ought to be loosed.

Jesus said that this woman ought to be healed because she was a daugh-ter of Abraham. If you're a son or a daughter of Abraham, you ought to be loosed. Galatians 3:29 says, *"And if ye be Christ's, then are ye Abraham's seed, and heirs according to the promise."* Galatians 3:7 says, *"Know ye therefore that they which are of faith, the same are the children of Abraham."* We're the seed of Abraham. We're the children of Abraham.

As a son of Abraham, and a seed of Abraham, I ought to be free. Jesus died to set me free, and, thank God, I'm free. I refuse to be bound. John 10:10 says, *"The thief cometh not, but for to steal, and to kill, and to destroy: I am come that they might have life, and that they might have it more abundantly."*

We see in this passage a contrast of two different works — the works of Jesus and the works of the devil. Jesus came to destroy the works of the devil (1 John 3:8). Jesus came to set us free.

Confession:

I am a child of Abraham, and I ought to be loosed. I refuse to be bound. I refuse to be sick. Jesus died to set me free from sickness and disease.

. . . *For this purpose the Son of God was manifested, that he might destroy the works of the devil.*

— 1 JOHN 3:8

Jesus Came To Destroy the Works of the Devil

A number of years ago, I knew a man in Texas who was in the healing ministry. When a tornado came along in the spring of the year, it blew down the tent in which he held revival meetings. He didn't have any insurance for the 20,000-seat tent, because no one would insure tents at that time.

So we took up an offering to help him buy another tent. During the service, I almost fell off the pew as this supposed great man of faith said, "I don't know whether the devil or God blew my tent down." Well, God is not out blowing Gospel tents down; He is putting them up.

No, God wasn't in that destruction. Floods, earthquakes, and other destructive acts are not acts of God. Where do things that hurt and destroy come from? The devil! The Bible says that when the devil is finally eliminated from human contact, or from the earth, there will be nothing that will hurt or destroy (Isa. 65:25; Matt. 25:41; Rev. 20:10). Get that settled in your mind.

According to First John 3:8, the Son of God came to destroy the works of the devil. What are the works of the devil? People think about lying, stealing, adultery, and murder as works of the devil. But the Bible says that although sin is behind them, these are works of the flesh (*see* Galatians 5:19-21). But what are the works of the devil? They are sickness, poverty, and spiritual death. Jesus came to destroy the works of the devil.

Confession:

Since Jesus came to destroy the works of the devil, and one of the works of the devil is sickness, then sickness does not come from God. Healing comes from God. I receive healing now.

Then enquired he [Jesus] of them the hour when he began to amend. . . .

February 28

— JOHN 4:52

Keep the Switch of Faith Turned On

Because healing is not always instantaneous, many people lose the beginning of their healing because they don't know that. Unfortunately, whenever I say that, people usually respond, "Well, Brother Hagin, under the ministry of Jesus, Jesus always healed everybody instantly." But I read in the Bible that under the ministry of Jesus, the nobleman's son began to "amend from that hour" (John 4:52). That means that he *began* to get better until he was finally all right.

Many people miss out on God's blessings because they don't receive an instant manifestation. But through the years, our ministry has had innumerable people healed of terminal cancer, and of all of those cases of healing, only one person was healed instantly.

I remember laying hands on a woman in Illinois as I ministered the healing power of God to her body. Eleven days later, as she woke up in the morning, she said to her husband, "I'm healed."

She said, "I usually wake up screaming with pain, but I don't have any pain." She waited three days, took no medicine, and no symptoms returned. She finally went to one of the doctors on the case, who ran every test he could run, but couldn't find a trace of the disease in her.

What happened? The power of God was administered to her, and it drove that cancer right out of her body. Now if she had said, "Well, I've still got my symptoms so it didn't work," she would have turned off the switch of faith and she would not have received her healing. But she kept the switch of faith turned on.

Confession:

I will keep the switch of faith turned on. I will believe that God's healing power is actively at work in my body effecting a healing and a cure.

59

February 29

Therefore if any man be in Christ, he is a new creature: old things are passed away; behold, all things are become new.

— 2 CORINTHIANS 5:17

We Died to Our Old Nature

When we were born again, we died to our old nature. We died to our diseases. And we rose in the fullness of life, free from our sins and diseases.

I was reading a sermon by a Methodist minister once. In his sermon, he shared the following story.

"I was in bondage to tobacco. I was in a large city at a Methodist conference and wanted a cigarette. So I went into the back alley and smoked a cigarette. [If any of the brethren had seen him, they would have taken his ordination papers away from him.] Afterwards, I felt so condemned. I said to the Lord, 'Lord, I've done my best. I know that I don't need that and I shouldn't be bound by anything. And yet, I'm under bondage. I've prayed and fasted sometimes as long as two weeks and I still go right back to it.' Then I heard the Lord say, 'That's the problem. You've tried to do it yourself. Don't you know that I delivered you from all bondage at Calvary?' I said, 'Yes, that's right. You did. Thank You, Lord. I'm delivered!'"

From that day on, he never wanted another cigarette. You see, he accepted God's deliverance and was set free!

In the area of healing, many people are struggling and trying to be healed. They don't realize that Jesus already delivered them from all sickness and disease at Calvary and that all they have to do is accept it and thank God for it.

Confession:

Thank You, Father, for delivering me from sickness and disease at Calvary. I accept it and thank You for it!

. . . they shall lay hands on the sick, and they shall recover.

— MARK 16:18

God Expects Something of You

As I was preaching one time in Pasadena, Texas, a man and his wife brought to the meeting their little girl who was afflicted. This eight-year-old girl didn't have much use of her body, and was even unable to feed herself. As I laid hands on her and prayed, I knew the power of God went into her, but she didn't seem to be any better. She was still helpless.

After the service, the family stopped to get some hamburgers before driving back to their home in Beaumont, Texas. When they ordered their food, they got a hamburger for the little girl. Ordinarily, the mother would feed her because the girl couldn't even handle a fork and had great difficulty swallowing. The mother would pinch off small bites of whatever she was eating, put it into her daughter's mouth, and coax her to swallow. But this time, to their utter amazement, the young girl reached for the hamburger and said, "Give me that." Then she started eating the hamburger! At this point, she was at least seventy to eighty percent better.

But because the mother and father didn't walk with God, this poor little girl lost the healing she had received. When the parents backslid, they said, "Well, she wasn't one hundred percent delivered, anyway." You see, they expected God to go ahead and complete the healing, but He was expecting something of them. He expected them to do their part, and their daughter paid for their decision not to believe.

Many times, God will initiate a healing, and a person will begin to feel better. And if that person will continue walking in faith, he or she will become perfectly well. But by backing up in their faith and even denying what has already occurred, many times people lose the whole healing.

Confession:

I will walk on with God and let the full manifestation of my healing come into being. It will come as I continue to believe.

61

So then faith cometh by hearing, and hearing by the word of God.

— ROMANS 10:17

Hearing the Word Over and Over

A denominational pastor I knew daily visited the home of a woman with terminal cancer to pray with her and read the Word to her. As this woman was bedfast, he would also bring her a different cassette tape every day to listen to.

He said to me, "I really didn't know or understand the leading of the Lord at the time. But something on the inside kept saying, 'So then faith cometh by hearing and hearing,' and it stopped right there [Rom. 10:17]. That went on over and over inside of me for three days, and on the third day, I finally decided that God was trying to get something across to me. I decided that God was trying to tell me that this woman needed to hear one tape over and over again, instead of me changing the tape each day."

When he asked the Lord which tape he should play over and over, he felt impressed in his spirit to play my tape, "God's Medicine." So he took the tape to her, and told her that he was not going to bring any more tapes because he wanted her to listen to this one tape over and over again.

In the process of time, the woman was completely healed of terminal cancer. I saw her some time ago, and she said to me, "Brother Hagin, you know I was on my deathbed, and the doctors said that they had done all they could do. But as I listened over and over again to your tape, 'God's Medicine,' it built faith in my heart. And I was completely healed."

Confession:

I am a doer of the Word. Faith is built in my heart by hearing and hearing and hearing the Word of God. Therefore, I hear the Word of God and then I act on the Word.

God Hears and Answers Prayer

A number of years ago, our ministry received a letter from a dear woman. A portion of the letter read: "I am a widow woman with only one son. He is fifty-seven years old, lives in Indiana, and has cancer and a heart problem. The doctors say that he will die. At my age, it's difficult for me to travel, so in talking to my daughter-in-law on the phone, I asked her if it would be possible to move him to a hospital closer to me so that I could see him one last time before he dies. My daughter-in-law talked to the doctors, and they said, 'No.' But my son wanted to see me. So after talking to the doctors many times, they finally said, 'Well, we don't believe he will make it, but if you want to try it, we'll put him in an ambulance and hook him up to the necessary equipment. We hope he gets there before he dies.' So they did."

When she wrote in asking us to pray, she wasn't even thinking about healing. She just thought, *If I could see him again, I would be satisfied.* She wanted us to pray that he would survive the ambulance trip so she would get to see him again. But, of course, we believed that God would heal the hole in his heart and the terminal cancer. So we prayed that he would live and not die.

Some time later, the mother said that when they got him to the hospital near her, the doctors couldn't find anything wrong with him. Since they had received all of his medical records from the previous hospital, they said, "You've either sent the wrong man or the wrong medical records. He doesn't have a hole in his heart or anything else wrong with his heart, and he doesn't have any cancer." That dear old mother rejoiced that her only son had been healed!

Confession:

The Lord hears me when I pray. I pray according to the Word of God. And God's Word says that I was healed almost two thousand years ago when Jesus hung on the Cross at Calvary. I agree with what God's Word says.

And Jesus went about all Galilee . . . healing all manner of sickness and all manner of disease among the people.

— MATTHEW 4:23

Healing Is the Will of God for You!

I know from more than sixty-five years' experience in the ministry that the thing that keeps most people from being healed is they do not know for sure if it is God's will to heal them. If they're sick, naturally, they want to be healed, especially if they have a terminal disease and medical science can't help them. So they look everywhere they can for help. I don't blame them. I did too when I was given up to die. And I found the answer in the Word of God.

Many times, people are just seeking in the dark, hoping something will happen. They say, "Well, I may or may not get healed. And if it doesn't happen, I'm going to die." They are prayed for many times, and hands are laid on them, but nothing seems to work. And under those conditions, nothing will, because they are uncertain that it is God's will to heal them.

One giant step towards receiving healing for your physical body is to settle the issue that healing is the will of God for you. What God provided in His great plan of redemption belongs to everyone, not to just a few of us. Let your faith solidly rest on the Word of God.

Knowing that healing is God's will for you doesn't come from just reading scriptures about healing or memorizing those scriptures. No, the revelation that it is God's will to heal you comes from meditating on scriptures about healing — thinking on them, turning them over and over in your mind until they become a part of your inner consciousness.

Confession:

It is God's will to heal me, for healing is in God's plan of redemption. I believe the Word, and according to the Word of God, it is His will to heal me, because God wants me well.

Who his own self bare our sins in his own body on the tree, that we, being dead to sins, should live unto righteousness: by whose stripes ye were healed.

— 1 PETER 2:24

Faith Is Based on Bible Facts, Not Theories

Faith is built on fact, not theory. A fact is a conclusion deduced from evidence. (My definition of a theory is a supposition established on ignorance of the subject under discussion!) Faith is based on the facts of God's Word, but theory about God's Word is based on suppositions.

It is a Bible fact that by Jesus' stripes, we were healed (1 Peter 2:24). It is a Bible fact that surely He has borne our sicknesses and carried our pains (Isa. 53:4). It is a Bible fact that Himself took our infirmities and bare our sicknesses (Matt. 8:17). These are Bible facts, not theories.

Start believing these facts — even while you still have the symptoms. Although your body may be telling you that you are not healed, continue to believe the facts of God's Word. I know it works. It has worked for me.

Confession:

I believe the facts of God's Word. I believe that by Jesus' stripes, I am healed. I am not going to be healed, because I am healed now.

How God anointed Jesus of Nazareth with the Holy Ghost and with power: who went about doing good, and healing all that were oppressed of the devil; for God was with him.

— ACTS 10:38

Jesus Is the Deliverer

What is another Bible fact? The fact that healing belongs to us, because sickness comes from Satan. Satan is the author of sickness and disease, not God. Could it ever be the will of God for a child of His to be under the dominion of Satan? Could it ever be the will of God for a child of His to have anything that comes from Satan? No!

Acts 10:38 says, *"How God anointed Jesus of Nazareth with the Holy Ghost and with power: who went about doing good, and healing all that were oppressed of the devil; for God was with him."* What did God do? He anointed Jesus of Nazareth with the Holy Ghost and power. Then Jesus went about doing good. What is the good that Jesus did? He healed people.

It is a fact that God is a healing God. Jesus said, "For he that hath seen Me hath seen the Father" (John 14:9). If you want to see God at work, look at Jesus. What did Jesus do? He went about doing good and healing. Whom did He heal? All those who were oppressed of the devil. And since all those He healed were oppressed of the devil, we know that sickness is satanic oppression.

So it is not the will of God that the children of God be oppressed by the devil, and we know that sickness and disease come from Satan; he is the author of them. Satan is the destroyer. He is the oppressor. Jesus is the Deliverer. He is the Healer. God doesn't want us to be oppressed or destroyed. He wants us to be delivered and healed.

Confession:

Jesus is my Deliverer and my Healer. He was anointed by God to destroy the works of the devil, which include sickness and disease. I believe that Jesus delivered me from sickness and disease.

A thing of Belial is poured out on him. . . .

— PSALM 41:8
(Young's Literal Translation)

The Author of Sickness

Second Corinthians 13:1 says, *". . . In the mouth of two or three witnesses shall every word be established."* So let's look at some more scriptures that tell us that sickness comes from Satan — that he is the author of it.

And ought not this woman, being a daughter of Abraham, WHOM SATAN HATH BOUND, lo, these eighteen years, be loosed from this bond on the sabbath day?

Luke 13:16

THE THIEF [Satan] COMETH NOT, BUT FOR TO STEAL, AND TO KILL, AND TO DESTROY: I [Jesus] am come that they might have life, and that they might have it more abundantly.

John 10:10

He that committeth sin is of the devil; for the devil sinneth from the beginning. For this purpose the Son of God was manifested, THAT HE MIGHT DESTROY THE WORKS OF THE DEVIL.

1 John 3:8

Confession:

Satan is the author of sickness and disease. According to Luke 13:16, John 10:10, First John 3:8, and Acts 10:38, sickness and disease come from Satan. So I refuse anything that comes from him, and stand my ground on the Word of God, which says that Jesus came to destroy the works of the devil and to give me life more abundantly.

March 8

But let it be the hidden man of the heart, in that which is not corruptible, even the ornament of a meek and quiet spirit, which is in the sight of God of great price.

— 1 PETER 3:4

Listen to Your Heart, Not Your Head

More than sixty-eight years ago when I was on the bed of sickness, I began to get a little glimpse of light from the Word of God concerning healing. So I began to talk to other Christians about it. They would tell me, "Well, yes, God did heal under the Old Covenant, but that was just for the Jews. That's not for us nowadays."

Now many might have responded by thinking, *Well, I guess that's a closed subject then. They're Christians, and they ought to know what they're talking about.*

But, you see, I was no longer religious. I wasn't just a church person anymore. I had become a Christian. There's a difference between the two. Unfortunately, many church people have been religiously brainwashed; they've never really been taught the Bible. So many times, they just accept what they are told about the Bible.

Now when these religious people would tell me that healing is no longer for us today, my head — my intellect — would want to accept that, because my head had been educated that way. My head had heard preachers and others say, "Yes, the Lord Jesus healed when He was here on the earth, and the apostles healed, all right. But the Lord did that just to get the Church established. When the last apostle died, all that ceased." I had heard that worn-out, washed-out theory over and over.

But my heart said, "That's not right." When I say "heart," I'm not talking about the physical organ that pumps blood. The heart of man is his spirit. The Bible also calls it "the hidden man of the heart" or "man's innermost being."

Something on the inside told me that I could be healed. I don't mean it was a voice; it was an inward intuition, an inward witness. Way down on the inside of me, I knew that what those religious people were saying was wrong.

Confession:

I listen to my heart, to my innermost being. And the Lord leads me and guides me into all truth.

He sent his word, and healed them, and delivered them from their destructions.

— PSALM 107:20

God Heals You Through Your Spirit

As you say the following confession, notice what happens on the inside of you: *God's Word works. Psalm 107:20 says, "He sent His Word and healed them," so I know He sent His Word and healed me. I no longer have* _____ [fill in the particular sickness or disease].

Did something start to leap and jump on the inside of you? That's your spirit getting excited. Your spirit knows you're on the right road.

Now your mind may not have grasped what you confessed. In fact, your mind may still be trying to get hold of what you said. Your head may be saying, "I don't understand it." But if you'll listen on the inside of you, you'll find that there's something down in there that's thrilled. Why? Your spirit knows the truth of your confession.

God's healing is spirit healing, not mental healing or physical healing as medical science teaches. God's healing is spirit healing, because He is a spirit.

God heals you through your spirit. He doesn't contact you through your mind, because He is not a mind. He doesn't contact you through your body, because He is not a man. He contacts you through your spirit. So when your head doesn't understand some things, your spirit will just be thrilled.

Confession:

Confession: God's Word works. Psalm 107:20 says, "He sent His Word and healed them," so I know He sent His Word and healed me. I no longer have _____ *(fill in the particular sickness or disease).*

March 10

My son, attend to my words; incline thine ear unto
my sayings.
Let them not depart from thine eyes; keep them in
the midst of thine heart.
For they are life unto those that find them, and
health to all their flesh.

— PROVERBS 4:20-22

Bible Principles Work

Begin to see yourself well and confess that you are well according to
Proverbs 4:20 through 22. What is not supposed to depart from your eyes?
God's words, which say that by Jesus' stripes, you *were* healed (1 Peter
2:24). The word "were" is past tense, so if that scripture doesn't depart
from before your eyes, you will soon see yourself well.

It's amazing to me how people out in the world will unknowingly take
Bible principles, put them into practice, and get results. I remember reading
about a new therapy technique some hospitals were using on cancer patients.
They would teach the patients to visualize themselves well. I don't know
whether or not they knew the source of that technique, but I know where I
learned it. The Bible teaches us to see ourselves well. And if hospital person-
nel can get that technique to work without God, Christians should get even
better results!

Another thing hospitals were teaching the patients to do was to meditate, or practice positive thinking. Remember that God told Joshua, "Do not
let the law [the Word of God] depart out of your mouth, but meditate
therein day and night, for then you'll make your way prosperous and you'll
have good success" (Joshua 1:8). If the world can take Bible principles and
get results by putting them into practice naturally, shouldn't we get better
results with the aid of the Spirit of God?

Confession:

*I do not let the Word of God depart from my eyes, but I meditate on it
night and day, because God's Word is life, health, and healing to all my flesh.
I see myself well and whole and healed.*

70

*s any sick among you? let him call for the elders of
the church; and let them pray over him, anointing
him with oil in the name of the Lord:
And the prayer of faith shall save the sick, and the
Lord shall raise him up; and if he have committed
sins, they shall be forgiven him.*

— JAMES 5:14,15

Healing in the New Testament

An inward intuition, that inward witness on the inside of me, told me that the answer was in the Book — in the Bible. And that was the difference between life and death for me. Most folks would have given up and died at fifteen years of age. But I got into the Book. I slept with it in my arms; I hugged it to my bosom; I hung on to it in the night. Praise God for the Book, for the Word of God.

I found out that God not only dealt with sickness in the Old Testament, but He also dealt with sickness in the New Testament, under the New Covenant.

Now I had read James 5:14 and 15 in the New Testament many times before. But one day it dawned on me that James asked the question, "Is there any sick among you?" The fact that James asked that question infers that there shouldn't be any sick people within the Church. In other words, James was saying that healing belongs to the Church, to us.

Confession:

I love the Word of God, for in it are all the answers I need. In the Word of God, I find that health and healing are for the Church, which means health and healing are for me.

March 12   . . . he [Jesus] *is the mediator of a better covenant,*
which was established upon better promises.

— HEBREWS 8:6

We Have a Better Covenant

Under the Old Covenant, the Israelites were *servants* of God; they weren't *sons* of God, as we are today. The Bible says concerning us, *"Beloved, now are we the sons of God . . ."* (1 John 3:2). Since God made provision under the Old Covenant for His servants to be healed and well, He has surely made provision for us as His sons. Under the Old Covenant, God said, *". . . I will take sickness away from the midst of thee. There shall nothing cast their young, nor be barren, in thy land: the number of thy days I will fulfil"* (Exod. 23:25,26). He made provision for their healing, saying, *". . . I am the Lord that healeth thee"* (Exod. 15:26).

God made provision under the Old Covenant whereby Israel could live out their full length of time down here on earth without sickness and disease. Now since He made that provision under the Old Covenant, and since we have a better covenant established on better promises, I wonder if our covenant includes health and healing (Heb. 8:6)? The better covenant includes all that the Old Covenant had and more, or it's not better.

Know this Bible fact: God has dealt with sickness and disease under the Old Covenant as well as under the New Covenant. Isaiah 53:4 and 5, Matthew 8:17, and First Peter 2:24 deal with the disease and sickness problem that faces the Church and the world today. And within those scriptures is God's cure. According to First Peter 2:24, by His stripes, we were healed.

Confession:

I am a child of God, a son of God. Since God provided health and healing for His servants under the Old Covenant, He has surely provided health and healing for us — His sons — today!

That it might be fulfilled which was spoken by Esaias the prophet, saying, Himself took our infirmities, and bare our sicknesses.

— MATTHEW 8:17

March 13

The Foundation for Healing

Our faith is not founded on what man says, but on what God says. In Isaiah 53:4 and 5, Matthew 8:17, and First Peter 2:24, God says that it is His will that we be well. So don't question that healing is the will of God!

I've found again and again in my dealings with people that the majority of people are hung up on this issue of whether or not it's God's will to heal them. Even though they're seeking healing and want to be healed, they're not really sure if it's God's will. Something lurks in the back of their minds that was probably put there by religious teaching. Even though they may have seen others receive healing, they still aren't sure that healing is for them.

And, of course, the devil will do his best to talk them out of healing. If he can get them to listen to him, he can rob them of the blessings of God. From my experience of more than sixty-five years of dealing with people, I found that this is one of the main points that needs to be made with people. They must understand that healing is God's will.

I've seen it again and again. As soon as people start believing that it's God's will to heal them, they are released from wrong thinking, and in just a little while, they are healed. Until then, all the prayers and laying on of hands seem to be in vain. The biggest part of the battle is won when people start believing that it is the will of God that they be well.

Confession:

It is not God's will that I be sick. It is God's will that I be well and whole.

March 14   Lay hands suddenly on no man, neither be partaker
of other men's sins: keep thyself pure.

— 1 TIMOTHY 5:22

Don't Lay Hands on Others Suddenly

In writing to Timothy, Paul said, *"Lay hands suddenly on no man. . . ."* If you read the whole context of this verse, Paul is not talking about laying hands on someone to do the person harm; he's talking about the doctrine of the laying on of hands. He is instructing Timothy not to be quick to lay hands on people and pray for them. I believe it is important that people are ready to receive when hands are laid on them.

I remember a woman who brought her daughter to me to be healed. The daughter was facing major surgery, and the woman wanted me to pray for her. Well, I endeavor to keep my spirit open to the Spirit of God, so before the mother said anything, I knew on the inside of me that the daughter didn't believe in divine healing and was just coming to please her mother. So I said to the two of them, "Well, let's just sit down and talk a little bit first."

"Oh, no," the mother said. "I already told you. I got up early this morning and drove two hundred and forty miles. After you lay hands on my daughter and pray, I'm going to take her back home. I want to get back before our church service tonight."

"Well, I don't want to be mean or ugly about it," I said. "But if that's the way it is, why don't you just go ahead, load her up, and take her back. Your daughter doesn't believe in divine healing, so there's really no point in me praying for her under the present circumstances."

The woman looked sort of startled and said, "Well, if that's the way you feel about it."

I told her that it had nothing to do with how I felt about it, but I knew there was no use for me to pray for her daughter under those circumstances. So the woman and her daughter agreed to sit down and talk with me.

Confession:

I believe in divine healing and keep myself ready to receive when hands are laid on me. Therefore, no man will lay hands suddenly on me, because I am always ready to receive from God.

74

Lay hands suddenly on no man, neither be partaker of other men's sins: keep thyself pure.

— 1 TIMOTHY 5:22

Do You Believe in Divine Healing? ✗

As I sat down to talk with the mother and her daughter, I said to the daughter, "Do you believe in divine healing?"

"Well," she said, "To be honest with you, no, I don't. I didn't want to hurt Momma's feelings, so I thought I would just go ahead and have you lay hands on me."

"That's the reason I'm not going to pray for you," I said. "You understand that God can heal you though, don't you?"

"No, no," she said. "We don't preach healing in our church. But I have great confidence in my pastor, because he's a man of God. And if divine healing were so, he would have told me about it."

I replied, "I'm sure your pastor is a good man who loves the Lord with all his heart and is walking in all the light he has, but there was a time I didn't see some things in the Bible that I now know to be true. Let me ask you a question. What if the Bible said, 'Himself, Jesus, took your infirmity — this serious condition you're facing — and bare your sicknesses?' Would that mean that healing is for you?"

"Why certainly, it would," she said.

I told her to pick up the Bible that was on the table next to her and open it to Matthew 8:17. I never will forget it. The minute she read the scripture, she looked at the cover of the Bible and said, "Why, it's just like my Bible! It's a Scofield too."

Then she said, "Go ahead and lay your hands on me. I'll be healed." I laid my hands on her and she was healed.

Now I could have laid hands on her earlier, but she wouldn't have received. Then she would have gone off saying, "It isn't the will of God." She had to establish in her mind and in her spirit that healing is the will of God for her before she could receive her healing.

Confession: ✗

I establish in my mind and in my spirit that it is the will of God for me to be well and whole.

March 16

How God anointed Jesus of Nazareth with the Holy
Ghost and with power: who went about doing good,
and healing all that were oppressed of the devil; for
God was with him.

— ACTS 10:38

Settle the Issue

I have read about Rev. John Alexander Dowie, a Congregationalist pastor in Australia in the 1870s, when a bubonic plague came to Australia. People were dying like flies during that epidemic. Rev. Dowie had already buried forty-three members of his congregation, and had four more waiting to be buried.

While sitting at the desk in his study one day, he began to cry out to God. "Dear God, is my whole church going to die? Did You send this plague? Is this Your will? Are You going to call them all home?" He didn't know who was to blame for it. He had read in the Old Testament how plagues could sometimes be stayed. Could this plague be stayed? He wept for the members of his congregation.

The Spirit of God spoke one verse of Scripture to his heart: Acts 10:38. Rev. Dowie said, in effect, "Like a flash, I saw it! The plague didn't come from Heaven — there aren't any plagues in Heaven. It didn't come from God. Satan is the oppressor — Jesus is the Deliverer. From Genesis through Revelation, scriptures began to come to me. I saw that it is the will of God that people be healed and live their full length of time out down here below and die without sickness and disease."

Then Rev. Dowie said to God, "Help me preach this to my people. Help me teach them so that they can see it and walk in the light of it. Give me the wisdom to share it with them."

Confession:

Jesus is the Deliverer — Satan is the oppressor. Sickness and disease don't come from God; they come from Satan. Therefore, I choose to live my full length of time out down here on earth and die without sickness and disease!

*How God anointed Jesus of Nazareth with the Holy
Ghost and with power: who went about doing good,
and healing all that were oppressed of the devil; for
God was with him.*

— ACTS 10:38

Sickness Is the Work of the Devil

Right after Rev. Dowie heard from the Spirit of God concerning the bubonic plague, there was a knock on his door. Three young men burst into his study. One of the young men said to Rev. Dowie, "Come quickly, Mary is dying, and Momma wants you to come." Mary was a twelve-year-old girl who had the bubonic plague.

Rev. Dowie jumped from his desk, hatless and coatless, and ran down the street with the young men. He ran into the house, where the little girl lay on the bed in convulsions. That's the way people died with the bubonic plague; they died in convulsions with bloody froth running out their mouth.

The doctor said to Rev. Dowie, "In what mysterious ways God moves, His wonders to perform."

Rev. Dowie, having just received this new revelation from God, said, "Doctor, how dare you call that the work of my God! My God wouldn't kill a twelve-year-old girl! Sir, I'll have you know that's the work of the devil!"

Rev. Dowie said to the mother of the girl, "Why did you send for me?" She said, "To pray."

Not knowing exactly what words to say, Rev. Dowie laid his hands on the little girl and said, "Jesus is the Deliverer. Satan is the oppressor." Then he quoted Acts 10:38 as well as other scriptures that began to come to him. While he was praying, the convulsions ceased, the bloody froth ceased, and the little girl fell into a deep sleep. When Mary opened her eyes, she looked at her mother and said, "Momma, I feel so good." She was completely healed.

Confession:

According to Acts 10:38, sickness and disease come from the devil, the oppressor. Healing comes from Jesus, the Deliverer!

I, even I, am he that blotteth out thy transgressions for mine own sake, and will not remember thy sins.

— ISAIAH 43:25

God Doesn't Remember Your Mistakes

What could be holding up your healing? The devil may be telling you that because you made some mistakes, because you sinned, you're paying for it now. The devil is a liar. That's not so! When you confessed and repented of those things, Jesus forgave you. He doesn't remember that you ever did anything wrong.

When my son Ken was small, he sometimes wanted to act up in church. I would say to him, "Now I'm going to punish you if you do that again. When we get home, I'm going to spank you." Well, often, I would forget that I said that, so I never did punish him. For me to punish him, I would have had to have remembered that I said I would.

God said, *"I, even I, am he that blotteth out thy transgressions for mine own sake, and will not remember thy sins"* (Isa. 43:25). For God to punish you, He would have to remember your sins, but He doesn't remember them. That's the devil talking to you, telling you that you're paying for some wrong that you committed. So don't listen to him. God is not punishing you — He wants to deliver you. Healing belongs to you.

Confession:

When I asked God to forgive me, He forgave and forgot my transgressions and my iniquities. I am clean before Him because of the blood of Jesus Christ. Because I refuse to dwell on any past mistakes or sins, I receive healing now!

— SOLOMON 2:15

A Minor Adjustment ✗

The Bible says that the little foxes spoil the vines. So sometimes, we just need to make a little adjustment to receive our answer to prayer. Then we'll receive our healing.

I remember a person who was seeking healing. Now, he was saved and filled with the Holy Ghost. But if people were automatically healed because they were saved and filled with the Holy Ghost, then all Spirit-filled people would be healed.

As I was talking with this person seeking healing, suddenly, he said, "That's it! That's it right there!" I really didn't know what he was talking about. He wasn't asking any questions; we were just discussing the Bible. But, all of a sudden, this person saw where he had failed to make the prayer connection. So he made the connection and he got results.

If you aren't getting results, the problem is not with God. Too many times, people think, *Well, maybe God doesn't want me to have that.* If the Bible says that He wants you to have it and if He has provided it for you, then He wants you to have it!

Instead of taking the time to see where they're missing it, many people say, "Well, If God wanted me to have it, He would give it to me. I guess I'll just do without it." They are playing right into the hands of the devil, and as a result, they are defeated.

Confession: ✗

If God's Word says something is mine, I believe it's mine. God's Word says that healing is mine. Father God, show me any adjustments I need to make in my life in order to receive my healing.

March 20

*If ye abide in me, and my words abide in you, ye
shall ask what ye will, and it shall be done unto you.*

— JOHN 15:7

The Problem Is Not With God

Many years ago, when I was pastoring a church, I was praying about a certain thing. I was praying just like everyone else does — leaving it more up to God than me — and God just dropped the following illustration down into my heart:

One day after church, my wife discovers that the diamond out of the engagement ring I gave her is gone. She knows it was there before she left for church because she noticed it. The diamond must have fallen out somewhere between the parsonage and the church. What do I do? I search for it. I go over the ground carefully and, if necessary, get down on my knees. I divide every blade of grass, going over the area carefully, because I know it has to be there somewhere.

Then I heard something on the inside of me say, "Similarly, it's in 'this' area that you're missing it in prayer." Do you know what I did? Spiritually speaking, I got down on my knees. I said, "It's in this area." So I began looking in that area in my life where the Lord led me. I hadn't been looking very far when I said, "That's it right there! I found it! That's it!" And I never had to pray about that thing anymore. It just came into being. And I had been praying for days and weeks about the same thing.

The problem was not with God. Jesus said in John 15:7, *"If ye abide in me, and my words abide in you, ye shall ask what ye will, and it shall be done unto you."* You see, whether or not your prayers are heard and answered rests more with you than it does with God. If you want to always get answers to your prayers, abide in Him and let His words abide in you.

Confession:

I abide in Jesus and let His words abide in me; then I can ask what I will, and it shall be done unto me. This is how I receive answered prayers.

Ask, and it shall be given you; seek, and ye shall find; knock, and it shall be opened unto you.

— MATTHEW 7:7

Healing Doesn't Just 'Fall' on You

I remember a man who wrote us from the penitentiary in McAlester, Oklahoma. He was in the penitentiary because he killed somebody. He was not only a murderer, but was also a gambler and a thief. He said in his letter, "I've tried it all and haven't found satisfaction. I don't know if there is a God or not, but if there is, I want you to help me find Him." Well, we were able to help him find God.

Now we didn't write and tell him, "You've murdered people. You've been living in sin and immorality. You'll have to wait for Jesus to die for you to purchase your salvation." No! God had already purchased this man's salvation through Jesus' death, burial, and resurrection. His new birth was waiting; it was wrapped up with his name on it. God was just waiting for him to accept it.

Salvation didn't just drop on him while he was in the penitentiary. It belonged to him, but it didn't just drop on him like a ripe cherry off a tree. He had to want it, to seek it, to look for it.

The same thing is true regarding healing. Healing is not going to just drop on you, even though you're saved. You have to find out what belongs to you and take it. Healing belongs to you; it's yours for the taking.

Confession:

Healing is mine because God provided it for me. He gave it to me, so I take it now.

March 22

Neither by the blood of goats and calves, but by his [Jesus'] own blood he entered in once into the holy place, having obtained eternal redemption for us.

— HEBREWS 9:12

You Must Be in Position To Receive

Because healing was purchased for us, it belongs to everyone, but not every person is in position to receive his healing. Sometimes we have to move people into position to receive what already belongs to them.

You know, sometimes we don't have as much sense when it comes to spiritual things as we do natural things. That's why Jesus used natural things to explain spiritual things. Sometimes people have the idea that if something belongs to them spiritually, it's just going to automatically fall on them, even though things don't automatically fall on us in the natural.

I want you to know that salvation belongs to the meanest person in your hometown just as much as it does to you or me. But he hasn't accepted it, and he may not even know about it. Yet it still belongs to him! Jesus died for him just as much as He did for you. Jesus shed His blood for him and has already purchased his salvation. All he has to do is accept it. It's already done! Jesus entered into the heavenly Holy of Holies once and for all with His blood to obtain an eternal redemption for that person.

If salvation belongs to everyone, why doesn't it just fall on him? Well, it's either because he doesn't know about it or he knows about it, but hasn't accepted what's been provided for him. After we became Christians, did all of God's blessings automatically fall on us? No. We had to find out what belonged to us and then receive it.

Confession:

It is through the blood of Jesus that salvation has come to all men. And just as I received salvation, I now receive healing. I accept what Jesus has already provided for me!

For an angel went down at a certain season into the pool, and troubled the water: whosoever then first after the troubling of the water stepped in was made whole of whatsoever disease he had.

— JOHN 5:4

God Initiates Some Healings on His Own

There is a difference between God initiating healing and you initiating healing. In John chapter 5, the Bible tells us that there was a pool called Bethesda in Jerusalem. And around this pool were five porches full of the weak, sick, and maimed. They were all waiting for an angel to come down periodically and trouble the water. And then the first person in would be healed. Everyone else had to wait until the angel came down again.

God initiated that on His own. He didn't ask you or me whether He could or not. He didn't ask the Sanhedrin or anybody else whether He could or not, because He is God. God can do whatever He wants to do, and we know that whatever He does will not violate His Word, because if He violated His Word, He would be a liar — just as you would be a liar if you violated your word. But we know that God cannot lie (Num. 23:19).

Well, of course, healing doesn't violate God's Word, because the Word teaches us that He is a healing God. Sometimes I think that God just did things such as troubling the waters every so often to let people know that He was still alive and doing well. I don't know for certain, because the Bible doesn't say, but I think God was trying to get the people to start believing what He had already told them.

God does initiate some things on His own, such as in the example of His sending an angel down to that pool. The healing at the pool of Bethesda was a healing initiated by God. Man didn't ask Him to do it; He just did it.

Confession:

Some healings are initiated by God, but I can receive healing anytime through faith in God's Word. I can stand on the Word of God and receive my healing.

And straightway the fountain of her blood was dried up; and she felt in her body that she was healed of that plague.

— MARK 5:29

You Can Receive Healing Anytime

Healings may also be initiated by man. In Mark chapter 5, we have the account of the woman with the issue of blood, who initiated her own healing. Notice verse 27: *"When she had heard of Jesus, came in the press behind, and touched his garment."* This woman started the ball rolling by doing something.

She said, *". . . If I may touch but his clothes, I shall be whole"* (v. 28).

Jesus responded to her and said, *". . . Daughter, thy faith hath made thee whole; go in peace, and be whole of thy plague"* (v. 34).

You, too, can initiate your own healing by acting on God's Word. You don't have to sit around like those at the pool of Bethesda and wait for God to initiate something. No, you can receive healing from God at any time by acting on His Word.

Confession:

I can reach out in faith and receive healing for myself, just like the woman with the issue of blood did.

For an angel went down at a certain season into the pool, and troubled the water: whosoever then first after the troubling of the water stepped in was made whole of whatsoever disease he had.

— JOHN 5:4

God Does Some Things as a Sign

I was preaching down in east Texas one time, and just as I closed my sermon, the word of the Lord came unto me, saying, "There's a sinner man standing outside this building, looking at you through those open doors. He has a double hernia. Call him in here and lay your hands on him, and the double hernia will disappear instantly."

Well, I just repeated what I had heard and that fellow came in. After I laid hands on him, some of the men took him into the back room and examined him, but they couldn't find the hernia. It had disappeared!

The next day, the pastor said, "Brother Hagin, nearly every man in this community knows this fellow, because he is the biggest landowner in this county. And if the governor of this state is running for re-election and wants to carry this county, he has to go through this man to get it. Since he's a very prominent citizen, everyone knows that this man has been operated on twice for a hernia."

You see, God does some things as a sign, such as in this situation and in sending that angel down to the pool of Bethesda. But I can't guarantee that He is going to do it for you or me. But, remember, you can initiate healing yourself by getting into the Word of God, finding out what God says, and then acting on His Word.

Confession:

I will get into the Word of God and find out for myself what God says. Then I will act on His Word, because acting on God's Word always produces results.

March 26

But all these worketh that one and the selfsame Spirit, dividing to every man severally as he will.

— 1 CORINTHIANS 12:11

As the Spirit Wills

The gifts of the Spirit are listed in First Corinthians 12. These gifts belong to the Church, and are manifested through individuals as the Spirit wills, not as man wills. I have had them manifest through me at times, and at other times, I would try to manifest these gifts myself. I would push every button, pull every lever, say everything I had said before, but nothing would happen. Why? Because the Spirit and the anointing weren't present to manifest these gifts.

First Corinthians 12:8 says, *"For to one is given by the Spirit. . . ."* No man controls the manifestation of the gifts of the Spirit; the manifestation is given *as the Spirit wills.*

I have been in meetings where people ministered with the word of knowledge or the gifts of healing. The minister would only call out four or five people, because he can't go beyond what the Lord says to him.

When I ministered to that sinner man in east Texas, the Lord initiated that. Well, why didn't the Lord initiate something else there to minister to others by a gift of the Spirit? I don't know; I'm not God. I don't know everything, but I'm going to stay open to Him and do my best to listen to Him.

I love it when the manifestation of the gifts of the Spirit operates through me. If it were up to me, I would manifest them more frequently. And that's just the reason God doesn't leave the manifestations up to us — we would be like kids with little red wagons! All we'd want to do is run up and down in front of the house, pulling our wagon and showing off. No, the manifestation of the gifts is as God wills, not as we will.

But if God doesn't initiate something on His own, I'm going to initiate something by telling people what the Word of God says. I can get them to initiate healing by their faith, because healing belongs to them.

Confession:

I'm so glad that healing belongs to me. I'm so glad that I can initiate healing through faith by acting on God's Word.

86

That your faith should not stand in the wisdom of men, but in the power of God.

— 1 CORINTHIANS 2:5

Divine Healing

Dr. Lilian B. Yeomans was a medical doctor who was born and raised in Canada and then moved to the United States. Her mother and father were doctors, and her grandfather had been a medical doctor too.

In her mid-forties, Dr. Yeomans practiced medicine in a large New York hospital. She began to take stimulants and narcotics to energize her and, eventually, became a dope addict. Other complications set in, and medical science of the day gave her up to die.

An older gentleman told her about divine healing. She knew something about medical healing, but she had never heard about divine healing. This older gentleman asked her if she wanted him to pray with her.

She said, "I'd better pray myself first, because I've gotten away from God. I knew God when I was a little girl, but I haven't known Him for years." She spent part of the night in prayer and got back on good speaking terms with the Lord. Then the older gentleman prayed for her, and she was healed by divine power.

Dr. Yeomans then quit her medical practice and spent the rest of her life practicing, preaching, and teaching divine healing. She also became an ordained Assemblies of God evangelist and minister.

Confession:

I believe in divine healing. My faith is in the power of God and I believe that the healing power is at work in my body now, effecting a healing and a cure.

March 28

He sent his word, and healed them, and delivered them from their destructions.

— PSALM 107:20

God Sent His Word To Heal You

Dr. Yeomans and her sister were both doctors and had a beautiful home in southern California — actually a two-story mansion — which they turned into a "faith home."

They would take patients into their home to get them healed by divine power, not by medicine. They could only handle four patients at a time because Dr. Yeomans traveled and taught most of the time. Her sister, Amy Yeomans, was the one who took care of the patients.

What did they do to get people healed? They simply taught them from the Word of God. It wasn't the Holy Ghost initiating anything, such as a gift of the Spirit (1 Cor. 12:9-11). The people were healed by initiating their own healing on the basis of their faith in the Word of God.

In Dr. Yeomans' day, tuberculosis was the number-two killer in America. As soon as a patient was healed, the next applicant would be notified to come in as a "patient" — if he or she hadn't already died, because these people were all terminal cases.

One particular woman who had tuberculosis was brought in and carried to an upstairs bedroom. Dr. Yeomans sat down by her bedside and said to her, "Just fold your hands and close your eyes and lie there. Relax and listen." Then she read to her from the Bible.

Confession:

God sent His Word to heal me. His Word is life to me and health and healing to all my flesh.

Christ hath redeemed us from the curse of the law,
being made a curse for us: for it is written, Cursed is
every one that hangeth on a tree.

— GALATIANS 3:13

You Are Redeemed From the Curse of the Law

Dr. Yeomans had every scripture on the subject of divine healing marked in her Bible. For two hours, she sat next to this woman who had tuberculosis and read those healing scriptures to her. Then at the end, she read Deuteronomy chapter 28 and Galatians chapter 3. She read them over and over again. Then she just read Deuteronomy 28:61 and Galatians 3:13.

Dr. Yeomans told the woman, "Every waking moment, say, 'According to Deuteronomy 28:61, sickness and disease is a curse of the Law. Tuberculosis is a curse of the Law. But according to Galatians 3:13, Christ has redeemed me from the curse of the Law. Therefore, I no longer have TB.'"

The woman said, "But I don't understand it."

Dr. Yeomans said, "That's all right. You just say what I told you to say."

The woman began saying, "According to Deuteronomy 28:61, TB is a curse of the law. But according to Galatians 3:13, Christ has redeemed me from the curse of the law. Therefore, I no longer have TB."

Confession:

According to Deuteronomy 28:61, _____ (fill in the particular sickness
or disease) is a curse of the Law. But according to Galatians 3:13, Christ has
redeemed me from the curse of the Law. Therefore, I no longer have
_____.

March 30

. . . he shall have whatsoever he saith.

— MARK 11:23

The Never-Failing Remedy of God's Word

The next morning, Dr. Yeomans and her sister fed their patients breakfast. Then Dr. Yeomans asked this particular woman if she had been saying what she told her to say. She said, "Oh, it seemed like I didn't sleep but ten minutes last night. I must have said it ten thousand times, but it doesn't mean a thing in the world to me. I don't understand it."

Dr. Yeomans said, "That's all right, honey. You just keep saying it over and over again, every waking moment."

If people would work at receiving divine healing like they ought to, it would work for them. But so many times, they only do it half-heartedly and then go on thinking about something else. In that case, it won't work for them. They have to get down to business.

Well, on the third day, Dr. Yeomans went to this woman's room again and read scriptures on the subject of healing to her for a solid hour. Then Dr. Yeomans said, "Are you still saying what I told you to say?"

She said, "Oh, yes, but it still doesn't mean a thing in the world to me. I'm not getting anything out of it." Dr. Yeomans again told her to just keep saying it.

At about 11:00 a.m. that same day, Dr. Yeomans and her sister were downstairs washing the breakfast dishes when they heard somebody upstairs shouting. They heard running footsteps, so they rushed out into the hall. And there was the woman who had come in only two days before. She was rushing down the stairway, yelling, "Dr. Yeomans, did you know I no longer have TB?"

"Yes," she said. "I've been trying to tell you that for three days."

You see, it got down in her spirit. That's when God's Word works for you. God's Word never fails. That woman initiated healing for herself.

Confession:

I can initiate healing for myself by putting my faith in the Word of God. God's Word says that I have been redeemed from all manner of sickness and disease.

Now all these things happened unto them for ensamples [examples]: and they are written for our admonition, upon whom the ends of the world are come.

March 31

— 1 CORINTHIANS 10:11

Possess the Land!

The Bible teaches us that what happened to those in the Old Testament happened as examples for us. For example, God delivered Israel out of Egypt, which symbolizes the world, and led them into Canaan's land. What does Canaan's land symbolize?

In the early years, I was taught that Canaan's land was a type or foreshadowing of Heaven. But how could Canaan's land ever symbolize Heaven since there aren't going to be any battles or enemies in Heaven? There are no giants there who are against us, no cities to take, and no battles to fight in Heaven!

I believe that Canaan's land is a type of the baptism in the Holy Ghost and of our rights and privileges in Christ Jesus, including divine healing.

God said to Israel, "I give you the land" (Joshua 1:2), and when they crossed over Jordan into Canaan's land, God said, "Every place that the sole of your foot treads shall be yours" (Joshua 1:3). Although God said that He had given the land to them, He also said they had to possess it by walking through it and taking it.

In the same way, God has given us as Christians the land — the blessing of God — but we have to possess it. Although He has provided healing for us, we must possess it.

You can read the Bible and find out what is legally yours — what actually belongs to you — but until you accept it, until you possess it, it will never become yours to enjoy. So first, read the Bible to find out what is legally yours. Then possess those things so that they become a vital part of your life.

Confession:

I know that healing belongs to me because Jesus paid for my healing nearly two thousand years ago. As I go in and possess the land, I receive the healing that Jesus provided for me.

91

He sent his word, and healed them, and delivered them from their destructions.

— PSALM 107:20

Jesus Is the Word of God

Under the Old Testament, the Word that God sent was spoken through the prophets. Under the New Testament, the Word He sent was the Lord Jesus Christ. John's Gospel says, *"In the beginning was the Word, and the Word was with God, and the Word was God. The same was in the beginning with God. All things were made by him; and without him was not any thing made that was made"* (John 1:1-3). Then verse 14 says, *"And the Word was made flesh, and dwelt among us. . . ."* The Lord Jesus Christ is called "The Word."

So how did God send His Word to heal you? He sent Jesus to take your infirmities and bear your sicknesses (Matt. 8:17). In the mind of God, you're already healed. First Peter 2:24 says, *". . . by whose stripes ye WERE healed."*

God sent His Word and healed you. If you need healing, I dare you to hold fast to that confession and not say anything to the contrary. Don't say, "Yeah, but I'm hurting." I guarantee you that if you'll hold fast to that one confession and not negate it by saying, "But I still have this and I still have that," you'll be all right. Your symptoms will disappear.

Now it won't work if you try it for a day or two. God's Word works by acting on it confidently and consistently. God's Word works by being a doer of it. Act like God's Word is so, because it is! Since He sent His Word and healed you, count it as done in your life and act like it!

Confession:

God sent His Word and healed me. Therefore, I no longer have _____ *(fill in the particular sickness or disease).* **He sent His Word and healed me!**

Who his own self bare our sins in his own body on the tree, that we, being dead to sins, should live unto righteousness: by whose stripes ye were healed.

— 1 PETER 2:24

The *Whole* Bible Is True

Church people everywhere believe that Jesus bore their sins. But many of them don't believe that He bore their sicknesses as well. The Bible says that Jesus bore our sins *and* our sicknesses. Matthew 8:17 says, *"That it might be fulfilled which was spoken by Esaias the prophet, saying, Himself took our infirmities, and BARE OUR SICKNESSES."* First Peter 2:24 says, *"Who his own self BARE OUR SINS in his own body on the tree, that we, being dead to sins, should live unto righteousness: by whose stripes ye were healed."* Jesus not only bore our sins, He also bore our sicknesses. That settles it!

Why look for a way around this great truth? Yet so many people do. But if Matthew 8:17 and First Peter 2:24 are lies, then the whole Bible is a lie. And if the Bible is a lie, then there is no God, and Jesus Christ is not the Son of God. He would be a fraud and a fake. Then, of course, the New Testament would not be true. And the Old Testament would be a fable. There would be no God, no Heaven, and no hell.

But, hallelujah, there is a God! And the Lord Jesus Christ is the Son of God! And the Old Testament is not a fable; it's true. And the New Testament is true. The *whole* Bible is true! Jesus not only bore our sins, He also took our infirmities and bore our sicknesses.

Confession:

Jesus bore my sins. It is the will of God for me to be saved and delivered from sin. Jesus also bore my sicknesses. Therefore, it is the will of God that I be healed and delivered from sickness!

There is therefore now no condemnation to them which are in Christ Jesus, who walk not after the flesh, but after the Spirit.

— ROMANS 8:1

Resist Sickness Just as You Resist Condemnation

Sickness doesn't have any right to impose itself upon us. And Satan, who is the author of sickness and disease, doesn't have any right to put sickness and disease on us. Why? Because we're free! And when symptoms of sickness or disease come, all we need to do is treat them exactly the same as we would treat our old sins. It's the easiest thing in the world to do.

You see, the devil may try to put you under condemnation by reminding you of your past sins. But you can say, "Satan, there is therefore now no condemnation to me, for I am in Christ Jesus." Jesus has dealt with those sins and put them away. And you can say to Satan, "You can't get them. Jesus put those sins away. He hid them in the depths of the sea – in the sea of forgetfulness."

God said, *"I, even I, am he that blotteth out thy transgressions for mine own sake, and will not remember thy sins"* (Isa. 43:25). The devil has brought pictures to my mind of things I've done in the past. He's said, "Look at what you did." And I've said to him, "Ha, ha, Mr. Devil. I sure did. You're right. But God forgave me and blotted them all out and put them as far away from me as the east is from the west" (Ps. 103:12).

But if you don't know the truth — that once you ask for forgiveness, you are cleansed from all sin — the devil will keep bringing pictures of your past mistakes, and it will rob you of faith and hold you under condemnation. But when you know the truth, you can laugh at the devil.

Confession:

Father, I resist symptoms of sickness and disease just as I resist condemnation. I know that sickness, disease, and condemnation all come from the devil. And I resist what comes from him and receive Your health, healing, and freedom today!

*He that committeth sin is of the devil; for the devil
sinneth from the beginning. For this purpose the Son
of God was manifested, that he might destroy the
works of the devil.*

— 1 JOHN 3:8

Healing Throughout the Bible

The works of the devil include sin and sickness. Jesus was manifested that
He might destroy the works of the devil. Jesus went about doing good and
healing all who were oppressed of the devil (Acts 10:38). Sickness does not
come from God. Sickness does not come from Heaven. There isn't any sickness
up there. No, sickness comes from the devil.

I remember a Baptist minister saying to me once, "You know, Brother
Hagin, I just read the New Testament through for the second time. I'm saved
and filled with the Holy Ghost. God is blessing me. I believe in healing and I
know God heals. I pray for the sick. But I can't see healing in the Bible like you
do. I just read it through twice and I can't see it."

I said to him, "Well, you know, it doesn't have to say *h-e-a-l-i-n-g*. I see
physical healing in almost every page of the Bible. For instance, in what we call
the Lord's Prayer, Jesus said, *'After this manner therefore pray ye: Our Father
which art in heaven, Hallowed be thy name. Thy kingdom come. Thy will be
done in earth, as it is in heaven'* [Matt. 6:9,10]. I see healing right there because
there isn't any sickness in Heaven. And Jesus said for us to pray that His will be
done on earth as it is in Heaven. If you're sick, you'd have to get healed for His
will to be done."

This Baptist minister decided to read the New Testament for the third
time. Afterward, he told me that he began to see healing in every chapter.
Praise God! It's in there!

Confession:

*Sickness doesn't come from Heaven. There isn't any sickness up there.
Healing comes from Heaven. And healing belongs to me!*

. . . And it came to pass, that, AS THEY WENT, they were cleansed.

— LUKE 17:14

Healing Is Not Always Instantaneous

Some people say, "When Jesus healed people, He always healed them instantly." Well, let's look and see if He did. The Bible says that the ten lepers were healed *as they went*. People are healed today just as they were in Bible days. Some of them are healed instantly. But some are healed *as they go*.

Years ago, a woman wrote me a letter after a meeting I held in Houston, Texas, at Brother John Osteen's church. She wrote, "Brother Hagin, I was carried to the meeting in Houston for you to lay hands on me and pray. I'd had two strokes and my left side was paralyzed. I couldn't walk. I was carried into the healing line. The doctor said that if I had a third stroke, it would probably kill me. He said that I could have one at any time.

"You laid hands on me and the power of God came on me. I fell on the floor under the power and lay there for a while. Then I began to move a little and make an effort to get up. I was helped to my feet, but I couldn't walk. I wasn't any better. Then I was carried out of the building."

She continued, "Some folks might have thought, *Well, that poor dear woman didn't get anything, because I saw her being carried in and carried out.* I was placed in the back seat of the car. We got about two blocks away from the church when, suddenly, there was a warm glow that went through the left side of my body. Then I had feeling in my left side and was all right."

You see, the power of God was administered to her at the church. The healing, or the manifestation, became evident later on. She was healed *as she went*.

Confession:

I keep the switch of faith turned on. As I go about my day, the healing power of God is working in my body to effect a healing and a cure.

Then enquired he of them the hour when he began
to amend. And they said unto him, Yesterday at the
seventh hour the fever left him.

— JOHN 4:52

You Can Get Better!

This is another instance of healing in Jesus' ministry. Notice that the healing wasn't instantaneous. The Bible says that the nobleman's son began to amend from that hour — at the same hour Jesus said, "Thy son liveth" (v. 53). What does that mean? That means he began to get better and better until, finally, he was all right.

On one occasion, I was preaching in an Assembly of God church in California. A woman was brought in an ambulance to the church auditorium. I never saw so much medicine and equipment keeping one person alive. She couldn't breathe without a machine. And a special nurse was with her all the time.

It took me a minute to find a place to lay hands on her, because she was nearly encased with various medical paraphernalia. I laid hands on her and prayed. I knew the power of God went into her. And I asked the nurse, "Can she hear?"

She said, "Yes, she can hear and understand what you say, but she can't talk."

So I said to her, "The healing power of God was administered to your body. I felt it flow out of my hands into your body. It will heal you. Believe that." Then I went on to pray for someone else.

They rolled her out. She didn't look any better. But from the moment the healing power of God was administered to her, she began to amend. Every day, she kept improving. And after three days, she was taken off all the equipment and could breathe without it. She was up and about, walking around the house!

Confession:

Every day I get better and better. Every day the healing power of God is
working in my body. Every day I am able to do more.

. . . they shall lay hands on the sick, and they shall recover.

— MARK 16:18

You Will Recover

Does this scripture in Mark say that all people who are prayed for will instantly get well? No. It says that they shall recover. As a Baptist minister, before I received the baptism in the Holy Ghost or ever spoke with tongues, I prayed for a woman in the hospital who was scheduled to have major surgery. The doctors said they didn't know whether or not she would make it.

I remember that as I was walking into the hospital, the Lord seemed to say to my spirit, "They'll lay hands on the sick and they shall recover. Just give her that verse and tell her she will recover."

This woman had not been taught about healing. She had just heard that I prayed for the sick. So she wanted me to come and pray for her. I simply read the verse of Scripture to her from my New Testament. Then I let her read it.

Then I said, "I'm going to lay hands on you and pray, and you will recover."

The doctors operated on her and said afterward, "We operate on people like this all the time. We've never seen anybody come out of it like she did." Now nature could have healed her up quickly enough, but there was something working here beyond nature.

She said to me afterward, "Why, I knew all the time that I would recover, because that verse says, 'You shall recover.' When the doctors said, 'You might not make it,' I just kept telling them, 'Oh, yes, I am going to recover.'" And she did.

Confession:

I am going to recover because Mark 16:18 says, ". . . they shall lay hands on the sick, and they shall recover."

The Laying On of Hands To Heal

There are many methods of healing. The laying on of hands is only one of them. When it comes to the laying on of hands to heal, there are some things to remember. One can be especially anointed as Jesus was. He was anointed with the Holy Ghost and power (Acts 10:38). Jesus can give a person a special anointing to minister to the sick.

Jesus appeared to me in a vision in 1952 in Rockwall, Texas, and laid the finger of His right hand in the palm of each one of my hands. He said, "I have called thee and have anointed thee. I have given thee a special anointing to minister to the sick. However, it won't work unless you tell people exactly what I told you. If they'll believe it and receive it, that power will flow from your hands into their bodies and heal them." Ministering with a special anointing by the laying on of hands is one way to minister.

However, any believer can lay hands on the sick in faith and it will work. I did that as a Baptist. And about halfway between the two — between laying hands on people in faith and laying hands on people with a special anointing — Spirit-filled believers charged with the power of God can lay hands on people. If any Spirit-filled believer will keep praying and wait on God long enough, he will become charged with that power and feel it flow out of him.

Confession:

According to the Bible, believers can lay hands on the sick and they shall recover. I am a believer. I can lay hands on the sick and they shall recover.

April 9

And [Jesus] said unto him, Go, wash in the pool of Siloam, (which is by interpretation, Sent.) He went his way therefore, and washed, and came seeing.

— JOHN 9:7

Some Instant Manifestations

The previous verse says, *"When he had thus spoken, he spat on the ground, and made clay of the spittle, and he anointed the eyes of the blind man with the clay"* (John 9:6). Jesus spat on the ground and made clay out of His "spittle" or saliva. He then rubbed it into the blind man's eyes and said, "Go wash it off in the pool of Siloam." The blind man obeyed and came out seeing!

Was this blind man healed instantly — was he healed right on the spot when Jesus ministered to him? No. Let me ask you another question. Would this blind man have been healed if he had not done what Jesus told him to do? No.

This blind man "went his way" — he went to the pool of Siloam as Jesus instructed — washed, and came out seeing. That infers that if he had *not* gone his way and washed, he would not have been cured. What if he had said, "Well, you know, there's an angel every now and then who troubles the water over at the pool of Bethesda. Why not go over there?" Would he have been healed? No.

I was holding a meeting one time, and a blind woman was sitting right in front of the pulpit. I laid hands on her, the power of God came upon her, and she fell on the floor under the power of God. When she got up, her face was shining like a new moon, like a neon sign at night! And she was yelling, "I can see! I can see!" She was instantly healed. I learned later that she had been totally blind for three or four years.

We should have some instant healings like this, because folks had them in the Early Church, as recorded in the New Testament. But, on the other hand, often if a person doesn't receive an instant manifestation, he might think that God was not in his laying-on-of-hands experience. But that's not so. He needs to "go his way" in obedience to the Lord; he needs to keep the switch of faith turned on.

Confession:

I choose to believe what the Bible says. Some people are healed instantly, and others are healed gradually. But, thank God, healing is for me!

Hold Fast to Your Confession

The same night that the blind woman was healed in my meeting, there was a young couple that brought their little boy to be healed. He had two clubbed feet. I'd never seen another child afflicted that way; I've seen children with one clubbed foot, but never two.

With the same anointing that I had when I laid hands on the blind woman, I laid hands on this little boy. I held those little feet in my hands. And I felt the power of God go into his feet. I opened my hands and looked at them, and they looked just as crippled as they had before I prayed.

I told the young couple, "Now I know that the blind woman received an instant healing. To encourage you, I can tell you what the Bible says and what God has said to me. I can't go beyond that. When Jesus appeared to me in a vision and laid the finger of His right hand in the palm of each one of my hands, He said to me, 'When you feel that power leave your hands and go into them, you'll know they're healed.' That means, as far as God is concerned, it's done! Keep believing and saying, 'The healing power of God was administered to my child's body and is working in him to heal him.'"

That was on a Thursday night. We closed the meeting that night and left. Some months later, we were holding a seminar in Tulsa, and this young couple was there. They came to the platform and asked the pastor if they could show the congregation their child's normal feet. Their testimony was that they did just what I told them to do. They held fast to their confession, and their child's feet were made just as perfect as they could be.

Confession:

I hold fast to my confession of faith. The power of God is working in me now to effect a healing and a cure.

. . . greater is he that is in you, than he that is in the world.

— 1 JOHN 4:4

Don't Try To Figure God Out

Many people jump over into the arena of reason and try to figure God out. For example, they'll think, *Why did God heal the blind woman instantly and not the little boy? I don't understand that.* They'll sit around and try to figure it out in their head and miss their own healing.

Don't ever try to figure God out. We can't figure Him out in our little peanut brain! We should just go ahead and rejoice in what He does do, whether it's instantaneous or over a period of time. The problem is not with God. In the case of the blind woman and the little boy, one of them probably took hold of healing instantly, and the other probably took hold of it gradually.

You see, oftentimes, the healing power of God is administered to a person, and the healing process becomes evident later on. Healing is by degrees and it is based on two conditions. First, it is based on the degree of healing power administered. Second, it is based on the degree of faith that gives action to the healing power administered.

Sometimes the healing power of God is administered to a person to such a degree that the person is supernaturally charged with the power of God, just as a person might be charged with electricity. And yet no real or final healing takes place until something happens that releases the faith of the individual.

Spirit-filled believers should be conscious of the healing power of God and the life of God that is in them (*see* First John 4:4). They can do it if they'll wait on God, meditate on His Word, and pray.

Confession:

The life of God is in me. Greater is He that is in me than he that is in the world!

Is any sick among you? let him call for the elders of the church; and let them pray over him, anointing him with oil in the name of the Lord.

— JAMES 5:14

Praying the Power Down

My wife and I had just moved into the parsonage of a Full Gospel church in the blackland of northcentral Texas. There was a knock on the door. I went to the door and a little cotton-headed — blond-haired — boy stood there. He said, "Momma wants you to come and pray for her. She's sick."

Well, I didn't recognize him. So I said, "Who is Momma?" He told me and I recognized the name. She was one of my Sunday school teachers. I said, "Son, you stand right there. I'll put on my tie and coat, and you can show me to your house." I was a stranger in town and I didn't know my way around. So he took me to his house.

I had a little bottle of olive oil in my pocket that I used to anoint people when I prayed for them. I took it out and anointed the woman's forehead. I knelt by the bed and prayed. Then I said, "In Jesus' Name. Amen," and I got up and started to go.

She stopped me, saying, "Brother B. [the former pastor of this Full Gospel church] always prayed until the power fell."

Well, I was new in Full Gospel circles. So I thought, *Maybe that's the way they do it.* So I got back down on my knees. I'd never prayed the power down before. I didn't even know you could pray it down. After about an hour and a half, the power of God fell on us. The whole room was energized with the power of God. The woman shook just like someone who was holding an electrical wire. I'd prayed down the power. So I got up and went home.

Confession:

It is scriptural for someone to anoint me with oil and pray the prayer of faith. James 5:15 says, "And the prayer of faith shall save the sick, and the Lord shall raise him up. . . ."

April 13

Is any sick among you? let him call for the elders of the church; and let them pray over him, anointing him with oil in the name of the Lord.

— JAMES 5:14

Put Your Faith in the Word First

The same day that I prayed for that woman, about the middle of the afternoon, there was another knock on my door. I went to the door and there stood that "cotton-headed" boy. He said, "Momma wants you to come and pray for her."

I said, "I thought she got healed this morning."

He said, "Well, she did, but she's hurting worse now."

I went back down to her house and prayed another hour and a half until I prayed the power down. I tried to get by just by anointing her with oil and laying hands on her, praying the prayer of faith, but she didn't believe. Her faith wasn't in God's Word. It was in the power. Well, the power of God certainly has something to do with healing, but a person's faith must be in the Word first.

This "praying the power down" for Momma went on and on — for four years! At least once a week for four years, I went to her home and prayed for her. But she never got any lasting results.

Confession:

When I put my faith in the Word of God first, I will see results. I will be healed!

Ask in Jesus' Name

One day I was at home in the parsonage getting ready for church. I heard my wife let someone in. Without even looking up, I knew who it was. It was that little cotton-headed boy. He came back to where I was in the house and said, "Momma wants you to come and pray for her."

Before I could say, "Will it be all right to wait until after church to come and pray for her?" the boy said, "She said to come over before church. She's hurting awfully bad!"

I looked at my watch. I didn't have much time. I had an automobile, but I thought it would be faster to run down the back alley. There was an old path down there. So I ran to her home, knocked on the door, and she said, "Come in."

By the time I got the door open, I had that little bottle of oil out of my pocket. There's no telling how many times I had anointed her — hundreds upon hundreds of times! I laid my hand on her forehead and anointed her with oil. I said, "God, heal this woman now in the Name of Jesus. You said to ask in Jesus' Name and You'd do it, so You've done it. Amen." I said those exact words real fast, because I was in a hurry. By the time I said, "Amen," I was heading for the door. As soon as I got the door open, she started to say something. What I said next surprised even me and changed everything for that dear woman.

Confession:

I ask in Jesus' Name. Jesus said that if I ask anything in His Name, He would do it.

April 15

And the prayer of faith shall save the sick, and the Lord shall raise him up; and if he have committed sins, they shall be forgiven him.

— JAMES 5:15

Release Your Faith

As this dear woman started to speak, I interrupted her, saying, "Wait a minute, sister; don't say a word." I realized later on that I was inspired by the Spirit of God to say what I did. I said, "I know you're hurting worse than you were when I came through this door a few seconds ago. [I don't know how I knew that. It surprised me that I said it.] But Jesus said, 'If you ask anything in My Name, I'll do it.' So He has done it. The next time I see you, you'll tell me it's so. Goodbye."

I hurried out, slamming the door behind me. I ran up the alley, across the street, and went in the side door of the church. I looked at my watch and it was exactly time to start church. I went to the pulpit and started the service. I said, "Let's have three testimonies before we begin the message." Three people stood up. Later, just as the third one was testifying, the front doors of the church burst open. This woman I had just prayed for came walking in! She walked down the aisle, picked up the microphone, and said, "Brother Hagin, it was just like you said. You hadn't been gone ten minutes when every pain left. I just got up and came to church."

And she was healed from then on. That chronic condition she'd had for four years was gone. The power of God had often come upon her and shook her until her bed rattled, but no real and final healing took place until something happened that released her faith.

Confession:

I release my faith. I believe God's Word, and I put it first place in my life.

. . . and the power of the Lord was present to heal them.

— LUKE 5:17

Healed by the Power of God

Back in the early 1950s, the Salk vaccine had just been discovered, and polio was still an epidemic. I was preaching in Hugo, Oklahoma, at a sectional camp meeting for the Assemblies of God organization. They put up a tent in the city park of Hugo and invited me to speak.

A woman brought her little boy who couldn't walk. He was almost five years old. When he was fourteen months old, he had contracted polio. Both of his legs were flopping around. When she would get tired of holding him, she'd hold him underneath her arm like a sack of flour. Those little legs were flopping just like a rag doll.

I was sitting in a chair on the platform as I laid hands on folks. In those days, that's the way I conducted my healing lines in larger meetings. I took that child from her and set him on my lap. I could feel the power of God go out of me into that child. I put him down, and he ran up and down the platform! He was instantly healed! Praise God! At sixteen years of age, he was a quarterback on his high school football team.

Confession:

God's power is present to heal. When I hook my faith up with the power of God, I will see results!

*Then touched he their eyes, saying, According to
your faith be it unto you.*

— MATTHEW 9:29

According to Your Faith

Just a few months after that boy was healed, we were in Beaumont, Texas, in the Lamar Assembly of God Church. A woman came up to the platform carrying her eight- or nine-year-old daughter, because she couldn't walk. She was a large-sized girl for her age. When I set her on my lap, her left leg just stood straight out; it was stiff. She had had polio when she was about four or five years old, and afterward, she had never walked another step.

I laid hands on her left leg, which was four or five inches shorter than her other leg and was encased in braces. It had never grown. As I laid my hand on the shorter leg, I knew the power of God went into it. I could feel it. I said to the mother of this girl, "All I know to do is tell you that Jesus told me, 'When you feel that power go into them, you'll know they're healed.' And I felt that power go into her."

Now I never tell anyone what to do unless the Lord tells me. When Jesus touched the two blind men's eyes in Matthew chapter 9, He said, "According to your faith, be it done unto you." So I'm not going to tell anyone to take his or her braces off unless I'm inspired by the Lord to do so. I'm not going to tell anyone to get out of a wheelchair unless I'm inspired by the Spirit of God to do so. Sometimes I have and they have gotten up. Sometimes I haven't told them anything, and they have still gotten up. We've had it happen!

I handed the girl back to her mother. She took her in her arms. She looked just the same. They went back and sat down. After I finished the healing line, we finished the service and dismissed everyone.

Confession:

It is according to my faith that I receive from God. I choose to walk by faith and not by sight.

And straightway the father of the child cried out, and said with tears, Lord, I believe; help thou mine unbelief.

— MARK 9:24

'Lord, Help My Unbelief'

The next morning, while I was getting ready for the morning service, I heard running footsteps. I heard the pastor's voice calling me. He came into the house and said, "Brother Hagin, that woman who was at last night's meeting with her little girl is at the church now, and her little girl is perfectly healed. The girl doesn't have any braces, and her left leg has grown out as long as the other one."

The mother shared, "By the time we got home, it was late and the child was asleep. I put her to bed. When I got up this morning and got my husband off to work, she was still asleep. As my custom is, I woke her up at eight o'clock to give her a bath, because she's helpless. I picked her up in her braces and carried her into the bathroom. I pulled off her braces. She wasn't any better.

"I put her in the bathtub and got down on my knees to bathe her. I said, 'Oh, Lord, why didn't You heal my baby?' Something on the inside of me said, 'Do you believe that Brother Hagin stood right there on the platform and lied? Do you believe he lied when he said that he felt that power go into this child and into that leg?'"

You see, she wasn't keeping the switch of faith turned on. But she changed. She said, "Lord, forgive me for my unbelief. I believe that Brother Hagin is a man of God. I believe that he told the truth when he said that Jesus appeared to him and placed the finger of His right hand upon each one of his hands and told him to tell people that the healing power is in his hands. I believe he told the truth when he said he felt that power go into my child's body. I believe that power is working in my child now to heal her."

When she said that, she heard something popping, like dry sticks breaking. She looked down in the bathtub, and that left leg straightened out right in front of her eyes! It grew to the same size as the other leg. She brought her daughter before the whole church and they saw that it was true. The girl was up and walking, and both legs were normal!

Confession:

I thank You, Father God, that Your healing power is working in my body right now. I thank You that I am well and healthy and whole.

109

April 19

Your Faith Can Make You Whole

Let's look at the woman with the issue of blood in Mark chapter 5.

MARK 5:25-34

25   And a certain woman, which had an issue of blood twelve years,

26   And had suffered many things of many physicians, and had spent all that she had, and was nothing bettered, but rather grew worse,

27   When she had heard of Jesus, came in the press behind, and touched his garment.

28   For she said, If I may touch but his clothes, I shall be whole.

29   And straightway the fountain of her blood was dried up; and she felt in her body that she was healed of that plague.

30   And Jesus, immediately knowing in himself that virtue had gone out of him, turned him about in the press, and said, Who touched my clothes?

31   And his disciples said unto him, Thou seest the multitude thronging thee, and sayest thou, Who touched me?

32   And he looked round about to see her that had done this thing.

33   But the woman fearing and trembling, knowing what was done in her, came and fell down before him, and told him all the truth.

34   And he said unto her, Daughter, thy faith hath made thee whole; go in peace, and be whole of thy plague.

Jesus said, "Thy faith has made thee whole" (v. 34). Some people think that it was the power that went out of Jesus that made her whole. Well, it was actually a combination of the two — her faith and His power. Notice that Jesus didn't even mention the power to her. He said that it was her faith that did it. And it is *your* faith that makes *you* whole! It is your faith that gives action to the power!

Confession:

If the faith of the woman with the issue of blood could make her whole, then my faith can make me whole. My faith gives action to the power of God!

And the whole multitude sought to touch him: for there went virtue out of him, and healed them all.

— LUKE 6:19

April 20

It's the Will of God To Heal Everyone!

On one occasion, I was preaching at the Oakcliffe Assembly of God Church in Dallas, Texas. After the Friday night service, several of us were in the pastor's office. There was a knock on the door. It was one of the ushers. He said that a couple wanted to speak to me. I followed the usher out of the pastor's office and into the main auditorium.

The usher introduced me to this couple. The husband said, "Brother Hagin, we've been listening to you on the radio. [I had been speaking on the subject of healing for a week or two.] About ten days ago as I was driving to work, I was listening to the radio. I was just changing the dials on the radio when I heard some beautiful singing, so I tuned into that station. The minute the singing stopped, you came on. You said, 'It's the will of God to heal everyone.'

"When I went home from work that night, I told my wife to tune in to that station. Every day she listened from home and I listened on my way to work. We've been listening for ten days now. I brought my wife with me. She's had two major operations and is facing a third major operation. The doctors have confided in me that they don't think she will be alive another six months. So I brought her for healing." This couple was now open to the fact that healing is the will of God for everyone.

Confession:

It is the will of God to heal everyone. It is the will of God to heal me!

All scripture is given by inspiration of God, and is
profitable for doctrine, for reproof, for correction,
for instruction in righteousness.

— 2 TIMOTHY 3:16

Locating People

I began to speak with this couple. You see, you can locate people, or find
out where they are in their faith, by asking them questions. People need to be
located before you pray for them. Now if I had had some manifestations of the
Spirit, I wouldn't have had to locate them, because God would have already
told me what to do. But I didn't have any manifestations of the Spirit. I didn't
sense any anointing.

To tell you the truth about it, I never felt so dead. I never felt so
unspiritual in all my life. If I had been going by feeling, I would have gotten
them to pray for *me*. But the Bible will work — whether it is quickened to
you or not.

For example, in the natural, I don't have to have some kind of feeling to
get the multiplication table to work for me. Is God's Word as true and as
workable as the multiplication table? Of course it is! The Bible will work for
you anytime because the Word is already anointed. The Word is already
inspired. The Word has been given by the Spirit of God. And it will work
when it's not quickened to you just as well as when it is quickened to you.

Some people think you have to have some particular feeling — that if
you have "goose-bumps," it will work. I've seen those people. Their faith is
in their goose-bumps and not in God's Word. As a result, they don't receive
from God. But God has given us His Word, and His Word will work for us
and profit us if we will trust and obey it.

Confession:

*The Bible is the inspired Word of God. It works whether it is quickened to
me or not. I believe what the Bible says.*

Then touched he their eyes, saying, According to your faith be it unto you.

— MATTHEW 9:29

Have Your Own Experience

As I said before, I never felt so dull, listless, and unspiritual in all my life as I ministered to this couple! If I had been going by feelings, I would have said, "No, I can't pray. There's no use in me praying." But, thank God, I know the Word. The Word of God works.

The husband said, "Ever since we heard you on the radio, we've been praying every night that if it is God's will to heal my wife, God would give us faith so that she can be healed." Well, that prayer is unscriptural.

If you'll learn to locate people and move them into a position to receive, you'll get results. I located this couple by what he said. I had already proven by giving scriptures on the radio broadcast that it was God's will to heal her and everyone else that is sick. But they hadn't quite caught that.

Now another thing was that the husband was doing all the talking. That is something that hinders many people. You can't speak for another person. For example, you can't get your wife healed because you believe in divine healing. Her unbelief can nullify the effect of your faith.

Also, you can't ride someone else's coattail. You can't get healed because someone else believes in divine healing. What do *you* believe about it? Sooner or later, you're going to have to have an experience of your own.

Confession:

I search the Scriptures to discover for myself what the Bible says about healing. I choose to believe what the Bible says. I choose to believe that healing is for me now.

That it might be fulfilled which was spoken by Esaias the prophet, saying, Himself took our infirmities, and bare our sicknesses.

— MATTHEW 8:17

Move People Into the Will of God

Based on what the husband said, I knew they weren't absolutely sure it was God's will to heal his wife. So I asked him, "How are you going to find out if it's God's will to heal her?"

He looked at me sort of startled and said, "I thought you'd lay hands on her and pray. And if it is God's will, He would heal her. And if it isn't, He wouldn't."

"No," I said, "I can't pray, because she wouldn't be healed."

"Well, what are we going to do? How are we going to find out whether or not it's God's will to heal her?" he asked.

I knew that I had to move them into faith. I had to move them into the will of God. So I said, "What if the Word of God said that Jesus took your wife's infirmities and bore her sicknesses? Would it be God's will to heal her?"

"Certainly it would," he said.

I turned to Matthew 8:17 and laid the Bible in his wife's lap. I told her to read the verse out loud. The minute she read it, her husband jumped off the altar and said, "The first half of my prayer wasn't any good, was it? We're going to have to throw it away." Well, I didn't tell him, but the whole prayer wasn't any good. He could throw the whole thing away.

He said, "The Bible says that Himself [Jesus] took our infirmities, and that includes my wife's infirmities."

I said, "You see that, but does your wife see it? You're not the one who needs healing."

I turned to his wife and she said, "I see it."

The husband said, "It's God's will then. We'll just have to throw the first part of that prayer away. All we have to do now is pray that God will give us faith so that she can be healed."

"No," I said. "I can't pray yet. Sit back there on the altar. We have to talk some more."

Confession:

Jesus took my infirmities and bore my sicknesses. By the stripes of Jesus, I am healed!

That it might be fulfilled which was spoken by Esaias the prophet, saying, Himself took our infirmities, and bare our sicknesses.

— MATTHEW 8:17

April 24

Praying for Faith To Be Healed

I asked this couple, "Are you folks Christians?"

"Yes, we've been born again," they said.

I asked the husband, "When you went down to that altar to get saved, did you pray, 'God, give me and my wife faith so we can be saved'?"

"No, the man just preached Jesus," the husband shared. "He said that whosoever shall call upon the Name of the Lord shall be saved [Rom. 10:13]. We knew before we went down there what the Lord would do."

"Good," I said. "That's exactly what I wanted you to say. You didn't have to pray for God to give you faith to be saved. Why then would you have to pray for God to give you faith to be healed?"

He jumped up and said, "You know, that whole prayer isn't worth a dime, is it? We're going to have to throw that whole prayer away!"

I said, "You see it, but you're not the one who needs healing. What about you, sister?"

She said, "I see it! I see it! I accepted Jesus as my Savior and I was saved. Now then, if I accept Him as my Healer, I'm healed!"

Confession:

I don't have to pray for faith to be healed. I simply accept Jesus as my Healer, just as I accepted Him as my Savior.

115

April 25

That it might be fulfilled which was spoken by Esaias the prophet, saying, Himself took our infirmities, and bare our sicknesses.

— MATTHEW 8:17

Accept Jesus as Your Healer

I said to the couple, "Now we can pray." I reached my hand out and laid it on top of the wife's head. I said, "Dear Lord Jesus, my dear sister has come for healing. She has seen that Jesus took her infirmities and bore her sicknesses. She accepted You as her Savior and was saved. Now she has come to accept You as her Healer, and she is healed. Thank You for it!"

Then I asked her, "Are you healed?"

She said, "I am."

I said, "How do you know you are?"

She said, "Because the Word said, 'Himself took my infirmities and bare my sicknesses.'"

"That's it! You've got it," I said. I turned and walked back toward the door to the pastor's office. I looked back and saw that she couldn't get up. Her husband lifted her up like a baby and carried her out of the building.

Two days after I prayed for the woman, she came back perfectly all right! The husband said there was no evidence of healing when they got home. But she pulled the brace off her back and threw it in the closet. She said, "Thank God, I won't need that thing anymore." When she went to bed, she had all of her symptoms. When she woke up the next morning, every symptom was gone. I saw her fourteen years later and she was still healed!

Confession:

I see that Jesus took my infirmities and bore my sicknesses. I accepted Jesus as my Savior and was saved. I accept Jesus as my Healer and am healed!

For I am not ashamed of the gospel of Christ: for it is the power of God unto salvation to every one that believeth; to the Jew first, and also to the Greek.

— ROMANS 1:16

The Gospel Is the Power

The Gospel is the power of God unto salvation to everyone who believes, to the Jew first and also the Greek. I have a footnote in my Bible that says the word "salvation" means *deliverance, safety, preservation, healing,* and *soundness.* In this Gospel of salvation, there is not only remission of sins and the New Birth, but there's also healing.

I heard about some meetings that Brother T. L. Osborn had in Africa. Blind people were instantly healed while he was preaching. He never prayed for anyone. He never laid hands on anyone. There were about seven or eight people in attendance who were chained like animals. They were down on all fours. Some of them were naked; they were making funny sounds like animals. They were demon-possessed.

Brother Osborn preached, "Jesus is the same today as He was when He was on the earth. When He was on the earth, He healed people. Jesus is alive and He is here in Spirit. He will heal people now, just as He did then."

You see, the Gospel is the power. No one touched or prayed for these men in chains. One fellow was on all fours barking like a dog. Suddenly, he lifted up his head and said, "Jesus, Jesus." Then he stood up like a man and was instantly all right. Every single one of them stood up and was instantly delivered.

What happened? The Gospel went forth. The Word of God went forth! The Gospel is the power of God unto healing. When the Gospel, the Word of God, gets into people, it will heal them.

Confession:

The Word of God is the power of God. As I read the Word and meditate on the Word, I am healed.

Who his own self bare our sins in his own body on the tree, that we, being dead to sins, should live unto righteousness: by whose stripes ye were healed.

— 1 PETER 2:24

A Fact, Not a Promise

By Jesus' stripes, you are healed. You don't have to pray. You don't have to have someone else pray. It's not necessary to pray when you know this fact as you ought to know it. Simply thank God for perfect deliverance.

The afflictions in your body were laid on Jesus. And He bore them. You do not need to bear them. All you need to do is recognize and accept the fact that Jesus has already borne your sicknesses and diseases. Therefore, you do not have to bear them. That's a fact, not a theory. It's a Bible fact.

I've heard people say, "Well, I know the Lord promised to heal me." No, He didn't. He didn't promise. First Peter 2:24 is a statement of fact. It tells you what happened. A *promise* tells you about something that's going to happen. A *fact* tells you about something you've already received or that's already happened. By Jesus' stripes, you are already healed!

Once you recognize this fact, then just refuse to allow disease in your body. Every believer should thoroughly understand that his healing was consummated in Christ. And if every believer thoroughly understood that, it would mean the end of chronic trouble in the bodies of believers.

Confession:

The afflictions in my body were laid on Jesus. My healing was consummated in Christ. And by His stripes, I am healed!

. . . Resist the devil, and he will flee from you.
— JAMES 4:7

April 28

Don't Accept Sickness and Disease

When I was a teenager, the doctors said I wouldn't live. But I proved them wrong! I had two serious organic heart troubles and an incurable blood disease. I was also paralyzed. The doctors said that my white corpuscles were eating up my red corpuscles faster than I could build them up and faster than anything could be done about it medically. They said, "We'll be honest with you. If you didn't have the heart condition, if you didn't have the paralysis, the incurable blood disease alone would prove fatal to you."

But it didn't prove fatal to me. In sixty-eight years, I have not had one single headache. I've proved God's Word works. The last headache I had was in August 1933. I'm not bragging on me. I'm bragging on what I learned from the Bible.

Someone might say, "What would you do if you had a headache?" Well, first, I wouldn't tell it if I did. And second, I'd resist it.

Some years ago, I was leaving the parking lot at RHEMA, and, all of a sudden, a pain hit me in my head. My head started hurting. I spoke up and said, "Oh no, you don't, devil! You don't put any headache on me! I don't have one! I'm not going to have it!" By the time I was heading down the road, it was all gone. You see, we make the mistake of ever accepting these things.

Confession:

I resist the devil and he flees from me. I resist sickness and disease. I refuse to accept anything that the devil brings my way!

He sent his word, and healed them, and delivered them from their destructions.

— PSALM 107:20

The Mercy of God

Let's back up a few verses.

PSALM 107:17-19

17 Fools because of their transgression, and because of their iniquities, are afflicted.

18 Their soul abhorreth all manner of meat; and they draw near unto the gates of death.

19 Then they cry unto the Lord in their trouble, and he saveth them out of their distresses.

God said this to the Israelites. He told them, "Walk in My statutes and keep My commandments, and I'll take sickness away from the midst of thee. The rest of your days will be fulfilled" (Exod. 23:25,26). But they were foolish. They sinned and broke their covenant with God. They took themselves out of the protection of God — out of His healing power. Verse 18 says that they drew near to the gates of death. They were almost dead.

Then they cried unto the Lord for help and He saved them! Isn't God wonderful to help them even though they were foolish enough to sin and do wrong, even though they got outside of His covenant and blessings? The mercy of God is so wonderful! God had mercy on them. He sent His Word and healed them!

Confession:

God sent His Word and healed me. Therefore, I no longer have sickness. He sent His Word and healed me.

And in that day ye shall ask me nothing. Verily, verily, I say unto you, Whatsoever ye shall ask the Father in my name, he will give it you. Hitherto have ye asked nothing in my name: ask, and ye shall receive, that your joy may be full.

— JOHN 16:23,24

Demand Your Rights

The word "ask" comes from the same Greek word that is translated "demand" and means *to demand something due.* In other words, Jesus was saying, "Whatever you *demand* in My Name, I will do it."

In Acts chapter 3, a crippled man was sitting at the gate as Peter and John were going into the temple. The crippled man was begging for alms. Peter said to him, "Silver and gold have I none, but such as I have, give I thee. In the Name of Jesus Christ of Nazareth, rise up and walk!" Peter took the crippled man by the hand and lifted him up. Peter demanded that the man get up in Jesus' Name.

Whatever you ask in Jesus' Name, He will do it! Our faith in the Name has been weak, but whatever we demand as our right in His Name, He will do it!

You have the right to use the Name of Jesus. If pain comes, you have the right to say, "In the Name of Jesus Christ, pain, leave my body!" The pain must go because you are master of your own body. You rule it!

Confession:

I ask in Jesus' Name, demanding my rights. And Jesus said that whatsoever I demand in His Name, He will do!

But let him ask in faith, nothing wavering. For he that wavereth is like a wave of the sea driven with the wind and tossed.

— JAMES 1:6

Don't Undo What God Has Already Done

Think about a carpenter. If he put the foundation for a house down one week and the next week took the foundation out, the house would never be completed. Christians are doing the same thing in their praying. They're undoing what they've already prayed, and they're wondering why their prayers aren't availing much.

Let me give you part one of a real-life illustration. I was invited to preach at a church in east Texas. Before I got up to speak, the pastor said, "We're going to receive an offering tonight for Brother Hagin." At that moment, a woman in the congregation stood up and said, "Pastor, before you pray over the offering, I feel like we should pray for Sister _____. She lives next door to me. The doctor came to visit her and said that she would not live past midnight." (It was eight o'clock in the evening.)

The pastor said, "Yes, let's all stand and pray for this sister." So we prayed.

Then the pastor said, "How many of you believe that God heard you?" Most of the people lifted their hands and praised God that He heard us.

Confession:

When I pray, I ask in faith, believing that God heard me. I refuse to waver. I refuse to have any doubt or unbelief. Instead, I praise God for hearing and answering me.

For let not that man [the man who wavers] *think*
that he shall receive any thing of the Lord.

— JAMES 1:7

Don't Waver in Your Believing

The next night, the same thing happened again. This particular woman stood up before the offering was taken and said, "Pastor, I feel that we should continue to pray for Sister _____. The doctor thought that she would die last night. You know, I live next door to her, and I was there at eight o'clock this morning when the doctor checked on her. He said, 'She's past the crisis. She has come out of it. Get her out of bed and let her sit in a chair two or three times a day. She's going to make it.'"

Because of our praying, God touched this woman who was given up to die. Now notice what the woman in the congregation said. She continued, "But she's still terribly weak. [Naturally, she would be. She's been bedfast and has just come through a crisis.] We know God touched her, all right. Let's pray that God would complete the work." (Remember, we prayed for a completed work the night before.)

Then the pastor said, "That's right. I was at her house to see her today. We know God touched her. Even the doctor admits that she's out of danger and she's going to make it. Let's stand up and pray for her again."

Confession:

I will not waver in my faith. I will not undo the effects of my prayers through doubt and unbelief. What God said, He will do, and I praise Him for it!

123

A double minded man is unstable in all his ways.

— JAMES 1:8

A Double-Minded Man

As soon as the pastor began praying, I heard the following in my spirit: "Now they've taken her out of My hands and she'll die. Within three days, she'll be dead." I knew it was the voice of the Lord speaking to me.

On the third day, the woman died, just as the Lord said. You see, we had placed her in God's hands and then we took her out of God's hands.

What should we have done? Instead of praying for her complete healing again, we should have stood in agreement and said, "We are going to stand up and agree that she is well. We are going to thank God for it." That way, we would have stayed in faith.

Many times, a whole church places a person in God's hands and then turns right around and takes him out of God's hands. God wants to heal the person, but He can't. Why? God operates on certain laws and principles.

Confession:

I cooperate with God and stay in faith. Instead of praying for my healing over and over, I agree that I am healed and whole. I thank God for it!

Find Someone Who Will Agree With You

Once a woman in Fort Worth said to me, "Brother Hagin, I realize that I haven't been standing in faith."

She had an incurable condition in her body. It wasn't terminal, but it was an incurable condition she'd had most of her life. Doctors in the Dallas/Fort Worth area had treated her. She and her husband had spent thousands of dollars.

She said to me, "I thought I had been standing in faith for nineteen years and the manifestation just hadn't come. But when I heard you teaching, I realized that I was praying for my healing over and over again instead of just agreeing that it was done. I decided to find someone to agree with me that I'm healed. And within three days, that incurable condition was gone! The specialists couldn't find a trace of it in my body!"

What happened? The Bible says that one can put a thousand to flight and two can put ten thousand to flight. So stay in faith and find someone to agree with you that you're healed.

Confession:

I agree with my brothers and sisters in Christ that I am healed and they are healed. We're not going to be; we are! According to the Word of God, it is done!

May 5

And his [Jesus'] name, through faith in his name, hath made this man strong, whom ye see and know: yea, the faith which is by him hath given him this perfect soundness in the presence of you all.

— ACTS 3:16

'Through Faith in His Name'

Smith Wigglesworth learned of a man in Wales known as Lazarus. He had worked by day in the tin mines and preached at night until he wore himself out physically. He contracted TB, and became bedfast for seven years.

Once as Wigglesworth was in Wales preaching, the Lord said to him, "I want you to go raise up Lazarus." Wigglesworth found other believers and went to Lazarus' house. They surrounded his bed and repeated the Name of Jesus until the power of God fell. Wigglesworth then said to the man, "There's your healing."

Lazarus began to speak faintly, so Wigglesworth drew closer to hear his words. The man said, "I've been bitter." You see, he once had believed in divine healing. Someone had anointed him with oil, but it didn't work. He was mad at God because he thought God hadn't healed him.

Wigglesworth told him to repent and God would forgive him. Lazarus began to cry, "God, forgive me for my bitterness. Healing is real and it's mine. I receive it."

Lazarus got himself out of bed, dressed, and walked down the steps into the living room. That night, he gave his testimony in an open-air meeting.

What impressed me was that they just gathered around the man's bed and repeated the Name of Jesus. I think it has never dawned on us the power that is in that Name.

Some people say, "Healing and miracles have been done away with. They are not for us today." Well, in light of Acts 3:16, that's tantamount to saying, "The Name of Jesus has been done away with and doesn't belong to the Church today. Faith in that Name is non-existent"! But, thank God, the Name of Jesus does belong to us today!

Confession:

I am made strong and whole through faith in Jesus' Name. Just as faith in Jesus' Name raised Lazarus up, faith in Jesus' Name will raise me up!

126

If ye shall ask any thing in my name, I will do it.
— JOHN 14:14

Ask in Jesus' Name!

As a believer, you have the right to ask God the Father for healing or any other blessing. And if you ask in the Name of Jesus, you have the absolute guarantee that God the Father will hear and answer your petition.

Many people add to the Scriptures or take away from them, because they have been religiously brainwashed instead of New Testament taught. Even in Charismatic circles, former religious teaching can hinder people. People have a tendency to revert to what they were taught early in life.

One time I awoke in the middle of the night and found myself praying about something. It was something I had been praying about for two or three weeks. I said to myself, *What's wrong with you? You know that kind of praying won't work.* You see, I had unconsciously reverted to a kind of praying I'd been taught years before.

I said, "That kind of praying won't work. Satan, I demand my rights." I had a scriptural right to what I was praying about. I had the Word of God for it. Well, it worked so fast, and I had been struggling with it for two or three weeks. It was done. I mean, it came into manifestation that day.

Jesus said, "Whatever you ask [in the Greek, that word means *demand*] in My Name, I'll do it." I'm not demanding it of God, because it's not God who is withholding it from me. He wants me to have it. He has made provision for me to have it. No, I'm demanding it of the devil. He's the one who's holding it back, not God. Religious people say, "Whatever I need, I know God will send. Just leave it up to Him. He knows." And that sounds good, but it's just not biblical truth.

Confession:

Whatever I need, God has made provision for me to have it. God is not withholding any of His blessings from me. He is a good God! And I simply ask for whatever I need in Jesus' Name.

> *The thief cometh not, but for to steal, and to kill,*
> *and to destroy: I am come that they might have life,*
> *and that they might have it more abundantly.*
>
> — JOHN 10:10

Take Back What the Devil Has Stolen!

Years ago, while I was holding a meeting in Port Arthur, Texas, a Methodist woman came up to me and said, "Brother Hagin, I don't know much about healing. For seventeen years I haven't been able to do my housework or cook breakfast for my husband. I haven't been able to function as a wife and mother because of bad health. And after spending thousands of dollars, doctors have admitted that they just can't help me. I've been in the prayer lines of some of the most outstanding healing evangelists of our day. But I didn't realize how important the Word of God was in receiving healing until I heard you teach today. I'm coming back tomorrow."

Well, she came back the third day and the fourth day. Every day she came, she got stronger. I never even prayed for her. She never got in the healing line. As far as I know, no one prayed for her. We eventually closed out the meeting and left.

About thirty days later, I received a letter from her that said, "I am the Methodist lady who told you that I didn't realize the reality of the Word of God and the Name of Jesus. I've been listening to tapes from your services and following along in my Bible. One day, I just suddenly stood up, lifted up my Bible in one hand, and said, 'Devil, it's you who has had me bound all these seventeen years. I haven't been able to do my housework. I haven't been able to function as a human being. I demand my rights! Get out of my house and leave right now in the Name of Jesus!'

"Brother Hagin, it's so wonderful! For the first time in seventeen years, I'm doing all my housework. I'm getting up every morning and cooking breakfast for my husband. I'm getting him off to work. I'm forty-six years old, but I've got the vim, vigor, and vitality of a sixteen-year-old. I'm so glad you came along and taught me!"

Confession:

The devil is the one who brings sickness and disease, not God. I take back what the devil has stolen from me! I demand my rights in the Name of Jesus!

Again I say unto you, That if two of you shall agree on earth as touching any thing that they shall ask, it shall be done for them of my Father which is in heaven.
For where two or three are gathered together in my name, there am I in the midst of them.
— MATTHEW 18:19,20

The Importance of Agreement

Jesus said that wherever two or three people are gathered together in His Name, He is there in the midst of them. What is Jesus doing there in the midst of them? He's there to make good on what they ask and agree upon, because He said in John 14:14, *"If ye shall ask any thing in my name, I will do it."*

Many times, though, people lack agreement. For example, if something you're agreeing on concerns another person, that other person will have to agree with you too. It won't work in disagreement. Get him or her to agree with you.

Notice that Matthew 18:19 says that it *shall* be done — not that it might be done or that there is a possibility of it being done. It *shall* be done!

I've had people come to me and ask, "Brother Hagin, will you agree with me?" Then they tell me what they want.

I say to the person, "All right, let's agree together. I'll pray. You listen and agree with it." You see, if both of us pray, one of us might go in one direction, and the other might go in another direction. Then we wouldn't be in agreement.

The majority of the time, after I pray and say to the person, "Is it done?" he or she says, "Oh, I sure hope it is."

Then I say, "No, it isn't, because I'm *believing* and you're *hoping*. There's no agreement here." Amos 3:3 says, *"Can two walk together, except they be agreed?"*

Confession:

There is power in the prayer of agreement. When another person and I agree in prayer, we can count it done! We can agree in prayer for health and healing!

Again I say unto you, That if two of you shall agree on earth as touching any thing that they shall ask, it shall be done for them of my Father which is in heaven.

For where two or three are gathered together in my name, there am I in the midst of them.

— MATTHEW 18:19,20

God Keeps His Word

The negative side of Matthew 18:19 and 20 is that if you *don't* agree, it *won't* be done. Isn't that simple? You see, we try to make the truth of God so complicated, but He has made it so simple. Time and time again, as I have acted on these verses of Scripture — as I have agreed with someone in prayer — such marvelous things have happened. And it will work for you too!

God said that He watches over His Word to make it good. Jeremiah 1:12 says, *". . . for I will hasten my word to perform it."* The margin says, "I watch over my Word to perform it."

If we would look for as many reasons for God to keep His Word and for it to work as we do for it *not* to work, God's Word would always work for us. Many times we are hunting around for something negative, saying, "Well, maybe it wasn't the will of God after all." Then why did Jesus say, "If two of you shall agree, it shall be done"?

Confession:

God keeps His Word. Jesus said that if two or three people gather together in His Name to agree on something, it would be done (Matt. 18:19). Thank God, He keeps His Word!

Agree and Then Don't Back Down!

In 1949 I was holding a meeting in Plainview, Texas, at the First Assembly of God Church. Christmas was coming up, and I needed some extra money for Christmas presents.

I wrote to my wife, "At three o'clock on Sunday afternoon, you open your Bible there in Garland, Texas, to Matthew 18:19, and I'll open my Bible here in Plainview. We'll agree that the offering will be a particular amount on Sunday night." You see, you can be in agreement in spirit and not be with the other person physically.

I preached on the last Sunday night before Christmas. And in all the hustle and bustle of special Christmas programs, the ushers forgot to count the offering. The pastor found the offering plates and brought them back to the parsonage. He dumped all the money out on the dining room table and said, "Let's count it."

He counted half and I counted the other half. He wrote down his amount, and I wrote down my amount. It was $23.12 short. He said, "My, my, I was hoping it would run as much as it has been running. I know Christmas is coming up. I'm so sorry."

I said, "Don't worry about it. My wife and I agreed."

It would have been easy for me to say, "Well, we missed it some-where." But my wife and I had agreed. I knew we had agreed. I mean if the Lord Jesus Christ Himself suddenly appeared and stood there and said, "Your problem is that you didn't agree," I would say, "Lord Jesus, You're lying about it. We did agree."

Confession:

When I agree in prayer with someone based on the Word of God, I don't back down. I stand my ground on the Word of God, believing that what God said is true!

Then said the Lord unto me, Thou hast well seen: for I will hasten my word to perform it.

— JEREMIAH 1:12

'If It's So, I'm Going To Have It'

I said to the pastor of that church, "I can't go home. My wife and I agreed that there would be a certain amount, and it's $23.12 short."

He said, "Well, bless God, if you agreed on it, it's here. We've made a mistake. Let's count it again."

So he counted his half again and I counted the other half. We came up with the same figure.

I said, "No, I can't accept that. My wife and I agreed. There has to be that much money."

You see, if we'd be persistent with the Bible like we are with other things, we'd get results. We counted those two piles of money four times! And we still came up with the same figure. We were $23.12 short.

I said, "My wife and I agree it's got to be here. That, or I've got to go back to every church where I've preached and tell them that Matthew 18:19 is a lie."

Now I don't know about you, but I'm that honest about it. If it's so, I'm going to have it. If the Word says something belongs to me, I'm going to enjoy the benefit of it. If I can't receive it after I know I've done what the Bible said, I'm just going to throw it away. That's what I said as a sixteen-year-old boy on the bed of sickness when I began to see what Mark 11:23 and 24 said. The Word works if we will work the Word properly — if we do what it says to do.

Confession:

God watches over His Word to perform it. What He said in His Word, I can have! I can have health, healing, and wholeness!

God is not a man, that he should lie; neither the son of man, that he should repent: hath he said, and shall he not do it? or hath he spoken, and shall he not make it good?

Refuse To Be Denied

When I was sixteen years old and on the bed of sickness, I said to the Lord, "Lord, if Your Word is so, I'm coming off this bed. If I don't come off this bed, it will be because You lied. And if the Bible is no good, I might as well throw it in the trash can and burn it up."

You need to settle on the integrity of the Word and then go after it "tooth and toenail." Do not be deterred. Don't let anything stop you. If the Bible said it, then believe it. That settles it.

After that pastor and I had counted that same offering three times, he said, "Let's count it again. We've missed it somewhere."

About that time, I remembered that I had an envelope in my pocket. A woman had given me the envelope at my book table. She had purchased a Bible for her husband and said, "I owe you $25.00 for the Bible, but I'm going to make out a check for more than that to include an offering for you."

I got out the envelope and looked at the check. There was $25.00 for the Bible and $25.00 for an offering! That was almost $2.00 over what my wife and I had agreed on. I said, "I can go home now."

Someone might say, "Well, what would you have done if you hadn't found it?"

I'd still be there counting it. More than fifty years later, I'd be right there! I wouldn't budge, because I refuse to be denied. God's Word works! You have to have that kind of determination to walk in the blessings of God. You have to refuse to be denied!

Confession:

God is not a liar. What He has said in His Word is truth. And I believe what His Word says. I believe that by Jesus' stripes, I am healed and made whole. I am determined! I refuse to be denied!

133

> But be ye doers of the word, and not hearers only,
> deceiving your own selves.
>
> — JAMES 1:22

Act on What the Word Says

There are a number of different methods whereby healing can be obtained through the Word of God. One way is to simply know what the Word of God says for yourself and then act on it. You don't have to pray. You don't have to get anyone else to pray. Simply act on what the Word says: *". . . by whose stripes ye were healed"* (1 Peter 2:24).

In February 1955, I held a meeting for a pastor. I stayed in the parsonage with him and his wife. One night, I was awakened at 1:30 with alarming symptoms in my body. The devil said to me, "Now this is one time you're not going to be healed."

You know, the devil will try every way in the world that he can to talk you out of healing. He'll try every way he can to rob you of any of the blessings of God.

Do you know what I did when the devil said that to me? I pulled the covers over my head and started laughing. I didn't feel like laughing. There is such a thing as laughing in the Spirit. It's easy to laugh when you're laughing in the Spirit. But I wasn't laughing in the Spirit. I was laughing in the flesh. I was making myself do it; I didn't feel like laughing.

Confession:

I am a doer of the Word. I act on what the Word says whether I feel like it or not. I receive what the Word says belongs to me. I receive health and healing.

But he was wounded for our transgressions, he was bruised for our iniquities: the chastisement of our peace was upon him; and with his stripes we are healed.

— ISAIAH 53:5

Jesus Already Obtained Our Healing!

While I was lying in bed at that pastor's home, the devil said, "Remember the doctors told you that nothing could help you. They said your symptoms would come back and you would die. This is one time you're not going to get your healing."

I just covered my head and started saying, "Ha, ha, ha, ha." I said that over and over again. I must have laughed that way ten minutes.

Then the devil said to me, "What are you laughing about?"

I said, "Mr. Devil, I'm laughing at you, because you said that I'm not going to get my healing." I laughed another ten minutes. And all the time, I was experiencing serious, alarming symptoms in my body.

The devil asked me again, "What are you laughing about?"

I said, "I'm laughing at you. You said that I'm not going to get my healing. I wasn't planning on getting it. Why would I want to *get* it? Jesus already got it for me! First Peter 2:24 says, '. . . by whose stripes ye WERE healed.' I don't have to get it. Jesus got it and because He got it, I have it. Now just gather up your duds and get out of here!"

Every symptom left! I didn't have to pray. I didn't have to get someone to lay hands on me. I just acted on the Word, because I knew what the Word said.

That's the best way to receive healing. But if your faith is not at that level, don't condemn yourself. Just hook up with another method and keep growing until you get to the place where you can act for yourself.

Confession:

I don't have to GET my healing. Jesus already got it. And because He got it, I have it. I am already healed!

135

. . . and the sheep follow him [the shepherd]: *for they know his voice.*
And a stranger will they not follow, but will flee from him: for they know not the voice of strangers.

— JOHN 10:4,5

Don't Listen to the Devil

I knew a preacher who had an outstanding healing testimony. In the early 1930s when tuberculosis was rampant, he was raised up from his deathbed.

He was a young married man. He and his wife had a little baby. And it was discovered that the man had tuberculosis. He requested prayer from every church where he'd ever held a revival. Every outstanding healing evangelist in the world laid hands on him. But he grew worse instead of better. Finally, he just came to the point where he couldn't go any longer; he became bedfast. He went to his in-laws' home to stay. They were farmers in Corsicana, Texas.

One day as he was lying in bed, he looked out the window and saw a clump of bushes and trees about a quarter of a mile away from the house. He said to God, "If You'll give me enough strength to get up and get to that clump of trees, I'll pray until I get healed."

He made an effort to get up, and he dragged himself to that clump of trees. Then he fell down, exhausted. Lying there on his back, the devil said, "Now you've done it! Nobody knows where you are. You're going to die right here behind these bushes. The only way they'll find you is when the buzzards lead them to you after you're dead."

This was not the voice of Jesus the Good Shepherd talking to this man. It was the voice of a stranger, the voice of the enemy, the devil. Thank God, this man finally recognized this voice as the voice of the devil.

Confession:

I know the voice of my Good Shepherd, Jesus. And the voice of a stranger I do not follow. I do not listen to the voice of the devil. He is a liar and the father of lies.

*And at midnight Paul and Silas prayed, and sang
praises unto God: and the prisoners heard them.
And suddenly there was a great earthquake, so that
the foundations of the prison were shaken: and
immediately all the doors were opened, and every
one's bands were loosed.*

— ACTS 16:25,26

Praise God for Your Healing

While lying there in the grass trying to get enough strength to whisper a prayer, this preacher started thinking about all the people who said they were going to pray for him. He figured that if they all prayed only five minutes a day, there's no telling how many hundreds of hours had gone up in prayer. He thought, *If all that praying can't get the job done, there is no use in me praying. I'm not going to pray at all. I'm going to lie here on my back and just praise God for my healing.*

He could have prayed and died; he would have been praying in unbelief. Prayer had already been made. He needed to "change gears" now. So instead of praying, he decided to praise God for his healing — because his prayer had been answered. He started whispering, "Praise the Lord." It took all the strength he had just to get a whisper out. Then he seemed to get enough strength to raise his hands. An hour and a half later, he was standing on his feet, hollering, "Praise God" so loud that someone heard him two miles away. He was healed!

He said to me years later, "Whenever I have my lungs X-rayed, the doctors say, 'You're the eighth wonder of the world. Did you know that you've got a hole in your lung and yet it's working? We don't understand it.' I always say to them, 'I've been that way all these years, and I'm still in good health. I'm just going to keep on enjoying it.'"

Confession:

I'm going to praise God for my healing. Thank You, Father, for providing healing for me. I am so thankful that I am no longer sick. I am so grateful that I am healed and whole.

*. . . because of unbelief they were broken off, and
thou standest by faith . . .*

— ROMANS 11:20

Stay in Faith

While I was holding a meeting in Pasadena, Texas, a woman called from
Canton, Texas, and said, "Brother Hagin, would it be all right for me to bring
my little daughter down there for prayer? She has epilepsy. Now by faith, my
prayer group has claimed her healing, but the manifestation hasn't come yet;
she still has the seizures. We don't want to get into unbelief. Would it be all
right for us to bring her down there for you to lay hands on her?"

I said, "Yes, but only under certain circumstances. I'll not be able to
counsel with you while you're here. I just don't have time. When you come
into the prayer line, say to the Lord, 'Now Lord, we're not coming down
here to receive healing like the rest of the people, because by faith, we
already believe that we have received healing. We're coming down here to
agree that she is healed.'"

Well, she came to the meeting and brought her daughter to the prayer
line and did what I told her to do. Two years later, I saw this woman at a
meeting we were having in Dallas. She testified that from that day we agreed
until then, the child never had another epileptic seizure.

Confession:

*I stay in faith. I stay in agreement with God. I agree with what God has said
in His Word. I agree that I am healed in Jesus' Name!*

How should one chase a thousand, and two put ten
thousand to flight, except their Rock had sold them,
and the Lord had shut them up?

— DEUTERONOMY 32:30

The Power of Agreement

After a meeting one time, a woman came up to me and said, "Brother Hagin, I have an incurable condition in my body. It isn't fatal; that is, it wouldn't kill me. But it might shorten my life five or ten years. And with the right medication, I can control it. But it is incurable.

"I've been believing God, trying to appropriate healing. But when you told the story about that little girl who stood in the healing line for agreement, it triggered something inside me. I thought, *I'm going down there for him to agree with me that I'm healed.*" So I prayed, agreeing with her that she was healed.

Some time later, this woman wrote a letter to me and said, "From the moment you agreed with me in the prayer line until now, I haven't had another symptom. In fact, I've been back to the same doctors, and they can't find a trace of the condition. It has disappeared!"

There is power in agreement. Deuteronomy 32:30 says, *"How should one chase a thousand, and two put ten thousand to flight. . . ."* One can put a thousand to flight, and two can put ten thousand to flight. There's power in agreement.

Confession:

There is power in agreement. Agreeing with another person based on God's Word brings about desired results.

. . . they shall lay hands on the sick, and they shall recover.

— MARK 16:18

Who Is Qualified To Lay Hands on the Sick?

We've looked at this scripture before in explaining that not all healings are instantaneous. Now let's look at the previous verse, Mark 16:17. *"And these signs shall follow THEM THAT BELIEVE. . . ."* These signs, such as laying hands on the sick, shall follow believers. Who shall lay hands on the sick? *Believers* shall lay hands on the sick.

You see, laying on of hands is more than a sign. It is also a New Testament doctrine. It's one of the fundamental principles of the doctrine of the Lord Jesus Christ. Hebrews 6:1 and 2 says, *"Therefore leaving the principles of the doctrine of Christ, let us go on unto perfection; not laying again the foundation of repentance from dead works, and of faith toward God, Of the doctrine of baptisms, and of laying on of hands. . . ."* The doctrine of laying on of hands belongs to the whole Church. Any believer has the right to lay hands on the sick in the Name of Jesus.

In 1963, I was preaching at a meeting in Tulsa, and a young Baptist couple came up to me. The wife said to me, "We're so glad we came. We've learned so much. You spoke about the laying on of hands a few nights ago. Well, my husband started mowing the lawn yesterday. I heard the lawnmower running, but I realized it wasn't moving. So I ran out and looked. My husband was lying in the middle of the front yard, flat on his face. The lawnmower had run up against the house and was still running. Ordinarily, I would have panicked and gone wild, but instead, I rushed out there and laid hands on him."

Confession:

The Bible says that believers, not just preachers, shall lay hands on the sick. I am a believer. I can lay hands on the sick, and they shall recover.

Of the doctrine of baptisms, and of laying on of hands . . .

May 20

— HEBREWS 6:2

Any Believer Can Lay Hands on the Sick

While the husband was lying on the ground, the wife said, "Lord, Mark 16:18 says that believers shall lay hands on the sick. I don't know what has happened to him, but in the Name of Jesus, I lay hands on him and expect him to be healed right now." She hadn't gotten those words out of her mouth when he suddenly revived.

He said, "What happened?"

She said, "I don't know. The lawnmower was running in one spot and you were lying in the front yard."

"Well," he said, "I felt myself getting sick and I just passed out. Right now, though, I feel so good. I've never felt better in my life." And he went on and mowed the yard.

The husband said to me, "You know, Brother Hagin, I feel so good. I believe I could just go to work without going home and sleeping tonight. I'm so refreshed and full of life."

Confession:

I lay hands on the sick according to Mark 16:18 and expect them to be healed.

I call heaven and earth to record this day against you, that I have set before you life and death, blessing and cursing: therefore choose life. . . .

— DEUTERONOMY 30:19

We Each Have Free Choice

In September 1950, there was a meeting in Rockwall, Texas. On a Thursday night, my wife and I went, but my children and my niece Ruth, who was living with us at the time, went to their local church. When the service was over, we stayed and prayed at the altar.

I heard an automobile outside. It was in the street in front of the tent. I heard all four wheels spinning to a stop. I looked up and saw a young person, a friend of my niece's, coming into the tent. He ran up to where I was kneeling at the altar and said, "Ruth had an attack of appendicitis. She fell off the pew at church. They prayed for her and then they took her home. Some of the Christians at the house prayed for her again. But she's getting worse instead of better. She's calling for you and your wife."

We rushed to the house, went into the room, and saw her with her knees drawn up to her chest. She was writhing in pain and clenching her fists.

My wife and I knelt by the bed and I said, "Now Ruth, do you want to go to the hospital?" You see, a person can't get healed just because *you* believe in divine healing. You cannot force your desires onto someone else. People have a will of their own. I said, "Ruth, if you want to, I'll take you to the hospital emergency room."

"No," she said. "I want to be healed. I want to believe God."

Confession:

I choose to believe God. But I cannot force my desires onto someone else. I must follow my heart and allow others to follow their heart.

Action Must Spring From Faith in Your Heart

My wife spoke to my niece, Ruth, and said, "Ruth, you know you're not our child. You don't belong to us. We can't make decisions for you. Also, you're eighteen years old. You're an adult now. You can make your own decisions. Don't say, 'I want to trust God' just because Uncle Ken teaches divine healing. Don't say that because you think that's what *we* want you to do. What do *you* want to do from your heart?"

You have to get action from people's hearts, not their heads. And it may take time to do this. People can mentally go along with you and say things, but their heart not be in it. And it won't work.

So my wife asked Ruth, "What do you want to do?" Ruth insisted that she wanted to trust God.

Then I said, "All right, let's get busy and get your healing or else go to the hospital." I knew, you see, that her appendix could burst at any time. I knew we had to work fast.

Confession:

My spirit is the candle of the Lord. I listen to my spirit, not my head. And I respond from my spirit, not my head.

Therefore I say unto you, What things soever ye desire, when ye pray, believe that ye receive them, and ye shall have them.

— MARK 11:24

Healing Must Be Received To Be Enjoyed

My wife and I laid hands on Ruth. I could feel the life of God pouring out of me. My wife sensed it too. We could both sense that life pouring out of us into her. I said, "Ruth, there's your healing. There's your healing." You see, I could administer the healing power to her, but I couldn't accept it for her.

Spiritual things are just as real as material things are. Many people think that if you have something, you can just give it to another person. But, no, the other person must accept it. If he doesn't, then he won't have it. The same thing is true in the Spirit. And you can know when people take hold and when they don't take hold.

My wife said, "There it is, Ruth."

Ruth said, "All right, I accept it. I receive it."

Instantly, Ruth's body relaxed and straightened out. That's when I saw that her hands were bleeding because her nails had dug into them as she clenched her fists in pain. She was instantly healed. And she never had another attack of appendicitis.

Every believer has the life of God abiding in him or her. It doesn't just belong to the preacher. Now the reason you may feel the life of God pouring into another person's body is, the life of God is in you. But it makes no difference whether there is a tangible manifestation of power or not. Whether you sense anything pouring out of you or not, if you go ahead and believe the Word of God, the healing will come into manifestation.

Confession:

Laying on of hands belongs to the whole Church. Laying on of hands belongs to me. I lay hands on the sick and they will recover whether I sense anything or not, because I believe the Word of God. The healing will come into manifestation.

While we look not at the things which are seen, but at the things which are not seen: for the things which are seen are temporal; but the things which are not seen are eternal.

— 2 CORINTHIANS 4:18

Don't Base Your Faith on What You Can See

I remember an Assembly of God woman down in east Texas who had double pneumonia. This was back in the late 1930s before miracle drugs. She just grew steadily worse. Of course, in those days, we didn't have the hospitals we have today. Doctors made house calls at that time.

Well, the doctor came and did what he could do. The doctor told the husband that unless there was a change, she would not live past midnight that night. The husband, who wasn't saved, decided to call the church and ask if some Christians could go over to the house.

The pastor and several members went to the house. They anointed the woman with oil, laid hands on her, and prayed. Now she had been almost unconscious, but she came right out of it and began to laugh and sing in tongues. She sat up in bed and said, "I'm healed. I'm healed."

The doctor who was expecting her to die that night came back to see her the next day. She was sitting up in bed talking. He listened to her lungs and said to the husband, "I don't understand it. Her lungs seem to be just as bad as they were. Sometimes I've seen people revive right before they die. She'll die soon."

He came back the next day and said the same thing. For three days, she sat up in bed, laughed, and talked. She told everyone she met that she was healed. On the third day, every symptom she had disappeared.

Now what if she had based her faith on what she saw or felt — or on what the doctor said? She would have missed it. But she chose instead to believe the Word.

Confession:

I base my faith on what God says in His Word. I don't base my faith on what I see, hear, or feel. Things in this sense realm are temporal and fleeting, but things in the spirit realm are eternal and everlasting.

As it is written, I have made thee a father of many nations, before him whom he believed, even God, who quickeneth the dead, and calleth those things which be not as though they were.

— ROMANS 4:17

'I'm Not Moved by What I See!'

According to this verse of Scripture, faith calleth those things that be not as though they were. Isn't it wonderful to believe God? I feel so sorry for those who walk by sight. I choose to walk by faith.

Now walking by faith means that you'll have to stand your ground sometimes. Don't be moved by what you see or feel. Rather, be moved only by what you believe.

The Bible never told you that you could have what you see. The Bible never told you that you could have what you feel. The Bible told you that you could have what you *believe*. Matthew 9:29 says, *". . . According to your faith be it unto you."*

The Bible doesn't say, "Go thy way and as thou hast *felt*, so be it done unto you." No! The Bible doesn't say, "Go thy way and as thou hast *seen*, so be it done unto you." No! I don't find it expressed like that in any of my Bibles! But I do find the expression, *". . . Go thy way; and AS THOU HAST BELIEVED, so be it done unto thee"* (Matt. 8:13).

Confession:

I'm not moved by what I see. I'm not moved by what I feel. I'm moved only by what I believe!

Then touched he [Jesus] their eyes, saying,
ACCORDING TO YOUR FAITH be it unto you.
— MATTHEW 9:29

May 26

You Receive 'According to Your Faith'

At a meeting in California, a seventy-two-year-old woman who wore a hearing aid approached me. She couldn't hear without her hearing aid. In fact, she said, "I can't even get half the message with my hearing aid on and sitting right under the speaker. I need to hear the Word."

I laid hands on her ears. Instantly, she could hear a watch tick out of either ear! That was quite obvious. She was there two more weeks in every service. She didn't need her hearing aid. She was talking to everyone in normal tones.

Now she had fallen and broken her hip some time before, so she used a walking stick to walk. As she walked away, I said, "Wait a minute!"

She turned and looked. I said, "Don't you want something else?"

She said, "No, I got what I came after."

I said, "What about that hip?"

She said, "Oh, I can live with that, but I really needed to hear."

I went back the next year and held a meeting in the same church. I saw the same woman a year later. She was hearing fine and talking to everyone in normal tones without a hearing aid, but she still had her cane.

Jesus said more than once, "According to your faith, so be it done unto you." Well, faith for healing for her ears was as far as this woman's faith went. And that's as far as she received.

Confession:

I receive according to my faith. Jesus said that according to my faith, it is done unto me.

The Spirit of the Lord is upon me [Jesus], because he hath anointed me to preach the gospel to the poor; he hath sent me to heal the brokenhearted, to preach deliverance to the captives, and recovering of sight to the blind, to set at liberty them that are bruised.

— LUKE 4:18

Jesus Is in the Delivering Business

I received a letter from a gentleman who had attended a meeting I held in Phoenix, Arizona, many years ago. This gentleman mentioned that he had been an officer in the United States Army. At the time of the meeting in Phoenix, he was retired and had just gotten out of the veterans' hospital for the third time. He had been in the hospital trying to be cured of alcoholism. But he came out drinking. He had also admitted himself into three different private hospitals trying to be cured of alcoholism.

He finally got down on his knees and began to pray. He said, "Lord, I knew You when I was young. Take me back. I'm a wayward child. Forgive me. Like the prodigal son of old, I'm coming back home."

After he prayed, that burden rolled off him just like a heavy load rolling off his chest. But he was still bound by alcohol. He couldn't stop drinking. A friend told him about our meeting in Phoenix and said, "There's a former Baptist preacher out there laying hands on people. They're getting healed and delivered."

He came to the meeting seeking help. I laid hands on him. A year later, I heard from him. He said, "Since then, I've never touched another drop of alcohol. I've never even wanted it."

Now in his letter, eight years had come and gone. He wrote, "The power of God came on me, surged through my body, and drove that alcohol demon right out of me. I've never had any withdrawal symptoms in all these years."

Isn't that just like Jesus? He wants to help people.

Confession:

Jesus came to set people free. He came to bring healing and deliverance to the world. Thank You, Jesus, for giving Your life so that I could be free!

Wherefore be ye not unwise, but understanding what the will of the Lord is.

May 28

— EPHESIANS 5:17

Should You Take Your Medicine?

People are always asking me if they should take their medicine or not. I tell them to wait until the Lord tells them to stop taking it. Don't stop taking your medicine because I told you to do it. I'm not going to tell you what to do.

I'm not opposed to doctors. Thank God for medical science. They're against the same things I'm against; they're fighting sickness and disease too. Nowadays, it's exciting that more and more doctors also believe in prayer and divine healing.

When people's faith is strong enough and they come to the knowledge of the truth, they may not need medical help. I was healed of two serious organic heart troubles, a body that was almost totally paralyzed, and an incurable blood disease. I never ran and played like other little children. I became bedfast at the age of fifteen. The doctors said that nobody in my condition ever lived past sixteen years of age.

As I read Grandma's Methodist Bible, I acted on Mark 11:23 and 24 and was healed. And in almost seventy years, I've never had so much as an aspirin. I haven't needed one. There's nothing wrong with taking aspirins if you need them, but I haven't had a headache in almost seventy years. I haven't had the flu in almost seventy years. I'm expecting to live and die without a headache. I'm expecting to live and die and never have the flu. Why? I found out about divine healing.

Thank God for natural healing. Thank God for what man can do. Doctors are fighting the same disease and devil we're fighting. Let's join hands with doctors and let them tell us when to stop taking our medicine.

Confession:

I thank God for doctors and the advances of medical science, but I am so glad that I know about divine healing. I am so glad that I know Jesus took my infirmities and bore my sicknesses.

149

And these signs shall follow them that believe; In my name shall they cast out devils; they shall speak with new tongues;
They shall take up serpents; and if they drink any deadly thing, it shall not hurt them; they shall lay hands on the sick, and they shall recover.

MARK 16:17,18

A Gradual Healing

Several years ago, I received a letter from a woman who had attended one of my meetings in Houston, Texas. She wrote, "I was healed of lung cancer at your meeting. Now I'm not saying that I was healed instantly; I wasn't. But the manifestation began the moment you laid hands on me. I am a thirty-two-year-old mother of two young daughters, and my condition was very serious. In fact, the doctors expected me to live only a few weeks. I had multiple malignant tumors in my lungs."

She continued, "Now I was skeptical of your tactics. Each night you laid hands on me [evidently, she got in the healing line every night], I felt nothing. And then the last night, you taught on Mark 16:15-18. I had never heard a sermon preached on that passage before. I believed what you said and asked God in the Name of Jesus to heal me. After that, I got in the healing line. And the moment you laid hands on me, I felt hot from the top of my head to the soles of my feet. [That was the healing power of God going into her.]"

The tumors were located in two places in her lungs. One tumor was large, and the other was smaller. A month after the healing power of God went into her, the large tumor was gone; the doctors couldn't find it. And in another two months, the other tumor was gone. The doctors were baffled. They couldn't understand it. But, you see, from the moment that hands were laid upon her, she began to amend (John 4:52). The rest of the letter stated that she was able to do all of her housework and mow the yard and that she felt wonderful!

Well, isn't that just like our wonderful Jesus? Once this woman accepted the deathblow to that cancer, she began to recover. And over the course of time, the healing was manifested.

Confession:

I receive the healing power of God into my body now, and I expect to recover. The healing power of God is working in my body to effect a healing and a cure.

*For verily I [Jesus] say unto you, That whosoever shall say
unto this mountain, Be thou removed, and be thou cast
into the sea; and shall not doubt in his heart, but shall
believe that those things which he saith shall come to pass;
he shall have whatsoever he saith.*

— MARK 11:23

The Principle of Faith

Once I invited a pastor to go with me to a preaching engagement in California. This pastor was fifty-six years old. At the age of thirty-nine, he discovered that he had diabetes. So for seventeen years, he had given himself a shot of insulin every day.

This pastor was a good man and had a wonderful church. But somehow, he had failed to grasp healing. Now I didn't talk to him personally. I think that sometimes people are sitting around waiting for God to initiate something. And sometimes God does initiate something on His own. But people don't have to just sit around and wait on Him.

I wanted to teach this pastor about the authority he has in Christ. I know the authority I have, and as long as a person is with me, I can exercise that authority. But when someone is on his own, he has to exercise his own authority. That's the reason things will happen many times in healing meetings — because people's faith is at a high and everyone is believing God. As a result, people get healed. But if people don't develop their own faith, they can lose their healing.

As we began our trip to California, I said to this pastor, "As long as you're with me, you'll not register any abnormal levels of sugar." I said that in faith. I didn't say that because I was led of the Lord to say it. I didn't say that because I was inspired to say it.

Many times people think that the Word will work if it is quickened to them. Well, sometimes God's Word is quickened to us, and it does work; that's true. But we make a mistake in thinking that's the *only* way it works, and that it always has to be that way.

I said that to my pastor friend because it is a faith principle. And faith principles work in the spirit realm just like natural principles work in the natural world. I don't have to get inspired to use the natural principle of the multiplication table. Three times three is nine. I know that. Similarly, I can use the principle of faith at any time to receive the blessings of God.

Confession:

Faith principles work! I exercise my authority in the spirit realm, and according to Mark 11:23, I can have whatsoever I say!

May 31

For verily I say unto you, That whosoever shall say unto this mountain, Be thou removed, and be thou cast into the sea; and shall not doubt in his heart, but shall believe that those things which he saith shall come to pass; he shall have whatsoever he saith.

— MARK 11:23

Have Faith in God

Several years ago, I was hemorrhaging from my body. I had serious pain symptoms. It was almost intolerable. The devil was giving me mental visions of cancer. I didn't have any kind of inspiration, and all the feelings I had were negative.

Now I learned the multiplication table many years ago. It still works. Three time three is still nine. I don't ever stop to think, *Will that work? Do you suppose three times three is still nine? Do you suppose the multiplication table will work today? I can't get it to work for me. I see it working for others, but it won't work for me.* No, if multiplication doesn't work for you, it's because you don't know the principle well enough.

I said to myself as I was lying in bed, "I learned what faith is. I learned Mark 11:23, which says, 'Whosoever shall say and not doubt in his heart, but shall believe that those things which he saith shall come to pass, he shall have whatsoever he saith.'"

So I just started saying, "According to the Word of God, I'm healed." In the face of pain, in the face of the most alarming symptoms, I said this. Every symptom began to abate almost immediately. And within two or three days, every symptom was gone.

Confession:

I say and do not doubt in my heart. I believe that those things that I say shall come to pass. Every day, I say, "According to the Word of God, I am healed!"

So shall my word be that goeth forth out of my mouth: it shall not return unto me void, but it shall accomplish that which I please, and it shall prosper in the thing whereto I sent it.

— ISAIAH 55:11

God and His Word Are One

I've never figured out how people think they're going to get God to do something for them apart from the Bible. You see, you can't separate God from His Word. The Bible is the Word of God. You can't separate someone from his or her word. In other words, a person is known by his or her word. God is known by His Word. He is everything the Word says He is, and He will do everything His Word says He will do.

If you want to find out who God is, go to the Word and find out. Sometimes people say, "Well, I don't know whether God will do that or not. I hope He will." If you want to find out what God will do, go to the Word.

I remember a man years ago who was in the healing ministry. He was saved, filled with the Holy Ghost, and was getting good results in his ministry. He wasn't praying in faith; the Holy Ghost was just manifesting Himself through him.

Now this man had missed it in a few places. I don't mean that he did some great wrong. He didn't rob a bank or kill someone. But he simply realized that he had missed God and failed to do what God wanted him to do. James 4:17 says, *"Therefore to him that knoweth to do good, and doeth it not, to him it is sin."* So he had sinned.

This minister said, "I hope the Lord will forgive me. I don't know whether He will or not." He was mightily used by God, yet didn't even know what the Bible teaches! The minute he said that, I automatically thought of what First John 1:9 says: *"If we confess our sins, he is faithful and just to forgive us our sins, and to cleanse us from all unrighteousness."*

This minister died early in life — before his time — right in the middle of his ministry. Some people said that the Lord just called him home. No, He didn't. This minister did go home to be with the Lord, but the Lord didn't *call* him home. He played into the hands of the devil, and the devil tripped him up and robbed him of what God intended for him to have. He should have learned that God and His Word are one. He should have still been alive and preaching.

Confession:

God and His Word are one. I line my words up with God's Word and see the results I've been longing for.

153

And whatsoever ye shall ask in my name, that will I do, that the Father may be glorified in the Son.

— JOHN 14:13

Exercise Your Authority

You have a right to freedom from pain and sickness. In Jesus' Name, you can command them to leave. Many people are always trying to get someone else to do it for them. Sometimes you can exercise your authority for someone else, and sometimes you can't. If you could always receive the blessings of God for others, that would relieve them of all responsibility. But the Bible teaches individual responsibility.

You have certain rights in the natural. For example, as a United States citizen, you have the right to vote in elections. I can't vote for you. You must be the one who exercises your rights, not someone else. That's also true in the spiritual. God the Father has given you authority over demon forces in the Name of Jesus. So you can use that Name to break the power of the devil, because sickness is caused by satanic oppression. You can use that Name to break the power of the devil over the unsaved and make it easier for them to accept Christ. They'll still have to do the accepting; you can't do that for them.

Confession:

I have the right to freedom from pain and sickness. I have the right to healing. And I exercise my rights. In the Name of Jesus, I command sickness and disease to go!

. . . they shall lay hands on the sick, and they shall recover.

— MARK 16:18

The Laying On of Hands Is a Point of Contact

When my wife and I moved to Oklahoma from Texas, we had to get Oklahoma driver's licenses. We picked up an Oklahoma driving manual, because in different states, the laws are a little different. Because we already had licenses, all we had to do was study the manual and take the written test; we didn't have to take the driving test. But I learn a whole lot more by driving — I personally learn a whole lot more by experience — than I do by reading the manual. Also, things I read in the manual come back to my remembrance when I'm driving.

The Christian life is the same way. We learn from our handbook, the Bible. But we also learn by experience.

The Bible teaches us about the laying on of hands. Any believer can lay hands on you without any anointing — without any kind of feeling — just because the Bible said it. The laying on of hands is a point of contact to release your faith. Now by that, I mean, that's the point where you start believing, "I receive my healing."

I've had people say to me, "Well, but what if I'm not healed?" They missed what I told them entirely. They didn't even get what I said.

If you'll believe that you receive it, you'll have it. But most people want to have it first, *then* they're going to believe they receive it. Well, there wouldn't be any faith to that! You wouldn't have to *believe* it then; you'd *know* it.

Confession:

When a believer lays hands on me, I release my faith. I start believing that I receive my healing.

For with the heart man believeth unto righteous-ness; and with the mouth confession is made unto salvation.

— ROMANS 10:10

Faith Is Not of the Head; It's of the Heart

Something that hinders many people is that they mentally try to believe they receive. They are just imitating someone else. With their mind, they say, "Yes, I believe."

You can usually tell when people are talking out of their mind or when they are talking out of their spirit. You see, your heart is your spirit, and your spirit is your heart. With the heart, man believeth. There will be a lack of conviction — a lack of assurance — when a person is speaking out of his or her mind. There will be hesitancy.

When I lay hands on people to be healed, I sometimes say to them, "Will you be healed now when I lay hands on you?"

Some people say, "Well, uh, yes, I believe." But I know they're not in faith.

I've had other people say, "I sure will! Just lay your hands on me and watch it! I'll be healed right now!" That's assurance. You can tell that right away. When I lay hands on them, it's like I am holding a live wire. The power of God just rushes out of me into them. Their faith becomes active. Their faith was at the place where they believed they received. Faith is not of the head; it's of the heart.

Confession:

Faith is of the heart. I believe I receive healing when hands are laid on me. I believe from my heart.

Trust in the Lord with all thine heart; and lean not unto thine own understanding.

Enter Into Rest

"Your own understanding" is *your own reasoning, your own thinking,* or *your own head or mind.* In other words, you could say, "Trust in the Lord with all thine heart and lean not to thine own *head*"! I think most Christians try to practice that in reverse. They trust in the Lord with all their head and lean not to their own heart. That's not what God said to do.

Hebrews 4:3 says, *"For we which have believed do enter into rest, as he said, As I have sworn in my wrath, if they shall enter into my rest: although the works were finished from the foundation of the world."* How can you tell if people are believing in their heart or just saying it from their head? The Scripture says that those who have believed "do enter into rest."

Remember, I said that the laying on of hands is a point of contact. That's the point where you start believing that you receive your healing. That's the point where you enter into rest about the situation. You're no longer frustrated. You're no longer fretting. You're not trying to get something. You believe that you have received it, and there is a rest on the inside of you. There is a rest in your spirit. Then you just sort of laugh to yourself, smile, and say, "I've got it; it's mine."

Confession:

I am not TRYING to get something. I believe that I have received. There is a rest on the inside of me. There is a rest in my spirit. I have healing; it's mine!

God is a Spirit: and they that worship him must worship him in spirit and in truth.

— JOHN 4:24

Healing Starts in Your Spirit

Healing starts in your spirit. Before it's ever manifested in your body, you believe you have it in your spirit. That's how I have received some of the greatest things that have ever happened to me in my life. I have received physical healing, finances, and many other things this way. I received them in my spirit first. I knew on the inside of me that I had "it" (whatever "it" was) before I ever saw it with my physical eyes.

I was calm; I was at rest. I had a peace, an assurance, a conviction on the inside of me. And when the devil came to my mind trying to make me question it, I would start laughing.

You may ask, "I want that kind of faith. How can I get it?" Romans 10:17 says, *"So then faith cometh by hearing, and hearing by the word of God."* If you'll meditate on the Bible, the Word of God, it will build conviction and assurance into your spirit. You'll not be moved. When the storms of life are raging, there will be a rest on the inside of you.

Confession:

The Bible says, "For we which have believed do enter into rest." I believe and, therefore, enter into God's rest. There is a conviction, an assurance, a "knowing" on the inside of me that what I have believed is mine now.

And said, Verily I [Jesus] say unto you, Except ye be converted, and become as little children, ye shall not enter into the kingdom of heaven.

— MATTHEW 18:3

Have Childlike Faith

At a meeting in Oklahoma, a gentleman came up to me and said that he was so hard of hearing that he couldn't hear it thunder without a hearing aid. Well, I laid hands on him and his ears were perfectly healed; he could hear.

I saw him five years later when he was seventy-seven years old, and he still didn't need a hearing aid. I saw him after another five years (when he was eighty-two years old), and he was still all right.

Not only that, but when I laid hands on him at the age of seventy-two, he could not walk by himself. He'd had a cane that he walked with, but he couldn't even walk with the cane anymore. He couldn't walk twelve or fifteen feet without falling. His daughter, who was with him, had to hold him up. The doctor said he should be in a wheelchair. The doctor told him at his last examination that he would go from his cane to a wheelchair, from a wheelchair to the bed, and from the bed to the grave. There was nothing medical science could do.

We laid hands on him in the Name of Jesus and believed God. He believed God too. We took the cane away from him, and he walked a steady, straight line.

At the age of eighty-two, he was still walking without a cane. I remember that when I dealt with him, it was almost like dealing with a child in that he believed everything I told him. We all need to have that kind of childlike faith.

Confession:

I believe what God's Word says. I am quick to believe God's Word. If God said it, I believe it, and that settles it!

Where is boasting then? It is excluded. By what law?
of works? Nay: but by the law of faith.

— ROMANS 3:27

The Law of Faith

At the same meeting in which I laid hands on the seventy-two-year-old man, I laid hands on his pastor. But the pastor did not receive healing. Five years later, he decided to resign his church. He said to me, "I've had this physical condition for so many years, and I just can't get healed. I feel like I'm doing the church an injustice because I can't do my job properly. I'm just going to retire." He was in his mid-fifties. He did retire and I never heard of him again.

Someone might ask, "Well, why could you get that church member healed, but not the pastor?"

I'll tell you exactly why. When I dealt with the pastor, I laid hands on him, prayed for him, and asked him the same questions I asked the man who was a member of his church. The pastor heard me talk to the man. He saw the man healed. He knew his physical condition. He knew that there was nothing that could be done from a medical standpoint — that it had to be supernatural. Yet the pastor sat right there and missed it.

Why? He was too much in the mental realm. Spiritual things were not real to him even though he was saved, filled with the Holy Ghost, and pastoring a Full Gospel church. Why didn't God just go ahead and heal him because he was such a good person? God operates by certain laws. One of those laws is the law of faith. This pastor didn't work that law. "

Confession:

I base my faith on what I know from God's Word. I don't base my faith on human reasoning or understanding. I operate out of my spirit, not my head.

— PROVERBS 3:5

The Hand of Faith

I said to this pastor when I laid hands on him, "Will you be healed now as I lay hands on you and pray?"

He said, "Brother Hagin, I sure hope so."

"Well," I said, "you won't be."

He responded, "I'm not going to say I'm going to receive something when I don't know whether I am or not."

I said to him, "Let me ask you a question." I held up a hymnal and said, "Let's say this songbook I'm holding is mine. And let's imagine that there are some songs in here that no other songbook has. You're a pastor and you'd like your congregation to learn some of these songs, but the songbook is out of print. So I decide to give it to you. It's yours. Would you say, 'I don't know whether I'm going to receive it or not. I hope I am'?"

"No, I'd just reach out and take it," he answered.

"Well, when it comes to spiritual things, you can't reach out your physical hand and take it," I said. "But there is a man living inside your physical body — your spirit man. The Bible calls him the hidden man of the heart, or the inner man. That inward man has a hand too. It's called the hand of faith."

He said, "Well, I'm not going to believe I have something I can't see or feel."

He wanted to see it first. He wasn't trusting in God with all his heart. Instead, he was leaning to his own understanding. He was relying on natural human reasoning.

I said to the pastor, "Well, you go sit down and do without healing, because you'll never get it as long as you're thinking that way." And he never did receive healing. Now if he had changed his thinking, his believing, and his talking, he could have been healed.

Confession:

I trust in the Lord with all my heart. I don't lean to my own understanding. I believe I receive healing before I ever see it with my physical eyes. I reach out and take healing with the hand of faith.

June 10

Even so faith, if it hath not works, is dead, being alone.

— JAMES 2:17

Act on Your Faith

Years ago, when my mother-in-law had a goiter, the Lord said to me, "Tell her to go to the altar at your church on Wednesday night, and I will fill her with the Holy Ghost and complete her healing."

Now if you stopped to analyze some things, you might talk yourself right out of God's blessings. Why did she have to go to the altar at the Full Gospel church on Wednesday night in order to receive? I didn't know why at the time, but I told her what the Lord told me.

On Wednesday night, we had a time of testifying and singing. I ministered a short sermon. My mother-in-law could tell that I was about to finish. She didn't even wait for me to say anything. She suddenly stood to her feet and said, "I can't wait." She came out from between the pews and just sprawled out on the altar. By the time her knees hit the floor, she was talking in tongues.

Later I learned why God had her go to the altar. She testified, "I'd always said, 'I'd like to have the Holy Ghost. I can see that it's in the Bible. But there's one thing I'll never do. You'll never catch me in the altar of that Full Gospel church.'"

You see, my mother-in-law was Methodist, but she was in the altar of that Full Gospel church that Wednesday night! And when she got up from the altar, the knot on her neck that was the size of a quarter was gone; it disappeared! Her healing was completed.

You'll find that very often healing will begin in people's bodies, but it won't be completed until something is done — until people act on their faith.

Confession:

I act on my faith. I believe God's Word. I obey the voice of the Spirit of God. I do what He tells me to do.

And Samuel said, Hath the Lord as great delight in burnt offerings and sacrifices, as in obeying the voice of the Lord? Behold, to obey is better than sacrifice, and to hearken than the fat of rams.

— 1 SAMUEL 15:22

June 11

It Pays To Obey God

I remember a dear, precious saint of God. She was saved and filled with the Holy Ghost. It was a joy to sit down and talk to her about the things of God.

I don't know how many times over a period of several years that I prayed with that dear woman for healing. I could help her momentarily, but I never could get her completely healed. She would be all right for a little while, and then she would lose it.

I wondered why she had been in such bad health for so many years. She was eighty years old, and for many years, she had never really lived. Sickness and disease had incapacitated her. One day while standing over her bedside, she said, "I never did what God asked me to do. I wasn't willing. God called me to be a missionary when I was twelve years old."

She loved the Lord, but she was never willing to obey Him. She was never willing to do what He wanted her to do. That hindered the flow of God's healing power. I understood it all then.

You see, disobedience opens the door to the enemy. Satan has a right to come in if the door is open. I've heard people talk about what it costs to serve God. It doesn't *cost* to go all out — it *pays*! But it will cost you to disobey God. It will cost you not to be in the will of God. It will cost you heartache and sadness. It will cost you sickness and disease. It will cost you money. Sometimes, it will cost you premature death.

If there is something you need to deal with, deal with it. If there is something hindering the healing flow, get it unstopped. Be willing to do anything God wants you to do.

Confession:

I am willing to do anything God wants me to do. Father God, show me any area of my life that is not right with You, and I will correct it. I will line my life up with You and Your Word.

163

June 12

Then Abraham gave up the ghost, and died in a good old age, an old man, and full of years; and was gathered to his people.

— GENESIS 25:8

You Can Die Without Sickness and Disease

Older people are eventually going to live their life out and go home to Heaven, but they don't have to die with sickness and disease. Grandma Jeffcoat is a good example of this. She had stomach cancer. She came to live with her daughter who attended my church. Grandma Jeffcoat had just come from Brother J.R. Goodwin's church. He was her former pastor.

Grandma Jeffcoat was so far gone physically that her family had already called Brother Goodwin to preach at her funeral. Her daughter said to me, "Brother Hagin, I want you to go see Mom."

Well, I began to talk to her mom, Grandma Jeffcoat, about healing. "Brother Hagin," she said, "Just leave me alone. I'm eighty-two years old, and I've suffered so with cancer of the stomach. Please leave me alone and let me die. I'm saved and ready for Heaven. Let me go on."

I said, "I'm not going to do it. Let God heal you and then die if you want to. It's not the will of God that you die with stomach cancer."

I knew that she was not going to be healed by my believing she was going to live while she believed she was going to die. There was no agreement there. I didn't pray for her healing on the first visit. I didn't pray for her healing on the *second* visit.

I just kept pouring the Word into her. I would kneel by her bed, lay my hand on her, and pray, "God, help Grandma not to cast away her confidence. She knows healing is right. Healing is the thing that brought her into the Pentecostal movement many years ago."

Confession:

I don't have to die with sickness and disease. No, God can heal me, and THEN I can decide if I'm ready to go home and be with Him.

164

God Has Promised You Long Life

We used to have divine healing services every Saturday night in our church, and Grandma Jeffcoat would be carried in. Sometimes she would have a spell, and we would think she was dead. Then somehow she would start breathing again. Those were some experiences!

That went on for about six months. We can get faith into people by teaching them, but we also need to get them into services where God is manifesting Himself.

One Saturday night, Grandma Jeffcoat was at the service, and as we came to the close, I had a little quick vision about her. I saw her out of her chair dancing. I looked over at her and told her it was her time. I walked down off the platform, laid hands on her, and prayed. At the moment, nothing happened, but ten minutes later, she let out a yell, jumped out of the chair, and started dancing. She was healed!

Several years later, my wife and I stopped by to visit her when she was ninety-one years old. Her daughter said that she was away visiting some people and that she was always busy running around. Grandma Jeffcoat's doctor had just examined her and said that he had never seen anything quite like it before. Her heart was perfect, and there wasn't a thing wrong with her! The doctor was fifty-five and said that he wished he was in as good a condition as she was!

Grandma Jeffcoat died when she was ninety-three, without sickness and disease! She just fell asleep in Jesus. I'm so glad I didn't let her die of that cancer.

Confession:

I will live a long life on the earth. And I will die without sickness and disease.

> Then came Peter to him, and said, Lord, how oft
> shall my brother sin against me, and I forgive him? till
> seven times? Jesus saith unto him, I say not unto thee,
> Until seven times: but, Until seventy times seven.
>
> — MATTHEW 18:21,22

God Is Willing To Forgive

I was holding a meeting in Houston, Texas, and a fine businessman came up to me and asked if he could talk to me.

I said, "I just don't have time right now. But I tell you what I'll do. I'll come thirty minutes early tomorrow night, and I'll meet you in the pastor's office. I can talk to you for thirty minutes, but that's all."

The next night as I was getting ready, the Lord said to me, "Do you think that I'd require you to do something that I wouldn't be willing to do?"

I said to the Lord, "Well, no, certainly not. That wouldn't be right. That would be unjust. And You are not unjust." The Lord asked me that question three more times, and I replied in the same way. The final time He asked me the question, He also said, "Remember, Peter came to Me and said, 'If my brother sins against me, how oft shall I forgive him? Till seven times?' And I said, 'Not seven times, but *seventy times seven.*' So I require you to forgive four hundred and ninety times in one day! Now if I require you to forgive, then would I be unwilling to forgive?"

I said, "Certainly not."

Then I heard these words in my spirit, *"Is any sick among you? let him call for the elders of the church; and let them pray over him, anointing him with oil in the name of the Lord: And the prayer of faith shall save the sick, and the Lord shall raise him up; AND IF HE HAVE COMMITTED SINS, THEY SHALL BE FORGIVEN HIM"* (James 5:14,15).

I drove up to the church and opened my Bible. I had read that passage in James hundreds of times, but I had never noticed that it said, "sins," *plural.* The moment I went into the pastor's office to talk to this man, I realized exactly what the Lord was doing; He was preparing me to help this man.

Confession:

God would not require me to do something that He wouldn't be willing to do. He tells me to forgive another person 490 times in one day. And He is willing to forgive me 490 times in one day! I receive His forgiveness, and I receive healing.

And the prayer of faith shall save the sick, and the Lord shall raise him up; and if he have committed sins, they shall be forgiven him.

Don't Dwell on Past Failures!

The doctors had told this businessman that he could fall dead any minute because of a severe heart condition. He also had high blood pressure and a severe kidney condition. The doctors said that if he would sell his business, stay on his medication, and just lie around, he might possibly live another two years. That's about the best they could offer. If he didn't do that, he could fall dead in his place of business any minute.

I asked him the question that the Lord had asked me: "Do you believe that God would require you to do something that He wouldn't do?"

"Why, no, certainly not," he said.

We turned to Matthew 18:21 and 22 and read where Peter asked how often he should forgive his brother. Then we turned to James 5:14 and 15 and read that if a person has committed any sins, they will be forgiven him. That is the thing that keeps many people's faith from working. They think that God won't heal them because they've failed.

Confession:

Father God, I ask You to forgive me for any wrong I've committed. I thank You for forgiveness. I thank You for health and healing.

There is therefore now no condemnation to them which are in Christ Jesus, who walk not after the flesh, but after the Spirit.

— ROMANS 8:1

'I Could Have Done More'

This businessman said, "You don't understand what I've done."

I thought from the way this man talked that he had committed some terrible sins. So I said, "Just what awful sins have you committed?"

"Brother Hagin," he said with tears, "It's not so much sins of *commission*. I don't know if I've done anything wrong. It's sins of *omission*. The Bible says, *'Therefore to him that knoweth to do good, and doeth it not, to him it is sin'* [James 4:17]. Now I'm a businessman and I've always had money. I have supported the church and paid tithes, but I could have given much more money. I could have prayed more. I could have been more faithful to my church."

I said, "I want to ask you a question. Have you committed the sin of omission four hundred and ninety times in one day?"

He said, "No, I haven't done that four hundred and ninety times in *thirty-six years!*" I got him to see that from those scriptures in Matthew and James. I laid hands on him in the office and prayed. He was healed.

Years later when he was in his seventies, I learned that he had just retired from business. Now he could have died in his mid-fifties, and someone would have said, "That was the will of God. God took him home." No! He could have gone home if I had not gotten his faith to work. If he hadn't accepted what I said to him, I couldn't have helped him. And if he hadn't done what the doctors said, he would have probably fallen dead.

Confession:

There is therefore now no condemnation to me who is in Christ Jesus. I forgive myself freely, because I know that God has forgiven me! I am qualified to receive the blessings of God, such as healing.

Obey the Laws of the Land

At the age of forty-two or forty-three, one of my uncles was working at a power plant north of McKinney, Texas. He was one of the two men who worked the graveyard shift from midnight to 8:00 a.m. The following was painted on a wall at the plant: DO NOT PULL THIS SWITCH UNLESS THE RUBBER MAT IS IN PLACE.

At about 4:00 a.m. one morning, my uncle stepped outside to get a little fresh air. The grass was wet with dew so his feet got wet. He came back in and pulled that switch without the rubber mat being in place. Hundreds of volts of electricity went through him.

The man upstairs heard him hollering. He ran downstairs, grabbed a pole to ground and protect himself from that powerful voltage, and knocked my uncle loose. Then he called an ambulance. My uncle was still conscious at the time. They put him in the ambulance and headed toward the hospital. He realized he was dying, but, praise God, he went home singing because he was a Christian.

Well, I'm glad he went to Heaven, but you couldn't say that God took him. He just went home early because he was careless. Various insurance companies and other organizations run safety programs at different workplaces, reminding them to be careful. Did you ever notice that when people abide by the safety rules, God doesn't take so many of them home! I said that jokingly. The point is, if we're not careful, we can put the blame in the wrong place.

Confession:

I obey God's laws set forth in His Word. And I also obey the natural laws of the land. As a result, I enjoy a long life on this earth.

> But whoso looketh into the perfect law of liberty,
> and continueth therein, he being not a forgetful
> hearer, but a doer of the work, this man shall be
> blessed in his deed.
>
> — JAMES 1:25

Put the Word Into Practice

I was asked to preach at a certain convention in California. They wanted me to come and teach on the subject of faith. I didn't have a "laying on of hands" service. I didn't have a "preaching" or a "ministering" service. I just taught on the subject of faith.

There was a woman there who was a member of the First Foursquare Church of Pueblo, Colorado. She had said, "I'll go to that convention and get Brother Hagin to lay hands on me." She had terminal cancer.

Well, she came, but I wasn't having a laying-on-of-hands service. I was simply teaching the Word. So she said to herself, *I'll just put that Word into practice myself.* She acted on the Word she heard and was completely healed.

Two years later, I happened to be at this woman's church in Pueblo, Colorado, and she was there. She gave her testimony. At first, her doctor just said that the cancer had gone into remission, but said that if she was still free of cancer after two years, it wouldn't come back; she'd be cured. She'd gone in for her final examination right before I arrived.

After her examination, the nurse came up to her and asked, "Are you a member of one of those churches that believes in divine healing and the power of God?"

"Yes," she said.

The nurse began to cry and said, "You know, the doctor and I already figured that out. We have your test results. This had to be a miracle of God!"

Confession:

I am not just a hearer of the Word. I am a doer of the Word. I act on what God's Word says, and I receive healing.

Fools because of their transgression, and because of their iniquities, are afflicted. Their soul abhorreth all manner of meat; and they draw near unto the gates of death. Then they cry unto the Lord in their trouble, and he saveth them out of their distresses.

— PSALM 107:17-19

Don't Be a Fool!

I remember praying for a sixteen-year-old girl who had a venereal disease. Now when she came up to the prayer line, I didn't know anything about her. I found out later that at the age of fifteen, she got involved with a gang. Now she was saved and filled with the Holy Ghost, but she had gotten involved in all kinds of sin and sexual immorality. At sixteen, the doctors wanted to take out all her female organs. They were damaged. Of course, if those organs were removed, she could never become a mother.

As she stood in the prayer line, the Spirit of God said to me, "Fools, because of their iniquities, because of their transgressions, are afflicted. Say to her, 'Confess, "I'm that fool," and you'll be healed.'"

So I just spoke that out to her. I said, "The Bible says that fools, because of their iniquities and transgression, are afflicted. Confess that you are that fool and you'll be healed."

I never laid hands on her. She threw her hands up and said, "I'm that fool," over and over again. She was instantly healed and never had to have that operation. In the process of time, she got married and became a mother.

Even since I've been saved, I've had to go to God and say, "I've been a fool. I acted foolishly. Forgive me." And, thank God, He did. If you've never done that, you probably need to start right now.

Confession:

Father God, I have acted foolishly. I ask You to forgive me and cleanse me from all unrighteousness. Thank You.

Of the doctrine of baptisms, and of laying on of hands . . .

— HEBREWS 6:2

Let God Do It His Way!

Let's read the following Bible account about a man named Naaman who had leprosy.

2 KINGS 5:1,9-14

1   Now Naaman, captain of the host of the king of Syria, was a great man with his master, and honourable, because by him the Lord had given deliverance unto Syria: he was also a mighty man in valour, but he was a leper. . . .

9   So Naaman came with his horses and with his chariot, and stood at the door of the house of Elisha.

10   And Elisha sent a messenger unto him, saying, Go and wash in Jordan seven times, and thy flesh shall come again to thee, and thou shalt be clean.

11   But NAAMAN WAS WROTH, AND WENT AWAY, AND SAID, Behold, I THOUGHT, HE WILL SURELY COME OUT TO ME, AND STAND, AND CALL ON THE NAME OF THE LORD HIS GOD, AND STRIKE HIS HAND OVER THE PLACE, AND RECOVER THE LEPER.

12   Are not Abana and Pharpar, rivers of Damascus, better than all the waters of Israel? may I not wash in them, and be clean? SO HE TURNED AND WENT AWAY IN A RAGE.

13   And his servants came near, and spake unto him, and said, My father, if the prophet had bid thee do some great thing, wouldest thou not have done it? how much rather then, when he saith to thee, Wash, and be clean?

14   Then went he down, and dipped himself seven times in Jordan, according to the saying of the man of God: and his flesh came again like unto the flesh of a little child, and he was clean.

Notice that the prophet Elisha did not even go out to minister to Naaman. Naaman, a mighty man of valor and captain of the host of the king of Syria, never did get to see Elisha. Instead, Elisha sent his servant to tell Naaman what to do. Naaman almost missed his healing by saying, "I thought surely the prophet would come out himself and call on the Name of the Lord on my behalf." You see, many people miss their healing because they want it done their way. Let's just let God do things His way and be blessed as we do.

Confession:

I don't want to miss out on my healing. God, I will obey You; I will do what You want me to do in the way You want me to do it so that I may receive my healing. Thank You, Father.

And herein do I exercise myself, to have always a conscience void of offence toward God, and toward men.

June 21

— ACTS 24:16

Don't Become Offended

A number of years ago, a mother and her sick little boy came to our Campmeeting. They stood in the healing line. Before I ever got to them, I got tired and turned the ministering to the sick over to others. Well, the mother almost missed it. She got mad and thought, *He doesn't care anything about us.*

People forget that I'm human. I'm still living inside a physical, mortal body. I get tired, just as anyone else does. And when a person gets tired, he can't yield to the Spirit of God like he can when he's rested. The devil told her, "He doesn't care." And she almost missed it.

I turned the healing line over to some RHEMA students who'd been working with me in Healing School. We found out later that the devil told the mother, "Now this young man's going to say that your boy is demon-possessed. He's going to make a scene right here in front of everyone." She became even more angry and offended.

This RHEMA student gently talked to the mother and boy. He didn't deal with any devil or demon at all. In fact, he told her that it wasn't a demon causing the boy's problem. He laid his hands on the boy and prayed, and the child was healed.

In the process of time, the doctors said that the boy was normal. They couldn't understand it. Before, they said he would never be normal — that he would never be right a day in his life. But they finally had to admit that he was normal.

I'm glad this woman didn't give place to the devil and his lies. It would have hindered the healing power in her son's life.

Confession:

I always exercise myself to have a conscience void of offense toward God and man. As a result, I keep myself open to the healing power of God.

But he [Elisha] said, As the Lord liveth, before whom I stand, I will receive none. And he urged him to take it; but he refused.

— 2 KINGS 5:16

You Can't Pay for God's Blessings

If we read this scripture in context, we'll find that Naaman wanted to pay Elisha for his healing. People try to do the same thing today. They would give thousands of dollars just to be healed. But they don't understand that they cannot pay for God's blessings.

One time in a healing line, a guy put a roll of bills in my hand. I don't know how many bills there were or whether they were all large or not. But he handed me a huge roll of bills with a rubber band around them. I said, "No, you take that back. I can't take that. No, sir. You take that money back. I can't take it." He did it because he was so thrilled that he had received healing. But ministers shouldn't take money in exchange for ministering healing to someone. Now if someone wants to put money in the offering, and the minister doesn't know about it, that's fine. But he or she shouldn't take any money from someone for ministering healing to him.

When the Lord appeared to me in a vision in 1950, He said, "There are two things to be careful of. One of those things is money. Just receive offerings as you have been doing. You shall make no charge for your ministry [1 Cor. 9:18]."

Over the years, we've gotten many little children delivered. We've seen children afflicted with polio healed and jumping up and down. The parents would have given thousands of dollars for the healing of their little crippled children. But the Lord said to me, "Make no charge. Only receive offerings. Be careful about money. Many on whom I've placed My Spirit and called to such a ministry have become money-minded and have lost the anointing."

Confession:

God's blessings are free. All I have to do is receive them. I don't have to work for them. I don't have to pay for them. All I have to do is thank God for them.

Afterward Jesus findeth him in the temple, and said unto him, Behold, thou art made whole: sin no more, lest a worse thing come unto thee.

June 23

— JOHN 5:14

'Go and Sin No More'

Very often, God will begin a healing in a person's life, but if he doesn't walk in obedience, he will lose it. I remember a Full Gospel businessman who had a daughter who was about nine years old. He and his wife came from ninety miles away to bring their daughter to our meeting. She had not developed right. I don't know whether the child had brain damage or something else was the matter with her, but she couldn't talk. All she could do was make sounds. She couldn't say one word that I could understand. And she couldn't use her hands, chew her food, dress herself, or even hold anything to feed herself. And she couldn't walk by herself.

After I laid hands on her, she didn't seem to be much better. I knew the power of God went into her. We did notice that she was standing up straight and walking better.

On their way home, they stopped at a drive-in to get a hamburger. Now the daughter couldn't even hold a hamburger. The mother would pinch off little bites and put them into her mouth. That was the way she had to feed her. They were sitting in the car, and it had only been about forty-five minutes since I had laid hands on her.

As the mother was pinching off the bites of hamburger for her daughter, suddenly, the little girl said, "Give me that." And she took hold of the hamburger and started eating. Within two or three days, she was ninety percent well. I saw her and talked to her. She hugged me and said, "I love you," several times.

But she lost that healing. She became worse than she ever was because her father and her mother backslid. I think they separated. If they had walked on with God, the healing would have been consummated. They were responsible; it was their child.

Confession:

I choose to walk with God. I make the decision not to live in sin anymore. A life of sin only produces troubles and hardships. But a life of godliness and holiness produces many rewards both in this life and the one that is to come.

And it came to pass, that, as they went, they were cleansed.

— LUKE 17:14

Instant Healings Can Be a Curse

I've observed many times that the Lord will begin a healing in a person's body, and as the person learns to walk in faith and walk close to Him, the healing will be completely manifested. The person receives a great spiritual blessing out of it as well as a physical blessing.

I'm inclined to agree with one minister who said that instant healings oftentimes are a curse to us. You see, many times people come to a healing meeting and are instantly healed. Many of them don't even know how they got it. Then they go away without consecrating or dedicating themselves to God, and they wind up with the same condition or something worse.

But in a gradual healing, people learn to walk close to God. They learn to exercise their faith. And they learn a great spiritual lesson in addition to having their physical healing.

Confession:

As I walk in faith, and as I walk close to God, the healing power of God drives out all sickness and disease in my body. I receive a complete manifestation of healing.

'I Shall Live and Not Die'

Years ago while I was ministering at a youth camp in the Sierra Mountains near Sonora, California, I received an emergency telephone call. The voice on the other end said, "Brother Hagin, do you remember Gary?" I did. The man was talking about his oldest boy who was nine.

"Well," he said, "he had a sore throat and we prayed about it. But it got worse. We carried him to the doctor, and the doctor said that the infection went to his kidneys. Now his kidneys have stopped functioning. The doctor said that he will be dead in a matter of minutes. He is in intensive care, and we want you to agree with us. We believe that Gary will live and not die."

I said, "I believe with you that he will live and not die."

I was at this youth camp for several weeks. Before I left, I received a little reel-to-reel tape recording in the mail. On it, the man said to me, "Brother Hagin, they would only let me in the intensive care unit for five minutes a day. I would say to Gary, 'You lie there and say, "Himself took my infirmities and bare my sicknesses." I'll live and not die.' That little fellow said that over and over again for two days and two nights. Suddenly, he was all right. We just brought Gary home, and he wants to say something to you."

Then I heard Gary say, "Brother Hagin, I want to thank you for bringing the truth to me. Dad has already told you, but I must have said those words over ten thousand times each night."

The doctors couldn't understand how that little boy had lived, but he did. God's Word works!

Confession:

I repeat the following to myself daily: "Jesus took my infirmities and bare my sicknesses. I shall live and not die, and declare the works of the Lord."

Afterward Jesus findeth him in the temple, and said unto him, Behold, thou art made whole: sin no more, lest a worse thing come unto thee.

— JOHN 5:14

Get Lined Up With God

When Gary was fifteen or sixteen years old, he left home. He got away from God and became involved in the hippie movement. He actually denounced God. And that same kidney trouble that he was healed of as a nine-year-old boy came back on him.

I went to Dallas to preach, and Gary came to my meeting. He wasn't right with God. I knew he wasn't. He tried to fake it, but he didn't fool me a bit. He was seventeen or eighteen years old at the time.

I said to him, "No, I'm not going to pray for you. You're not going to get healed under the present conditions, because you're just faking it. You haven't made things right with God."

He admitted I was right. He said, "You've told the truth about it. I haven't. There are a lot of things in me that should not be in me. I'm not right with God, and I *know* I'm not right with God. But I don't want to die. And the doctors say I'm going to die. They say I haven't got much longer to live."

I said, "Well, you have to get lined up with God."

You know, Gary refused to do that until he got right down to death's door. It cost him his life, but I'm glad he did get back into fellowship with God during the last few minutes of his life. He died praising God. But if he had done that six months ahead of time, he would have been healed.

It is important to walk with God. God doesn't put on any half-price sales. It's all or nothing with God. Make Jesus your Lord. Let Him dominate your life. Purpose to walk with Him.

Confession:

I purpose in my heart to walk with God. He is Lord of my whole life! I let Him dominate my life. I let Him have His way in my life.

Divine Healing Is Spiritual

Divine healing, though it is manifested in the physical, is spiritual. It is not mental, as Christian Science and other metaphysical teachers claim. Now don't misunderstand me. People get some results through mental science. The mind does, to a great extent, control the body, and a person could get some results that way.

I know people who seemed to be miraculously healed through metaphysical cults. And I've heard people say, "If they're healed, God must have done it."

But, no, not necessarily. If it's mental healing, their minds produced it. I would rather stay sick and not be healed than to be healed through some unbelieving cult.

Metaphysical religions such as Christian Science are not biblical. They believe that God is mind, and, in effect, that their mind is God. They believe that Jesus Christ is an idea in the divine mind of God and that He did not actually come in the flesh. And if you hold that idea in your mind, they say, it will produce certain results.

First John 4:2 says, *"Hereby know ye the Spirit of God: Every spirit that confesseth that Jesus Christ is come in the flesh is of God."* When I talk about the Lord Jesus Christ, I'm not talking about some idea; I'm talking about the Son of God! Jesus Christ of Nazareth came in the flesh and walked the shores of Galilee. When I talk about God, I'm not talking about my mind or your mind or someone else's mind! I'm talking about a divine Personality — the Father of our Lord Jesus Christ.

Divine, scriptural healing is not mental as Christian Science and other metaphysical teachers think; it's spiritual. Neither is it physical, as the medical world teaches.

Confession:

Jesus Christ came in the flesh. He is the Son of God. And He died for me to redeem me from sin, sickness, and disease. I am free because Jesus came to this earth and died on the Cross for me. Thank You, Jesus!

179

June 28

For we know in part, and we prophesy in part. But when that which is perfect is come, then that which is in part shall be done away.

— 1 CORINTHIANS 13:9,10

Doctors Help Nature Do Its Job

Now I'm not opposed to medical healing. But doctors have just learned by experimentation what kinds of medicines will help nature do its job. God put into the human body what we call "nature." Naturally, any body — whether the person is saved or not — will help heal itself. And most doctors will tell you that.

I've had more than one doctor say, "I don't know of any medicines that will heal anyone of anything, and no other doctor does. We help nature do its work. If nature doesn't respond, there's nothing we can do."

I'll never forget when my father-in-law lay in a hospital room dead. The surgeon performed an operation on him that had never been done before in the region where he lived. (Today, they do that kind of operation all the time.) The surgeon who performed the surgery had a type of diploma in surgery that only three other men in the world had. He was one of the world's greatest surgeons.

The surgeon said to me, "I hated to lose him. Now you seem to be more intelligent than the average person. I can say this to you and you'll understand me. You see, this procedure may have been what killed him. That sounds harsh, but all we know is what we've learned by experimentation. The only thing that gives me any ease is knowing that we may learn from him. Although we lost him, we may save a dozen other people because of him."

Well, thank God, for what doctors can do. But I believe that God can beat that. When man heals, either he must do it through the mind that is governed by the physical senses, or he must do it through the physical body. But when *God* heals, He heals through the human spirit. You see, man is a spirit being. He has a soul and lives in a body (1 Thess. 5:23). And life's greatest forces are spiritual: love and hate; faith and fear; joy and grief. All are of the spirit.

Confession:

Doctors know in part. They can help my body naturally heal itself through medicine and other means, but only God can heal me through my spirit.

And Jesus said unto the centurion, Go thy way; and as thou hast believed, so be it done unto thee. And his servant was healed in the selfsame hour.

— MATTHEW 8:13

Jesus' Healings Were Spiritual

It's a remarkable fact that when Jesus came on the scene as Healer, He demanded faith again and again. To the woman with the issue of blood, He declared, "Thy faith has made thee whole" (Mark 5:34).

To the man who came with his lunatic son, Jesus said, "...*If thou canst believe, all things are possible to him that believeth*" (Mark 9:23). You see, the man came to Jesus and said, "If thou canst do anything, have mercy on us and help us" (Mark 9:22). Jesus said to him, in so many words, "It's not so much a matter of what I can do as it is of what *you* can *believe*. All things are possible to him that believeth."

To the nobleman who came on behalf of his son, Jesus said, "...*Go thy way; thy son liveth...*" (John 4:50). The man believed the word that Jesus spoke unto him, and he went on his way. He believed the words of Jesus, and his son was healed.

All of these scriptures prove this fact: Jesus' healings were spiritual. He demanded faith, and faith is born of the spirit.

Confession:

Jesus demands faith of the person desiring to be healed. I meditate on God's Word. I build up my inner man, my spirit man. And I receive healing by faith in God's Word.

But let it be the hidden man of the heart, in that
which is not corruptible, even the ornament of a
meek and quiet spirit, which is in the sight of God of
great price.

— 1 PETER 3:4

The Hidden Man of the Heart

In my prayer lines, I sometimes have to say to people, "God's healing power went into you, because I'm conscious of that power being administered to you. But it came right back out of you. I can sense it. I can feel it coming right back into my hands. You didn't take hold of it."

You see, they tried to receive mentally, rather than spiritually. Faith is of the heart. Your heart is your spirit. Peter calls it the hidden man of the heart (1 Peter 3:4).

Then I say to them, "Keep your mind quiet and on Jesus. You cannot contact God with your mind. He is not a mind. He is a Spirit. Jesus said in John 4:24, *'God is a Spirit: and they that worship him must worship him in spirit and in truth.'* God is not a mind. You can't come to Him mentally. God is not a man. Numbers 23:19 says, *'God is not a man, that he should lie. . . .'* You can't contact God with your physical body. You can contact me with your physical body, because I live in a physical body. I can reach out and shake hands with you. But God is not a mind or a body. He is a Spirit. It's the human spirit that contacts God. God, who is a Spirit, contacts you through your spirit."

I've found healing to be the simplest thing in the world when I can get action from people's spirits. I tell them, "Now begin to believe on the inside of you. And on the inside of you, in your heart, say, 'I am receiving my healing. I do receive my healing.' Start believing it." Instantly, when they do this, I can feel that power flow out of my hands right into them, because their faith becomes active.

Confession:

I keep my mind on Jesus. I believe on the inside of me — in my heart, in my spirit — that I receive my healing now.

While we look not at the things which are seen, but at the things which are not seen: for the things which are seen are temporal; but the things which are not seen are eternal.

— 2 CORINTHIANS 4:18

Healing Works From the Inside Out

Healing starts on the inside and then it appears or manifests on the outside. Everything you receive from God works that way. It starts on the inside and then moves to the outside.

When people are born again, it's their spirit that is reborn. You can't tell they're a new creature in Christ by looking at their body. You can't even tell by looking at them right at the moment they appear to have an experience with God. Many times, I've seen people come to the altar and get emotionally stirred up — they jump up and down the aisles hugging everyone in sight. Then I never see them again. They didn't get a thing in the world, but some kind of emotional high.

I've had other people come to the altar and I've thought to myself, *Dear God, they never got a thing. They're so unemotional.* Yet many of them became some of the best Christians I ever had in my church. Why? There was action from their spirit. The same thing is true with healing.

You receive from God with your heart, your spirit, on the inside. That's the reason you can know something on the inside of you before you ever see it with your physical eyes. For example, I've known that I had the money I was believing for, yet didn't have a dime in my hand. I could see it inside of me. I'd just laugh and say, "Glory to God. It's mine; I know I've got it." I knew God had answered my prayer. I had the answer in my spirit. And then it materialized.

I've also known in my spirit that I had healing. I didn't know it because I saw that my body was well. I knew it in my spirit, because that's where we get it first.

Confession:

I am a believer. Healing belongs to me. God sent His Word and healed me. I see myself well. Thank You, Lord Jesus.

For to one is given by the Spirit the word of wisdom; to another the word of knowledge by the same Spirit.

— 1 CORINTHIANS 12:8

The Word of Knowledge

A woman in New York found out that she had a rare disease. At the time, only seven or eight people in the world had ever had this disease. There was no cure for it. The disease wouldn't kill her the next day, but the doctors said to her, "We have no way of knowing how fast it's going to progress. Don't expect to live more than ten years, although you could die sooner because the disease could progress faster."

Someone told her about Kathryn Kuhlman's meetings in Pittsburgh, Pennsylvania. Some of her friends took her to Pittsburgh. And in the very first service she attended, Miss Kuhlman began to minister and pointed in her direction. She said, "There's a woman over here who has a very rare disease. In fact, doctors have told you that only seven or eight people in the world have ever had the disease."

That was the word of knowledge in operation. Well, the woman was perfectly healed. The doctors couldn't find a trace of the disease afterward. It had all disappeared.

Confession:

I thank God for the gifts of the Spirit. And I thank God for His Word. I don't have to have a gift of the Spirit in operation to receive healing. I can stand on God's Word anytime and receive healing.

When the unclean spirit is gone out of a man, he walketh through dry places, seeking rest; and finding none, he saith, I will return unto my house whence I came out.

— LUKE 11:24

How To Keep Your Healing

In 1970 while I was at a meeting in New York, I met this woman who had been healed in Pittsburgh, Pennsylvania, of the rare disease. She said to me, "Brother Hagin, I haven't said one word to my husband about it, but it's all come back on me. In fact, every symptom I ever had has come back. I'm worse than I ever was. Can you help me?" You see, people must develop a faith of their own in order to keep their healing, or else it will come right back on them.

I said, "Yes, I can help you. Just be present in these daytime teaching services." I knew the Word would do it. I was there for several weeks. Before I left, she came to me and said, "I'm perfectly well. Every symptom has disappeared. And this time, I got it by my own faith. I know now how to keep it."

You see, people often receive healing through the gifts of the Spirit in operation. Or they get into a mass meeting where there is mass faith and things happen. But when they get back on their own, they're alone and don't know how to stand in faith.

The Bible plainly teaches that the devil is the author of sickness and disease (*see* Acts 10:38). The Bible plainly teaches that an unclean spirit will go back into the house that it came out of (Luke 11:24). The devil will go right back in where he left if people let him. That's the reason we need to teach people how to resist the devil and hold fast to their healing. This woman learned. She received her healing and *kept* it.

Confession:

God is not the author of sickness and disease. The devil is! I resist the devil, and he must flee from me. I hold fast to the Word of God. I keep my healing!

> *Behold, I come quickly: hold that fast which thou hast, that no man take thy crown.*
>
> — REVELATION 3:11

Hold Fast to What Belongs to You!

I remember a man who was marvelously healed in one of my meetings in Oklahoma. He couldn't walk by himself, but he was instantly healed and could walk just as good as anyone. Also, he couldn't hear without a hearing aid. He couldn't even hear it thunder. He hadn't heard for seven years without his hearing aid. Instantly, his ears were opened and he could hear.

About ten days later, the same man was back in my meeting. He couldn't walk by himself, and he couldn't hear without his hearing aid. He'd lost it all. Now he had maintained it for ten days and was perfectly all right. But, you see, without good teaching about what belonged to him and how to hold fast to it, he lost his healing.

Matthew chapter 12 gives us an example of a man who was delivered but then became worse than he was to begin with.

MATTHEW 12:43-45
43 When the unclean spirit is gone out of a man, he walketh through dry places, seeking rest, and findeth none.
44 Then he saith, I will return into my house from whence I came out; and when he is come, he findeth it empty, swept, and garnished.
45 Then goeth he, and taketh with himself seven other spirits more wicked than himself, and they enter in and dwell there: and the last state of that man is worse than the first. . . .

It is necessary that we study the Word and get the Word of God in us. We must be filled up with the Word and give no place to the devil. It is important that we know who we are in Christ, what we have in Him, including healing, and how to hold fast to it.

Confession:

I study the Word. I get the Word of God in me. I learn who I am and what I have in Christ Jesus. Then I hold fast to it!

And he [Jesus] said unto them, Take heed what ye hear: with what measure ye mete, it shall be measured to you: and unto you that hear shall more be given.

July 5

— MARK 4:24

Learn the Word for Yourself

Dr. Lilian B. Yeomans was a medical doctor. She was healed and raised up from her deathbed. Then she devoted the rest of her life to teaching the Word of God on healing.

I remember Dr. Yeomans saying that it made her mad when she was teaching on an important subject like healing, and some people just sat there and thumbed through the songbook or looked out the church window. Well, the same dear people who are so nonchalant and unresponsive are going to need help some day. They're going to run around trying to find someone to help them and God won't allow it, because they could have learned for themselves. But they didn't learn.

You know, you can get things for people on your faith the first time if they don't know any better. But the next time around, they'll have to do it on their own faith. I have prayed death off many of my close relatives. But I couldn't do it the second time. God wouldn't let me.

Confession:

I take heed to the Word of God I hear. I learn the Word for myself. I apply the Word to my own life. I exercise my faith and see results, because the Word works!

But the righteousness which is of faith speaketh on this wise, Say not in thine heart, Who shall ascend into heaven? (that is, to bring Christ down from above:)

Or, Who shall descend into the deep? (that is, to bring up Christ again from the dead.)

But what saith it? The word is nigh thee, even in thy mouth, and in thy heart: that is, the word of faith, which we preach.

— ROMANS 10:6-8

God's Word Must Be in *Your* Mouth and *Your* Heart

My own sister died with cancer at the age of fifty-five. Now five years before, when she was only fifty years of age, she had a different type of cancer. The doctor said that there was no connection between the two cancers.

When she had cancer at the age of fifty, I prayed about it. The Lord said to me, "Because you asked Me, I'm going to heal her. I'm going to give her five more years. But she's going to have to do something herself then."

She was saved and filled with the Holy Ghost. She was a Sunday school teacher in a Full Gospel church. But that doesn't guarantee that you'll never have any tests or trials in your body, or that you'll just automatically receive healing.

So the next time she had cancer, God began to tell me two years ahead of time that she was going to die. Well, I did my best to change it. I fasted and prayed, but I couldn't change it. She was the one who had to change it. She had to believe God's Word in *her* heart. She had to speak God's Word out of *her* mouth. I could no longer do it for her.

Confession:

I cannot rely on another person's faith to get things done in my own life. I must believe God's Word in my own heart. I must speak God's Word out of my own mouth.

Repent ye therefore, and be converted, that your sins may be blotted out, when the times of refreshing shall come from the presence of the Lord.

— ACTS 3:19

July 7

You Must Change the Situation

In the Old Testament, we read that God told Isaiah, "You go tell Hezekiah to set his house in order because he's going to die" (Isa. 38:1). Well, Hezekiah turned his face to the wall and repented. He cried and prayed. Before Isaiah got out of the courtyard, the Lord said to him, "You go back and tell Hezekiah that I'm going to give him fifteen more years" (v. 5).

That sounds like a paradox to the casual reader. One time God said Hezekiah was going to die, and the next time He said that he was going to live. Did God change? No. He wanted Hezekiah to live to begin with. God simply told Isaiah what was going to happen *under the circumstances.* And notice that Isaiah, the prophet of God, couldn't change it. Only Hezekiah could change it. That doesn't mean that it was God's will, His highest and best, for Hezekiah.

The Lord told me concerning my sister, "She's had five years. You're on the radio in her city, and she's never listened to your radio program one single time. She's never read one of your books. She's never listened to one of your tapes. She didn't do one single thing to build up her own faith or to try and help herself. She depended on someone else to do it. You can't do it for her anymore."

What happened? She died. I'm glad she went to Heaven, but she shouldn't have gone so soon. That wasn't God's best. The time will come in every Christian's life when he will have to believe God for himself. Someone else won't be able to carry him any longer.

Confession:

I build up myself on the Word of God. I feed on the Word of God so that my inner man becomes strong. And when opposition comes, I am able to stand up and resist it with the Word in my mouth and in my heart!

July 8

Therefore I esteem all thy precepts concerning all things to be right; and I hate every false way.

— PSALM 119:128

Reverence the Bible

The reverence we have toward the Bible, the Book of life, could mean the difference in our own life between life and death. God spoke to me while I was praying at the altar one time. He said, "After you preach your next meeting, you'll go into the city of Dallas for a meeting. After you preach that meeting, you'll come back to a certain place [He named the place] for a meeting. While you're there, a pastor from hundreds of miles away will call and want you to come. I want you to go there to him."

I wrote it all down, dated it, and put it in my billfold. I didn't say a word to my wife or anyone about it. Well, everything came to pass exactly as the Lord had spoken to me. Now the pastor who called me wanted me to come and minister to his wife who had terminal cancer. I did just that, but she didn't get healed. Now it would seem that since God so miraculously led me there, she would have been healed. But she wasn't.

She was a Bible teacher and people loved her. She used to be a school-teacher before she married this preacher. The congregation would rather hear her preach than her husband, because she was such an expert on the Bible. She said to me, "I've studied every subject in the Bible except faith and healing. I've never studied one thing about those two subjects."

When I left her, I went down the road weeping because I knew she had failed to receive. I knew she would die at forty-three years of age. I said to the Lord, "You led me in such a miraculous way. I thought she would be miraculously raised up."

He said, "I sent you there to endeavor to get truth in them [her and her husband], but they didn't listen. And when they stand before Me, as all Christians must stand before the Judgment Seat of Christ, they can't say they didn't know, because I'm going to point out to them that I moved on them miraculously to contact you. They didn't even know you. I just moved on them by My Spirit. And I did My best to help them, but they wouldn't listen."

Confession:

Father God, I reverence Your Word. I esteem all Your precepts highly. I put them first place in my life.

Christ hath redeemed us from the curse of the law, being made a curse for us: for it is written, Cursed is every one that hangeth on a tree.

— GALATIANS 3:13

The Curse of the Law

The Bible says that Christ has redeemed us from the curse of the Law. What is the curse of the Law? Well, the term "the Law" actually refers to the first five Books of the Bible. Deuteronomy is one of the first five Books of the Bible. Let's read what Deuteronomy says about the curse of the Law.

DEUTERONOMY 28:20-22,27-29,35,58-61

20 The Lord shall send upon thee cursing, vexation, and rebuke, in all that thou settest thine hand unto for to do, until thou be destroyed, and until thou perish quickly; because of the wickedness of thy doings, whereby thou hast forsaken me.

21 The Lord shall make the pestilence cleave unto thee, until he have consumed thee from off the land, whither thou goest to possess it.

22 The Lord shall smite thee with a consumption, and with a fever, and with an inflammation, and with an extreme burning, and with the sword, and with blasting, and with mildew; and they shall pursue thee until thou perish. . . .

27 The Lord will smite thee with the botch of Egypt, and with the emerods, and with the scab, and with the itch, whereof thou canst not be healed.

28 The Lord shall smite thee with madness, and blindness, and astonishment of heart:

29 And thou shalt grope at noonday, as the blind gropeth in darkness, and thou shalt not prosper in thy ways: and thou shalt be only oppressed and spoiled evermore, and no man shall save thee. . . .

35 The Lord shall smite thee in the knees, and in the legs, with a sore botch that cannot be healed, from the sole of thy foot unto the top of thy head. . . .

58 If thou wilt not observe to do all the words of this law that are written in this book, that thou mayest fear this glorious and fearful name, the Lord thy God;

59 Then the Lord will make thy plagues wonderful, and the plagues of thy seed, even great plagues, and of long continuance, and sore sicknesses, and of long continuance.

60 Moreover he will bring upon thee all the diseases of Egypt, which thou wast afraid of; and they shall cleave unto thee.

61 Also every sickness, and every plague, which is not written in the book of this law, them will the Lord bring upon thee, until thou be destroyed.

Notice that there are eleven specific diseases mentioned. Then "all the diseases of Egypt" were added (v. 60). Verse 61 says, "Also every sickness and every plague not written in the Book of this Law." Well, that includes *all* sickness. We can readily see from these scriptures that sickness is a curse of the Law.

Confession:

Sickness is a curse of the Law. But Jesus redeemed me from the curse of the Law. Therefore, I do not accept any sickness or disease in my life.

191

Also every sickness, and every plague, which is not written in the book of this law, them will the Lord bring upon thee, until thou be destroyed.

— DEUTERONOMY 28:61

Does God Put Sickness on People?

All the dreadful diseases enumerated in Deuteronomy chapter 28 are a part of the punishment for breaking God's Law. It says so in verse 61. Well, they should come upon us, because we have all sinned: *"For all have sinned, and come short of the glory of God"* (Rom. 3:23). Those diseases should come upon us, but, thank God, Jesus took our place. He became sin for us. He became sickness for us. He took our place to redeem us from sickness!

In the *King James Version,* one would be led to believe that God Himself puts sickness and afflictions upon His people. For example, Deuteronomy 28:22 says that the Lord will smite thee. But you can't just skim across the surface of the Bible and find out what it is saying. In *Hints to Bible Interpretation* by Dr. Robert Young, he points out that the Old Testament was written in Hebrew. In the original Hebrew, the verb is in the permissive sense rather than the causative sense. Actually, it should have been translated something like this: "The Lord will *allow* you to be smitten. The Lord will *allow* these plagues to be brought upon you."

Where would God get the sickness to put on you, anyway? There isn't any sickness in Heaven. He would have to steal it first, before He could put it on you, because He doesn't have any.

Confession:

God does not put sickness and disease on people. He doesn't put sickness and disease on me. I resist sickness and disease because it does not come from God.

Permission Versus Commission

There are many verbs in the Old Testament that are translated in the causative sense in the *King James Version*. But the original verbs are in the permissive sense. Let's look at a few of them so you can understand what I'm saying.

In Isaiah 45:7, God said, *"I form the light, and create darkness: I make peace, and create evil: I the Lord do all these things."* Does God create evil? No. If you know your Bible well enough, you know that the Bible doesn't teach that. Well, this verse said that He does.

If God creates evil, then that would make God a devil. The Bible teaches that the devil is responsible for all that's evil. God may *permit* evil, but He doesn't *create* it. And when you understand, as Dr. Robert Young pointed out, that the verb is in the permissive sense rather than in the causative sense, you'll see that God doesn't cause evil. He merely permits it.

Let's look at another verse of Scripture. Amos 3:6 says, *"Shall a trumpet be blown in the city, and the people not be afraid? shall there be evil in a city, and the Lord hath not done it?"* Again, if God commits evil, then He has no right whatsoever to judge man for sinning. But God does not commit evil.

You see, this verse says, "Shall there be evil in the city, and God has not done it?" Has any evil happened in the town in which you live? Has anyone killed anyone else? Has anyone robbed a store? Well, yes, of course. Did God do it? This verse said He did. But you know that can't be right, because God didn't do it Himself and He didn't *commission* anyone to do it. He didn't commission anyone to go out and rob a store or burn down a building. No, God does not do evil. He only permits evil. There is a vast difference between permission and commission.

Confession:

God doesn't create evil. He only permits it. Because I have a free will, I can choose to obey God or I can choose to go against God. I choose to follow God and enjoy all of His many benefits.

The last enemy that shall be destroyed is death.
— 1 CORINTHIANS 15:26

Death Is an Enemy

I remember hearing about a woman who was saved and went to church, but her husband was unsaved. Their four-year-old son was sick. He was the only child they had. The unsaved husband would say to the wife, "You go on to church. I'll keep the boy."

The child grew worse until, finally, the doctor said, "I'll just be honest with you. I don't know what's wrong with this child. I can't find out what's the matter with him. I don't know what to do, but he's going to die if he keeps going the way he is."

Well, the child surprisingly got better, and the husband told his wife one night, "Go on to church. I'll stay here with him. He's doing fine."

When the service was over, they were praying around the altar and someone came to the pastor and said that the little boy had just died. So the pastor went over to where the wife was kneeling and told her about it. Then the pastor and several of the church members went with her to the home.

When they walked in the door, they saw this dear man sitting on the bed with his only child, dead in his arms. He had such a look of agony on his face. He was sobbing, crying his heart out. He was reaching out for help from somewhere. Because he was unsaved and didn't know God, he didn't have the Comforter within him.

Many of the church people tried to help him. Some of them said, "God took your boy so you'd get saved."

The man suddenly straightened up, laid the little boy down on the bed, wiped his tears, and said, "I want to tell you folks something. If God did that, to hell with Him." Then he stomped out of the room.

I watched this man over a period of thirty to forty years. No one could reach him. He thought God robbed him of his four-year-old boy. No one had enough sense to sit down on the bed by this man's side and say, "The devil did this. But your son's spirit has gone to be with Jesus. He can't come back to you, but you can go to him some day." The man would have gotten saved.

Confession:

God is not the author of death. The Bible says that death is an enemy. It's the last enemy that will be put under foot. I'm looking forward to that day. Death is an enemy, not a friend. God is a friend.

*The thief cometh not, but for to steal, and to kill,
and to destroy: I am come that they might have life,
and that they might have it more abundantly.*

— JOHN 10:10

The Devil Doesn't Heal People

Many years ago, a healing evangelist was holding a meeting in Phoenix, Arizona. One of the ranchers there had a foreman who had a little girl who was lame. Well, this rancher started attending the evangelist's tent meetings. Then the rancher went to his ranch and got his foreman, his foreman's wife, and their lame little girl. He brought them to the meeting, and the twelve-year-old girl was healed.

The rancher owned five different ranches and was very wealthy. He attended one of the churches there in town. After the rancher told several people about the little girl who was healed, his pastor decided to get up and preach on it. He said, "I don't doubt that the child got healed, all right, but the devil did it."

After the service, the wealthy rancher went up to the pastor and said, "I want to get this clear, Pastor. Do you mean to tell me that the devil healed my foreman's daughter?"

The pastor said, "Yes, exactly, because healing's not for us nowadays. And the devil will heal people to mislead them."

The rancher said, "I'll tell you one thing. If the devil did it, he's a pretty good devil. And I'll tell you another thing. I won't be back here, because I'm going where the things of God are real and where they are esteemed." He had enough sense to leave. Actually, he went over to an Assembly of God church where they preached divine healing and people got healed.

Confession:

The devil is a liar, a thief, and a destroyer. Jesus is the Healer. It is through Him that I have life more abundantly. I receive the healing that Jesus bought and paid for me to have. Healing is for me today.

For they [God's words] are life unto those that find them, and health to all their flesh.

— PROVERBS 4:22

Don't Let the Word Depart From Your Eyes

Another thing that God said in Proverbs chapter 4 is, "Let My words, My sayings, not depart from before your eyes" (v. 21). If you don't let Matthew 8:17 — "Himself took our infirmities, and bare our sicknesses" — depart from before your eyes, you're bound to see yourself well. If you don't see yourself well, then that Word has departed from before your eyes, and, that being the case, you no longer have any guarantee of an answer.

I was preaching in a church in Fort Worth, Texas, and the pastor said to me, "Brother Hagin, I want you to go with me to visit a dear eighty-two year old woman. She used to be an Assembly of God evangelist. This dear woman is one of the greatest soul-winners I've ever met in my life. I came into the family of God under her ministry. Many people who are preaching the Gospel today came in under her ministry. But she has cancer. She was operated on more than two years ago, and doctors don't understand how she has lived this long."

We went to visit her. She was bedfast at her daughter's home. With so many cancerous tumors in her stomach, she looked like she was pregnant. And the rest of her body had wasted away. Her hands were tissue-thin. I began to share my testimony with her. And I felt led to share Proverbs 4:21.

Confession:

I keep the Word of God before my eyes. I see myself well and whole and doing what God has called me to do.

For they [God's words] *are life unto those that find them, and health to all their flesh.*

— PROVERBS 4:22

See Yourself Well

In May 1958, I was at a meeting in Fort Worth, Texas, and was straightening up my book table when I saw two women coming. I didn't recognize either one of them, so I kept on with my work. About that time, a woman threw her arms around me and hugged me.

I pushed away from her, surprised, and she said to me, "You don't recognize me, do you?"

I didn't recognize her. When she told me who she was, I threw my arms around her, and we just had a "hallelujah" spell right there! She was the 82-year-old evangelist I had ministered to several months earlier! She who had been bedfast and given up to die now looked so young and pretty!

She said, "I'm sure glad you didn't let me die! It would have been the easiest thing in the world for me just to die and go on to Heaven. But I started thinking after you left. And every time I looked at that huge stomach, I saw it flat. I saw myself winning souls and preaching again. I saw myself well. Within two or three month's time, I saw my stomach go down. And in the process of time, my stomach flattened out and all the symptoms left me."

Confession:

I see myself well. I see myself _____. (Fill in the blank with whatever you see yourself doing.)

As it is written, I have made thee a father of many nations, before him whom he believed, even God, who quickeneth the dead, and calleth those things which be not as though they were.

— ROMANS 4:17

Call Those Things That Be Not as Though They Were

Faith calls those things that be not as though they were. After teaching on the subject of faith for the past sixty-five years, I have learned that there is nothing quite so hard for Christians as calling those things that be not as though they were. Many honest, sincere, good people think they would be lying if they did this, so they fail to do it. But I want you to consider for a moment that the Bible tells us that God cannot lie (Num. 23:19). And God calls those things that be not as though they were!

I've had people say to me, "That's all right for God to do that." Well, if it's all right for God to do it, it's all right for *you* to do it! The children of God should act like God (Eph. 5:1). And God calls those things that be not as though they were, because He is a faith God. We are faith children of a faith God. We should act like God.

Romans 4:17 says that God made Abraham a father of many nations. You see, Abraham had to call those things that be not as though they were. And God tells us to follow in the footsteps of Abraham (*see* Romans 4:12). Because God calls those things that be not as though they were and because He tells us to do it, then it's impossible for it to be wrong in the least degree.

Confession:

I call those things that be not as though they were. In the face of sickness, I call my body healed. I call my body well. I say that I am able to do things I couldn't do before! Praise God!

As it is written, I have made thee a father of many
nations, before him whom he believed, even God,
who quickeneth the dead, and calleth those things
which be not as though they were.

— ROMANS 4:17

Limiting God in the Faith Walk

Let me give you some examples of God calling those things that be not as
though they were. Revelation 13:8 says, *"And all that dwell upon the earth
shall worship him, whose names are not written in the book of life of the
Lamb slain from the foundation of the world."* The Bible speaks of Jesus as
the Lamb slain from the foundation of the world. And yet, Jesus did not hang
on the Cross until thousands of years later.

Ephesians 1:4 says, *"According as he hath chosen us in him before the
foundation of the world, that we should be holy and without blame before
him in love."* We were chosen in Christ before the foundation of the world.
We weren't even born yet. Well, was God lying when He said that? No, He
wasn't.

Sin is disobeying God. And holiness is simply obeying and pleasing God in
all things at all times. One way to obey and to please God is to walk by faith.
Hebrews 11:6 says, *"But without faith it is impossible to please him: for he
that cometh to God must believe that he is, and that he is a rewarder of
them that diligently seek him."*

God is pleased when you call those things that be not as though they
were. This attitude honors God, because you are believing His Word without
any outward evidence. It also puts you in an attitude of faith to receive great
things from God.

Confession:

*God is pleased when I walk by faith. God is pleased when I call those things
that be not as though they were, because I am believing His Word without
any outward evidence.*

Blessed be the God and Father of our Lord Jesus Christ, who hath blessed us with all spiritual blessings in heavenly places in Christ.

— EPHESIANS 1:3

The Eye of Faith

Faith is the hand, so to speak, that takes from God. In the natural realm, if someone offers you something, you can reach out your physical hand and take it, because you can see it. In the spirit realm, you have to see with the eye of faith. You can't see in the spirit realm with the physical eye. You can only see physical and material things with the physical eye. But we know from God's Word that there are things available to us in the spirit realm.

For instance, in the spirit world, there is healing. It has already been purchased. It has already been paid for. God already has it wrapped up with your name on it. It's just waiting for you to take it.

Well, how are you going to see that? You can't see it with your physical eye like you would a birthday gift all wrapped up and packaged for you. So how do you know it's there? *You know it's there because the Bible said so.*

Jesus not only purchased your salvation — the remission of sins and the New Birth — but He also took your infirmities and bore your sicknesses (Matt. 8:17). And He is waiting for you to reach out and take healing. He is waiting for you to see it with the eye of faith — faith that is based on the Word.

Confession:

With the eye of faith, I see healing. And with the hand of faith, I reach out and take my healing. It's mine; I have it now. Even when it doesn't seem like I have it, I know that I have it. I call those things that be not as though they were.

Now Faith Is . . .

This scripture gives us God's definition of faith. Notice that faith is present tense: It is the substance of things hoped for, the evidence of things not seen. *The New English Bible* says, "Faith is giving substance to things hoped for." You see, hope doesn't have any substance. Hope has to be there, but faith is what gives substance to the things hoped for.

How does faith give substance to the things you're hoping for? In Mark 11:23, Jesus said, *"For verily I say unto you, That whosoever shall say unto this mountain, Be thou removed, and be thou cast into the sea; and shall not doubt in his heart, but shall believe that those things which he saith shall come to pass; HE SHALL HAVE WHATSOEVER HE SAITH."* It is by believing in your heart and speaking with your mouth that you see those unseen things manifest before your eyes.

Let's continue reading in Mark. *"Therefore I say unto you, What things soever ye desire, when ye pray, believe that ye receive them, and ye shall have them"* (v. 24). Before you ever see something manifest on the outside, you have to "see it" on the inside first. This is faith — the substance of things hoped for and the evidence of things not seen.

I've preached Mark 11:23 and 24 so much that some people jokingly say that I wrote it! But I didn't. I got it out of the Bible. Jesus said it. And after sixty-five years, I'm still just as thrilled when I read it. Way down deep inside of me, in my spirit, something starts turning somersaults. That's when the Word of God works for you — when you get thrilled with it!

Confession:

Faith gives substance to the things I'm hoping for. I need hope, but I also need faith. As I believe in my heart and speak out of my mouth, I shall have whatever I say.

> And the prayer of faith shall save the sick, and the Lord shall raise him up; and if he have committed sins, they shall be forgiven him.
>
> — JAMES 5:15

The Prayer of Faith

Notice that this scripture says, "The prayer of faith will save the sick." It's not the anointing with oil that does it. It's not the elders' hands or even the elders. It's the prayer of faith that does it. You can pray that prayer as well as anyone can.

Many people reason that if they don't get healed after someone lays hands on them, anoints them with oil, and prays, then the person who ministered to them didn't pray the prayer of faith. What is the prayer of faith?

Let's substitute God's definition of faith in Hebrews 11:1 for the word "faith" in this scripture. In other words, "The prayer of *the evidence of things not seen* will heal the sick." Or we could substitute Romans 4:17 in there: "The prayer *that calls those things that be not as though they were* will heal the sick." That's what the prayer of faith is. It's the prayer of the evidence of things not seen.

The prayer of faith doesn't say, "Look and see if you're healed. If you are, that's how you'll know if you prayed the prayer of faith." No, the prayer of faith sees with the eye of faith and counts it done. Faith calls those things that be not as though they were.

I saw this as a Baptist boy, and I started preaching it as a Baptist boy. And I got results. Then the Full Gospel people came to town, held a revival, and built a church. I found out that they believed in divine healing, and I was thrilled about it. I had people to fellowship with around faith and divine healing.

Confession:

I can pray the prayer of faith and get results. I can pray the prayer of "the evidence of things not seen" — the prayer that calls those things that be not as though they were. I can call my body well and whole in Jesus' Name.

. . . God, who quickeneth the dead, and calleth those things which be not as though they were.

— ROMANS 4:17

July 21

Turn Your Faith Loose

When I was a Baptist minister, I had an interesting experience that will help you in your own faith. I went to bed one Sunday night after church feeling fine. But I woke up on Monday morning, and the right side of my face was paralyzed. It was numb. I could reach up there and pinch it without feeling a thing. I tried to wrinkle up my forehead, but the right side wouldn't wrinkle. The right side of my mouth wouldn't move, either.

I said to myself, *I know what I'll do. I'll go down to the Full Gospel Tabernacle on Wednesday night and have the pastor anoint me with oil. He can lay hands on me and I'll be healed.*

So on Wednesday night, I went down to the Full Gospel Tabernacle. They weren't having a healing service, but when the service was over, I stood up in the back and said, "Pastor, I want you to pray for my healing before we go." Now when I opened my mouth to say that, the left side of my mouth sort of ran all the way around to my ear, but the right side of my mouth didn't move!

The pastor told me to come down to the front and he would pray for me. I walked right down the aisle, stood in front of the pulpit, and he anointed me with oil on my forehead. He laid his hand on my head and prayed. I don't remember one word he said. I didn't pay any attention. I was waiting to hear him say, "Amen." That's when I turned my faith loose. In other words, that's when I started calling those things that be not as though they were.

Confession:

I turn my faith loose. I call those things in my body that be not as though they were. I call myself well. I call myself healed. I speak to every part of my body to function as it was designed to function.

And being fully persuaded that, what he had promised, he was able also to perform.

— ROMANS 4:21

Act in Faith

When the pastor said, "Amen," I said in faith, "Thank God, it's gone." What does it mean to say something in faith? It means to call those things that be not as though they were. Many honest Christians are afraid to act because they don't know what faith is.

Someone might ask, "Well, was the paralysis gone?"

"No, the right side of my face was still dead."

"You were lying, then," someone might respond. No! I was acting on the Word.

After the service, everyone rushed up to me. They said, "Did the Lord really heal you when Pastor laid his hands on you and anointed you with oil?"

I said, "He sure did."

"Well, you don't look any different. Do you feel any different?" they asked.

"Not that I can tell," I said.

They said, "If you don't *look* any different and you don't *feel* any different, what makes you think the Lord has healed you?"

I said, "I don't *think* He has; I *know* He has."

What was I doing? I was acting in faith. I dare you to do it. We used to say in Texas, "I double-dog dare you!" I challenge you to act on the Word. Are you afraid that maybe God lied? No, He didn't lie. You have to be convinced in your own spirit, though. It won't work just out of your head. It won't work *trying* to do what I did. I didn't *try* it. I *did* it!

Confession:

I act in faith. No matter what I see with my eyes, no matter what I feel in my body, I act on the Word in faith. I believe that I receive when I pray.

*And the prayer of faith shall save the sick, and the
Lord shall raise him up; and if he have committed
sins, they shall be forgiven him.*

July 23

— JAMES 4:15

Talk About Your Faith and What the Lord Has Done for You

I was a single man at the time I experienced this paralysis in my face. I had walked a young woman named Imogene to church. As I was walking her back home, several of the young people who were walking with us said, "Kenneth, did the Lord really heal you?"

I said, "He sure did."

"Well, we noticed when we passed under the street light and you laughed, that one corner of your mouth ran all the way around to your ear. Do you feel any different?"

"Not that I can tell," I said.

"What makes you think you're healed?" they asked

I said, "I don't *think* it. I *know* it."

"We can see you're not healed, and you admit you don't feel any better. Aren't you lying about it?"

I said to them, "No, I'm talking faith. Faith calleth those things that be not as though they were. Jesus said that when you pray, believe that you receive, and you shall have it. The next time you see me, you'll admit it's so yourself." Now why did I say that? Because I knew that I had received it, and that my healing had to manifest.

Well, we got to Imogene's house. She brought her mother into the living room, put me under a light, and said to her mother, "Look at Kenneth's face." I couldn't keep from laughing, and my face only smiled on one side.

Imogene said, "*Mama* admits you don't look any different. *You* admit you don't feel any different. What makes you think the Lord healed you?"

I said, "I don't *think* He did. I *know* He did. Faith calls those things that be not as though they were. According to the Word of God, I'm healed. The prayer of faith — the prayer that calls those things that be not as though they were — heals the sick."

She said, "Well, Pastor didn't pray the prayer of faith for you. If he had, you'd have it. And I can see you don't have it."

"Yes, he did," I said. "And I've got my healing."

Confession:

According to the Word, I'm healed. I talk about my faith and what the Lord has done for me. I call those things that be not as though they were. And then I see the manifestation.

That your faith should not stand in the wisdom of men, but in the power of God.

— 1 CORINTHIANS 2:5

Healed by *Faith*-Power

Imogene's mother, Mrs. Alexander, finally spoke up and said, "Imogene, I'd be careful if I were you. Maybe Kenneth knows something that we don't know. When he was bedfast, I remember the doctor said, 'That young man has the strongest willpower of any person I've ever seen in my life. He should have been dead months ago. I don't know how he's lived. I'll give him ninety days at the most.'"

Well, those ninety days have stretched into more than sixty-five years! I wasn't healed by willpower. I was healed by *faith*-power. Don't substitute willpower for *faith*-power. You can go a while on willpower if you're strong-willed, but it will break sooner or later.

I do know something about faith. It has worked for me for more than sixty-five years. It's not that I'm so smart. I just read it in the Bible. And I can share what I've learned with you.

I went home that night and went to bed praising God because I was healed. I got up the next morning, and my face was straight. I went to the Alexanders' house and had a bowl of cereal for breakfast. I was grinning from ear to ear!

Imogene said, "Oh, I see you got your healing."

I said, "Yes, I got it last night when Pastor anointed me with oil and prayed."

She said, "Well, you didn't have it when you left here."

You see, if I had been walking by that kind of faith, it never would have materialized. Her kind of faith does not call things that be not as though they were.

Confession:

I don't base my faith on what I see or feel. I don't base my faith on what other people think. I base my faith on God's Word. There is power in the Word of God.

Faith Will Prevail

The following is a word that was given to me by the Spirit of God:

I've found a secret.
It's revealed in the Word.
It's not hid from a soul that's willing to hear.
And you can say from your spirit, down here, "I have heard and I know, for His Word has spoken and it cannot fail."
Faith will prevail.
Speak it out when all hell against you assails.
Shout it out when symptoms and sickness and disease belie the truth.
And you'll see that all that troubles thee will dissipate and disappear.
And you'll rise up victorious and shout and give glory to Him.
Your health shall spring forth speedily, and you'll be a blessing unto those around about,
Because you've learned what faith is all about.
Hear with the ear of faith.
See with the eye of faith.
Take with the hand of faith.
Speak with the Word of faith.
Shout with the joy of faith.
Rejoice in the goodness of faith.
For the Lord your God, your Father, is a faith God.
And ye being faith children of a faith God, walk, act, and talk like God.
That's what the Spirit is saying.

Are you ready to act on God's Word? Are you ready to call those things that be not as though they were? Shut your eyes and say the following from your heart. Let your heart agree with it. Say it out of the inside of you. Listen to your voice say it.

Confession:

He sent His Word and healed me. Therefore, I no longer have sickness. My faith prevails.

So we see that they could not enter in because of unbelief.

— HEBREWS 3:19

Don't Miss God's Best

Doubt and unbelief can rob you of the blessing God intended you should have. Doubt and unbelief will cause you to receive something less than God's best. Let's look at an example of this in the Bible.

MATTHEW 14:25-31

25 And in the fourth watch of the night Jesus went unto them, walking on the sea.

26 And when the disciples saw him walking on the sea, they were troubled, saying, It is a spirit; and they cried out for fear.

27 But straightway Jesus spake unto them, saying, Be of good cheer; it is I; be not afraid.

28 And Peter answered him and said, Lord, if it be thou, bid me come unto thee on the water.

29 And he said, Come. And when Peter was come down out of the ship, he walked on the water, to go to Jesus.

30 But when he saw the wind boisterous, he was afraid; and beginning to sink, he cried, saying, Lord, save me.

31 And immediately Jesus stretched forth his hand, and caught him, and said unto him, O thou of little faith, wherefore didst thou doubt?

Now in the case of Peter, the Lord intervened by His divine sovereignty and saved him. Jesus kept Peter from sinking. But Peter still missed the best that God had for him.

Notice that Jesus rebuked Peter. He said in verse 31, *". . . O thou of little faith, wherefore didst thou doubt?"* In other words, He was saying, "Why did you doubt?" Doubt robbed Peter of the best that God had for him. His life was saved, but Peter missed God's best.

Confession:

I don't want to be robbed of God's best for my life. I choose to believe and not doubt. I choose to act on God's Word. And as a result, I experience God's blessings in my life.

Walk on the Water

In Matthew 14:28, Peter said, *". . . Lord if it be thou, bid me come unto thee on the water."*

Jesus said, "Come."

Peter stepped out of the boat and walked on the water to go to Jesus. Notice that he walked on the water. Don't ever criticize Peter until you can walk on the water without sinking! If you can walk on the water and not sink, then we'll accept your criticism. But don't criticize Peter. At least he did walk on the water.

On the other hand, you have no excuse to hide behind Peter, so to speak, and make excuses for why we fail to receive from God. The Bible tells us exactly why Peter began to sink. If we'll listen, we won't have to sink when our faith is tested.

Jesus didn't intend for us to sink as we're walking on the sea of life, and He didn't intend for Peter to sink. Jesus said to Peter, "Come." And as long as Peter acted on Jesus' word, he walked on the water.

Verse 30 says, *"But when he [Peter] saw the wind boisterous, he was afraid; and beginning to sink, he cried, saying, Lord, save me."* Peter got his eyes off Jesus and onto the wind and the waves. Peter didn't actually see the wind, because no one can see the wind. But he got his eyes on what the wind was doing. He saw the waves that were boisterous. He was afraid and began to sink. He cried out to the Lord, and Jesus reached out His hand and saved him.

Confession:

As long as I act on God's Word, I will walk on the water of life. I will enjoy health and healing. I won't sink when the storms of life come, because my faith is grounded in the Word of God.

And immediately Jesus stretched forth his hand, and caught him, and said unto him, O thou of little faith, wherefore didst thou doubt?

— MATTHEW 14:31

Don't Let Doubt Rob You

Many times a miracle begins in a person's life, and then doubt robs him or her of the full blessing. A miracle began in the life of Peter. He was walking on the water. But that miracle was never consummated. That miracle never came into full fruition. Why? According to Matthew 14:31, he let doubt get in.

I was preaching along this line one time, and an Assembly of God pastor said, "I understand something now that I didn't understand before. As a young preacher, there were two women in my church. Both of them had cancer of the liver. By the time they both found out about it, they each had only a few weeks to live.

About that time, a healing evangelist came to the church. He prayed for the sick by the laying on of hands. And both women were gloriously and marvelously healed.

At the time this pastor spoke to me, fifteen or twenty years had passed since the women had been healed. Only one of them was still alive. The other had died. All her symptoms were gone for several months. Then she got up at a prayer meeting and said, "I want you all to pray for me. Those symptoms of cancer have come back on me." Well, they prayed, but she let doubt get in. She grew steadily worse until she died.

Confession:

I refuse to let doubt rob me of the blessings of God. I shut the door on doubt. I choose instead to believe God's Word. I act on what God's Word says about me.

*. . . When he [the devil] speaketh a lie, he speaketh
of his own: for he is a liar, and the father of it.*

— JOHN 8:44

Don't Believe the Devil's Lies

After the woman died, this Assembly of God pastor said to me, "When
the doctors performed an autopsy on her, they couldn't find any trace of
cancer in any way, shape, or form in her body. Her liver was just as perfect
as anyone else's liver. They couldn't find a trace of cancer. They don't know
why she died."

I know why she died. She began to doubt. She let the devil in and began
to believe that she had cancer. She began to believe his lies. The doctors said,
"We can't find any reason why she died."

A miracle began in her life, yet she was robbed of the best that God had
for her, because of doubt. I think if Jesus had been there to talk to her personally, He would have said, "O thou of little faith, wherefore didst thou
doubt?" In fact, I've had Him say that to me. And when He did, I straightened up and got right.

Doubt robbed Peter of the best God had for him. Remember, Peter was a
man who walked with Jesus. He was part of the inner circle that followed
Him. Yet Peter was robbed of God's best. I wonder how many more of
those who walk with Jesus are robbed of the blessings God intended they
should have.

Confession:

*I refuse to believe the lies of the devil! I believe God's Word. I believe that
according to His Word, I am healed, whole, and healthy in Jesus' Name.*

And he could there do no mighty work, save that he laid his hands upon a few sick folk, and healed them. And he marvelled because of their unbelief. . . .

— MARK 6:5

Unbelief Will Keep You From the Blessings of God

Let's look at a city that was robbed of God's best. According to Mark 6:5, when Jesus left the city of Nazareth, He left people languishing on beds of sickness and disease. These were people who could have been healed and should have been healed. It was the will of God to heal them.

Now many people say, "God is all powerful and if He wanted to heal them, He could have."

Well, wasn't Jesus God in the flesh? Yes! Jesus said, "He that has seen Me has seen the Father. If you want to see God working, look at Me" (John 14:9). Yet Jesus didn't heal these people. Why? It was because of their unbelief.

The unbelief of that city robbed them of the blessings of God. Unbelief robbed them of the healing God wanted to bring to them.

Confession:

It is God's will to heal me. But I have a part to play. I have to believe God's Word and refuse to doubt in order to receive the healing that Jesus bought and paid for me to have.

And he marvelled because of their unbelief. And he went round about the villages, teaching.

— MARK 6:6

The Cure for Unbelief

After I left the last church I pastored in 1949, I primarily held meetings in Full Gospel churches until 1962. Again and again, I had pastors say to me, "Brother Hagin, I don't want to hinder you. I'm so full of unbelief. I'll just get completely out of the way and sit in the back of the auditorium." And some of them got completely out of the church services. Isn't that a tragedy?

I've laid hands on people with the pastor standing behind me and breathing the hot breath of unbelief down my neck. But God sent me to help them. And I tried to help them. When they come before the Judgment Seat of Christ, they can't say, "We didn't know."

You see, doubt and unbelief have not only robbed individuals and cities, but doubt and unbelief have also robbed entire churches of the blessings God intended they should have.

My wife once said to me, "Honey, it just dawned on me while you were teaching this morning, that in twelve years of pastoral work, we never did bury one church member." Now I realize that eventually people live their lives out and go home. But I taught them that they could live their lives without sickness and disease and just fall asleep in Jesus.

Now God didn't love our church any more than He did a neighboring church. Well, what's the difference? I knew how to get rid of unbelief. Let's read what Jesus did about unbelief: *". . . he marvelled because of their unbelief. And he went round about the villages, TEACHING."* He taught the people.

Confession:

I feed on the Word of God. I listen to good teaching based on the Word of God. And I receive the blessings God intended me to have, including healing.

And when he [Jesus] *had called unto him his twelve disciples, he gave them power against unclean spirits, to cast them out, and to heal all manner of sickness and all manner of disease.*

— MATTHEW 10:1

We Have Power – Faith Activates the Power!

In Matthew chapter 17, we read that Jesus took Peter, James, and John to what became known as the Mount of Transfiguration, where Jesus was transfigured before them. The only disciples on the mountain with Jesus were Peter, James, and John. During this experience, the other nine disciples were at the foot of the mountain, where a man brought his son for them to minister to the boy, but they failed. Let's pick up with verse 14.

MATTHEW 17:14-16
14 And when they [Jesus, Peter, James, and John] **were come to the multitude, there came to him a certain man, kneeling down to him, and saying,**
15 Lord, have mercy on my son: for he is lunatick, and sore vexed: for ofttimes he falleth into the fire, and oft into the water.
16 And I brought him to thy disciples, and they could not cure him.

The nine disciples had ministered to this man's son, but they could not cure him. Jesus had given all twelve of His disciples power to cast out unclean spirits, as we see from our text (Matt. 10:1). So you couldn't say that they didn't have power. You couldn't say they were without authority. You couldn't say they didn't have it, because Jesus said they did, and I believe Jesus told the truth.

Why weren't the nine able to help this boy? Jesus gives the answer in Matthew 17: *"Then Jesus answered and said, O faithless and perverse generation, how long shall I be with you? how long shall I suffer you . . ."* (v. 17). Jesus called the disciples "faithless." Then Jesus rebuked the devil, and the child was cured from that very hour.

The disciples had power, and we have power too. But our faith must activate the power, or we will be rendered helpless.

Confession:

Jesus gave me power over all sickness and disease. Therefore, I use my faith to activate that healing power. I will not be faithless, but believing.

August 2

— MATTHEW 17:19

Faith Gives Action to the Power

In Matthew 17:19, the disciples asked Jesus why they couldn't cast the devil out of the boy. They were troubled because they had been casting devils out and ministering successfully to others. So why couldn't they do it this time? It wasn't because they didn't have the power, because they did. Jesus gave it to them in Matthew 10:1, and they had been ministering to the sick and casting out devils with that power. If they hadn't been, they wouldn't have asked, "Why could we not cast *this one* out?" The disciples had a reputation of ministering to people.

Jesus said unto them, *"Because of your unbelief: for verily I say unto you, If ye have faith as a grain of mustard seed, ye shall say unto this mountain, Remove hence to yonder place; and it shall remove; and nothing shall be impossible unto you"* (Matt. 17:20).

I want you to notice something. This is an area in which practically the whole Pentecostal movement has missed it: emphasizing power over everything else. They've said, "If we've got the power, we can do it." Well, these disciples had the power, and they *couldn't* do it.

People have said, "If nothing happened, it's because we didn't have the power." But that's not where the problem is. It's not a power problem; it's a faith problem. Every failure is a faith failure. These disciples had the power. Jesus said they couldn't cast the devil *out because of their unbelief*. Power doesn't work by unbelief. Power works by *faith*. Faith gives the power action. Faith puts the power to work!

Confession:

My faith gives action to the power of God. My faith puts the power of God to work. I use my faith to receive healing from God.

And these signs shall follow them that believe; In my name shall they cast out devils. . . .

— MARK 16:17

A Christian Can't Be Demon-Possessed

Almost twenty years ago, the Lord appeared to me in Rockwall, Texas, and laid the finger of His right hand in the palm of each one of my hands. Afterward, my hands began to burn as if they had a coal of fire in them. Then Jesus gave me instruction for ministering to the sick in those days. He said, "When you minister to the sick, lay one hand on one side of their body and one hand on the other side of their body."

I would always lay my hands on the body wherever the problem was. If it was a woman needing ministry, I would have my wife help me. And if she wasn't with me, some older women in the church would lay her hands on the woman's body, and then I'd lay my hands on her hands.

Jesus said, "If the fire in your hands jumps from hand to hand, then there is a demon or an evil spirit in the body." Notice that Jesus didn't say the demon or evil spirit would be in the *spirit*; it would be in the *body*. And as I obeyed the Lord in ministering to the sick, I did find that on those occasions when an evil spirit was present, the fire would jump quickly from hand to hand like heat waves.

Now if I cast a demon or an evil spirit out of someone in a healing line, people would get all confused and walk away saying, "Why, that beats all I've ever seen! One of our Sunday school teachers had a devil in him," or "One of the deacons had a demon in him."

No, the devil can't get in a Christian. The spirit, the inward man, is born again. A Christian can't have a demon in his spirit. He could have one in his soul, because his soul — his mind, will, and emotions — hasn't been renewed with the Word of God. He could start worrying and open the door to the devil. And certainly we know that a demon could get in and oppress a person's body (although all diseases aren't the work of an evil spirit). But a Christian can't be demon-possessed.

Confession:

I keep the door closed to the devil. I guard my heart and my mind. I meditate on the Word of God. I meditate on truth, not lies.

— 1 THESSALONIANS 4:4

Your Body Is the 'House' in Which You Live

Your body is the house in which you live. Your body hasn't been redeemed yet. To explain further, let's say that, in the natural, you live in a house at 405 South Elm Street, and someone says, "That house has termites." Well, just because that house has termites in it is no sign that you, the resident of that house, have termites *in you*. You just live in that house. You don't have termites *in you*, but you can do something about the termites in your house. You can get someone to help who knows how to get rid of the termites, or you can do something about them yourself.

Well, your body is the "house" in which you live. The real you is the spirit man who has been born again. And if you don't know how to keep the devil out of your "house," he'll get in.

You see, it's not a matter of casting the devil out of a person's *spirit*. The devil is cast out of a person's *body*. Can a Christian have a demon? Certainly. Can a Christian be demon-possessed? Certainly *not*. When we talk about demon-possession, we are talking about a demon taking over a person's spirit, soul, and body. And if one were fully demon-possessed, he would be crazy or insane; his mind would be gone.

But a born-again, Spirit-filled Christian can have a demon in his body or even his mind, his soul. You might think, *How can that be? If my body is the temple of the Holy Ghost, how can the devil get in?* You can *let* him in.

Confession:

I am a spirit, I have a soul; and I live in a body. I refuse to let the devil into my soul or body. I keep him out by feeding on the Word of God and resisting his lies.

August 5

How God anointed Jesus of Nazareth with the Holy Ghost and with power: who went about doing good, and healing all that were oppressed of the devil; for God was with him.

— ACTS 10:38

Jesus Heals All Those Oppressed by the Devil

There was a twelve-year-old boy in one of the churches my wife and I pastored who virtually grew up in the church. After I left pastoring to go out on the evangelistic field, my wife and I went back to that church to hold a meeting.

A young man about eighteen years old came up in line during one of the services for prayer. He had just graduated from high school. I asked him what was wrong with him, because I usually asked people, "What am I praying for?" I wanted to find out whether to pray for healing or the baptism of the Holy Spirit, because I put everyone in the same line and called it a prayer line.

He said, "Brother Hagin, when you were the pastor here, I never had any problems. But after I got out of high school, I began to have epileptic seizures. I tried to enlist in the military, but they wouldn't take me because of the epilepsy." He wanted to be delivered.

That was before Jesus appeared to me in the vision and said, "Put one hand on one side of their body and one hand on the other side of their body. If the fire jumps from hand to hand, then there's a demon in their body." But the word of knowledge operated in me. I knew the minute I touched him that an evil spirit was causing the epilepsy. I cast the spirit out of him.

Now this young man was saved, filled with the Holy Ghost, and a member of the Assembly of God church. Did he have a devil in him? Yes. Was he demon-possessed? No. Was he delivered? Yes!

Confession:

Jesus specializes in delivering people. He goes about doing good and healing all that are oppressed by the devil. Jesus heals me!

Give No Place to the Devil!

Now about a year later, I was at a church for just one service on a Saturday night. As I was sitting on the platform and looking the crowd over, my eyes fastened on this young man who just a year before had been delivered from epilepsy.

The Spirit of God said to me, "After you cast that spirit out of him, he didn't have one single epileptic seizure for a whole year. But in the last thirty days, he has had three attacks. And they have all come on him in the nighttime while he was asleep. The reason that he woke up in a seizure is that he went to bed afraid. Now cast that thing out of him again and teach him how to stand against the devil."

Well, I got up to preach and told the young man to come down to the front. He came down, and I said, "When I was here last year, you were healed of epilepsy. That thing left you for a solid year. You did not have one epileptic seizure. But in the last thirty days, you've had three attacks. You woke up out of a deep sleep in a seizure."

He said, "That's right."

I said, "I'm going to cast that thing out of you. And I'm going to tell you why it came back on you. You see, you went to bed afraid."

He said, "Yes, I did. All three times, I did. Before I was able to get rid of that fear, I fell asleep."

"You went to sleep and left the door open," I said. "If you were to go to sleep in your house and leave the front door open, there's no telling what would get in your house. A cat, a dog, or even a thief might get in. The devil is a thief and he is looking for doors. When you fear, you open the door. And when you go to sleep with the door open, that thief, the devil, will come running in."

I cast the devil out of him the second time. Then I taught him about resisting the devil. I saw the young man years later and he told me, "I've never had another attack, Brother Hagin." He learned how to keep the door shut.

Confession:

I keep the door shut on the devil; I give him no place. I resist fear. God has not given me a spirit of fear, but of power, love, and a sound mind.

August 7

And he [Jesus] did not many mighty works there because of their unbelief.

— MATTHEW 13:58

Unbelief Is an Enemy!

At a meeting in Broken Bow, Oklahoma, years ago, a man stood in the healing line. I asked him, "What did you come for?"

He said, "I have TB of the spine. My spine is as stiff as a poker; I don't have any movement."

This man couldn't move his back. He could move his neck just a little bit. I laid one hand on his chest and one hand on his back. I felt that fire jump from hand to hand, so I knew his body was oppressed by a demon.

I said, "I command you, foul spirit, that oppresses this body to come out of him [I meant out of his body.]." The man had been saved, filled with the Holy Ghost, and was a member of a Full Gospel church. The demon was not in his spirit. It was in his body. His back was as stiff as a board.

After I said, "Come out of him in the Name of Jesus," I missed it. Remember, Peter missed it after he stepped out of the boat onto the water, and unbelief robbed him of God's best; he started sinking in the water. The nine disciples missed it, and unbelief robbed them of God's best; they couldn't cast the devil out of the boy.

I missed it when I said to the man, "See if you can stoop over and touch your toes." Well, he couldn't. I mean, he could barely move his head.

I put my hands on his chest again, felt that fire jump from hand to hand, and said, "Come out of him, you foul spirit, that oppresses this man's body. I command you to come out of him in the Name of Jesus."

Then I missed it again. I said, "See if you can stoop over and touch your toes." He couldn't move. His back was as stiff as a poker. I did the whole thing again for the third time, and he still couldn't touch his toes.

Well, I thought that three times should be enough to minister to a person. I had given him more attention than anyone else. He walked back to his seat without having been helped. I didn't realize that I'd allowed unbelief to creep in.

Confession:

I'm not going to let doubt or unbelief defeat me. Doubt and unbelief are of the devil. Faith and love are of God. I walk in love. And I walk by faith.

If ye shall ask any thing in my [Jesus'] name, I will do it.
— JOHN 14:14

August 8

Healing and Deliverance Come by Faith

When this man with TB of the spine walked back to his seat, I wondered why what I'd done didn't work. I walked back behind the pulpit, and, suddenly, Jesus stood right in front of me. I saw Him just as plain as I saw the pulpit. It was an open vision. No one but me saw Him.

Jesus put His finger right up under my nose and said, "*I said*, 'In My Name, the demon or demons will have to go!'" No one else saw or heard Him (although they did hear what I said in reply), but I saw and heard Him.

I said, "Lord, I know You told me to call them out in Your Name and the demon or demons would have to go. I told it to go, but it didn't leave."

Jesus again put His finger right up under my nose and almost touched it. He said, "*I said*, 'In My Name, call them out! In My Name, the demon or demons will have to go!'"

I said, "Lord, I know You said that. It hasn't been thirty days since You appeared to me in Rockwall, Texas, and laid the finger of Your right hand upon each one of my hands and told me to lay hands on the sick. You said that if that fire jumped from hand to hand, it meant there was a demon or demons in the body. Then you said to call them out in Your Name and they would have to go. I know You said that. And I told it to leave, but it didn't go."

Then Jesus stuck His finger right up to my nose and said, "Yes! But I said it *would*!" Then He disappeared. When He said that, I got it.

I told the man to come down to the front again. I put one hand on his back and one hand on his chest. I said, "Devil, I told you to go and now you're gone." Then I said to the man, "Stoop over, brother, and touch your toes."

When I said that, over he went! I mean, he touched his toes in an instant! Where was this man's healing? It was in the faith realm. My doubt robbed me. I'd been saying, "*See if you can* touch your toes." My unbelief robbed me. Unbelief robbed the disciples. Don't let doubt and unbelief rob you.

Confession:

The devil is a liar and a thief. I'll not let him defeat me. I'll not let the devil rob me of the blessings of God. Instead, I will walk by faith.

August 9

Nevertheless I tell you the truth; It is expedient for you that I go away: for if I go not away, the Comforter will not come unto you; but if I depart, I will send him unto you.

— JOHN 16:7

The Executive of the Godhead

The Holy Spirit is the only executive of the Godhead on the earth today. In other words, He's the One who's here to carry out the orders of God. You have to cooperate with Him in your prayer life, because the Holy Spirit is the One who helps you. And when it comes to healing, the Holy Spirit is the One who executes the healing in your body that Jesus bought and paid for on your behalf.

According to First Peter 2:24, Jesus already purchased your healing: "By whose stripes you *were* healed." You're not *going to be* healed; you *were* healed. That means that in the mind of God, you were healed back when the stripes were laid on Jesus' back. In the mind of God, you're already healed. In the mind of Jesus, you're already healed, because He remembers when the stripes were put on Him. In the mind of the Holy Spirit, you're already healed, because He inspired Peter to write First Peter 2:24.

The Holy Spirit is on the earth to execute, to put into motion, the healing in our body when we believe and claim it — when we accept that Jesus has already purchased it for us and then believe it.

Confession:

Jesus already purchased my healing. According to First Peter 2:24, I WAS healed. And the Holy Spirit is working effectively in my body to bring about that healing for me.

Now faith is the substance of things hoped for, the evidence of things not seen.

— HEBREWS 11:1

Don't Be Moved by What You See

Back when we were pastoring, I remember a woman who brought her mother from another county to see us.

Margene brought her mother, who was sixty-seven years old and had been in the asylum at Wichita Falls, Texas, because she had lost her mind. Margene explained to us that the state authorities had contacted her and her two sisters to see if one of them would keep their mother. The state said they would pay for the daughter to keep her mother.

The mother had not responded to institutional care. Those at the institution told Margene, "We can't help your mother. Her mind will never be right." She was unsaved and not expected to live much longer. She was going to die and go to hell.

When I looked into the mother's eyes, I noticed that they didn't look right. They were dull and listless. Margene shook her mother, put her hand on her shoulder, and said, "Now, Mama, come on, get up now. We've got to go home, because I've got to get back in time to cook supper."

When Margene shook her that way, she suddenly blinked her eyes and looked at me. Then she said the only sensible thing she had said all day. She said, "Will I ever be any better?"

I immediately thought of Mark 11:23: *"For verily I say unto you, That whosoever shall say unto this mountain, Be thou removed, and be thou cast into the sea; and shall not doubt in his heart, but shall believe that those things which he saith shall come to pass; he shall have whatsoever he saith."* I pointed my finger at her and said, "Yes, you will, in the Name of Jesus." That's all I said.

Margene bundled her mother in the car and took her home. Now she didn't look a bit better. She still looked as crazy as she ever did. But to me, that settled it. I said that to her in faith. Faith is not moved by what it sees. Faith is not moved by what it feels. Faith is not moved by what it hears from the natural standpoint. Faith is moved only by what the Word says.

Confession:

I am not moved by what I see. I am not moved by what I feel. I am not moved by what I hear from the natural standpoint. I am moved only by what the Word says.

223

Cast not away therefore your confidence, which hath great recompence of reward.

— HEBREWS 10:35

Cast Not Away Your Confidence!

After I said that to Margene's mother, my wife would say, "I wonder what happened to Margene's mother?"

I would always answer, "I'll tell you exactly what happened to her. She was healed. Her mind was restored."

She would say, "Well, we haven't heard anything."

I would say, "I don't have to hear anything. I spoke it. That's it. That's all I need."

About a month after I spoke with Margene and her mother, my wife received a letter from Margene. It read, "Brother and Sister Hagin, I would like to come down and have you all pray with me about something, if that's all right with you." So my wife wrote back and told her to come.

Margene didn't say anything about her mother in the letter. When she drove up in front of the parsonage, we went out there to greet her. My wife and I both said at the same time, "What ever happened to your mother?"

She said, "Brother and Sister Hagin, let me tell you. I took her home, and the next day she wasn't any better. The third day at 3:00 p.m., we were in the living room in my house, and, all of a sudden, her mind was all right. It happened in an instant! She got down on her knees and wanted me to pray with her. The Lord saved her and filled her with the Holy Ghost!

"Then, my dad, who also lives with us, got saved and filled with the Holy Ghost. He had claimed that he was an infidel, but when he saw what God had done for Mama, he got down on his knees and said to me, 'Put your hand on my head and pray.' God saved Dad and filled him with the Holy Ghost too!"

Later, Margene's mom and dad lived in their own house. Her mama began doing all the housework and the cooking. Years later, they were both in good health. They were in church every Sunday morning and every Sunday night. They paid their tithes and supported the house of God.

Confession:

I cast not away my confidence, for it hath great recompense of reward!

We Will Either Doubt or Have Faith

We checked up on Margene's mother and father several years later when her mother was eighty-nine years old. She still did all her housework. She had a better, clearer mind than even her daughters had! At sixty-seven, she was sitting around, out of her mind, making funny, unintelligible sounds. But at eighty-nine, she had a sharp mind and was able to function just fine.

How can you receive the best that God has for you? Well, first, be hungry and thirsty for God and His best. Resist doubt constantly. The only cure for doubt is faith in God's Word. Act on the Word. Believe it for what it says. Act on the Word of God and receive all of its promises. There is no other way.

The Spirit of God said through James, *"But let him ask in faith, nothing wavering. For he that wavereth is like a wave of the sea driven with the wind and tossed. For let not that man think that he shall receive any thing of the Lord"* (James 1:6,7). Now you can have either doubt or faith. It's up to you. You're the one who makes that choice. Which one do you want?

Confession:

I'm not a doubter. I'm a believer. I am a child of God. God is my very own Father. I am His very own child. I am born of God.

August 13

But without faith it is impossible to please him: for he that cometh to God must believe that he is, and that he is a rewarder of them that diligently seek him.

— HEBREWS 11:6

Keep the Door Open to God

I've had many people say to me over the years, "The doctor told me that I will be dead in three months." Some of them were healed of incurable diseases, such as cancer. Others died in three months. Did God show favoritism? No! God is not a respecter of persons (Acts 10:34). What happened, then?

Some of them opened the door and said, "Come on in, God." And He came in. Others kept the door shut on God. God's hands were tied, so to speak; He couldn't come in and help them. Some were in doubt, and the others were in faith.

Read this prayer aloud and let your heart agree with it:

Heavenly Father, thank You because You're my Father and I'm your child. I have been born again. I am born of You. You are my very own Father, and I am Your very own child. Hallelujah! It is written in Your Word that "my God shall supply all my needs according to His riches in glory by Christ Jesus" [Phil. 4:19]. I believe that in my heart. You supply my physical needs — that is, healing for my body — for it is written in Matthew 8:17, "Himself took our infirmities, and bare our sicknesses." Jesus took my infirmities. He bore my sicknesses. What He bore, I need not bear. Because He bore them. I'm free; I'm healed. I believe that in my heart. I say it with my mouth. It's mine. I have it now. He meets all my needs. My spiritual need is met. My financial need is met. Every material need is met. All my needs are met. I believe it in my heart. Because I believe it in my heart, I say it with my mouth. It is done.

*And when Jesus departed thence, two blind men fol-
lowed him, crying, and saying, Thou Son of David,
have mercy on us.*

August 14

— MATTHEW 9:27

Prayer Alone Will Not Heal You

Jairus' little daughter had just been raised up from the dead and healed. Two blind men followed Jesus from Jairus' house, crying and saying, "Thou Son of David, have mercy on us."

Even though these two men cried and prayed, they were still in the same boat they were in to begin with. They were still blind. One account I read said that these two men were still blind after crying and praying because they addressed Jesus as the Son of David. But Matthew wrote his entire Gospel to prove that Jesus was the Son of David! Jesus was the Son of David; the blind men were addressing Him correctly. And by calling Him the Son of David, they were acknowledging that He was the One who was to come. They were acknowledging that He was the Messiah.

But even though the blind men were correct in calling Him the Son of David — even though they were correct in their praying — they didn't get an answer. That proves one thing to us: Prayer alone will not save you. And prayer alone will not heal you. Mere prayer will not save your spirit or heal your body. These men followed Jesus from Jairus' house crying and praying. But their prayers alone brought no reply.

Confession:

Jesus is the same today as He was over two thousand years ago when He walked the earth. Since crying and praying alone didn't get the two blind men healed, crying and praying alone won't get me healed today.

August 15

And the prayer of faith shall save the sick, and the Lord shall raise him up; and if he have committed sins, they shall be forgiven him.

— JAMES 5:15

Pray in Faith

Many people have been praying for years and are in the same boat they were in when they first began praying. Things haven't changed at all. Some people have been praying for forty years, and it seems they're no nearer to the answer now than when they first began praying.

I am not belittling prayer, because prayer is important. But prayer alone will not save your spirit or heal your body. Some people have been praying all their lives and are still not saved. I prayed for years. I can't remember the first time I prayed. As far as I know, I've been praying all my life. I do not have any conscious moment of not praying. Yet in all those years of praying, I wasn't saved. Now I know exactly when I did get saved, because it took more than prayer to save me. And it takes more than prayer to save you or heal you.

You see, some people imagine that if they can get enough people to pray, God will answer them. Many have prayed for years and received no answer. Well, there is a reason why. You see, if they had prayed in faith, they would have gotten an answer. And if they had prayed in faith, they wouldn't have prayed so long!

Confession:

When I pray, I pray in faith. I don't pray in doubt. And I receive answers to my prayers.

*And when Jesus departed thence, two blind men fol-
lowed him, crying, and saying, Thou Son of David,
have mercy on us.*

The Presence of God May Not Heal You

If you stopped reading this story at verse 27, you could hold up the two
blind men as a perfect example of people who prayed but did not receive an
answer. And verse 28 says, *"And when he* [Jesus] *was come into the house,
the blind men came to him. . . ."* Even though the blind men were in the
Presence of Jesus, they were still blind. That illustrates this fact: Merely coming into the Presence of God will not save or heal you.

Today people seem to think that just going to meetings, or just getting
under certain spiritual influence, will bring them their blessings. Well, those
are steps in the right direction. But if people just stop there, they haven't
gone far enough.

Many even present themselves at the altar for salvation or healing and are
still no better; they do not receive from God. When I was a Baptist pastor,
people would come to the altar for salvation, the baptism of the Holy Spirit,
and healing. Some received what they came for; others did not. That dis-
turbed me. None of them should have gone away without salvation or the
baptism of the Holy Spirit. And not one of them should have gone away
without healing.

Yet some of these people who left without salvation, the baptism of the
Holy Spirit, and healing were just as sincere and honest as some who left
with their prayers answered. Why didn't they receive? Notice that the Lord
didn't say in Mark 11:24, "Therefore, I say unto you, whatsoever things you
desire, *if you are sincere*, you'll have them."

Confession:

*Merely coming into the Presence of God will not heal me. Just going to meet-
ings where the Spirit of God is moving will not heal me. It takes faith to be
healed.*

August 17

*. . . Jesus saith unto them, Believe ye that I am able
to do this? They said unto him, Yea, Lord. Then
touched he their eyes, saying, According to your
faith be it unto you.*

— MATTHEW 9:28,29

The Great Law of Faith

Notice that Jesus didn't say to the two blind men, "Well, because you are sincere and honest, go your way and see." No, He didn't say that.

You see, although people should be sincere and honest, they must also act in faith. These two blind men who followed Jesus from Jairus' house, crying, "Thou Son of David, have mercy on us," were still blind after calling out to Jesus.

All your crying and praying is of no avail unless you definitely believe that God does for you what He claims He does. That is so important. Jesus asked these two blind men a question, "Do you believe?" In other words, He asked, "Do you believe that I'm able to heal you?" If you don't believe God is able to meet your need, you are wasting your time taking any further steps.

You see, God operates on laws or principles, just as the natural world operates. Paul said in Romans, *"For the invisible things of him from the creation of the world are clearly seen, being understood by the things that are made, even his eternal power and Godhead; so that they are without excuse"* (Rom. 1:20). This seen world operates on certain laws. For instance, there are certain natural laws that must be in place in order for electricity to be produced. The same is true of God's power.

After Jesus asked the blind men if they believed, He was able to heal them. Jesus uttered the great law of faith: "According to your faith, be it unto you" (Matt. 9:29). The law of faith determines for every one of us the measure of our blessings. Then Jesus touched the blind men's eyes and sight was restored to them. They went out into the day, able to see the glorious light.

Confession:

According to my faith, be it done unto me. Just as the natural world operates according to certain laws, the spiritual world operates according to certain laws. One law, the great law of faith, determines the measure of my blessing.

When he was come down from the mountain, great multitudes followed him.
And, behold, there came a leper and worshipped him, saying, Lord, if thou wilt, THOU CANST make me clean.

God Will Heal You

Notice what the leper said: "Thou canst." We would say today, "You're able to." You see, he already believed that Jesus was able to do it. But he wasn't sure if Jesus was *willing* to do it. Then Jesus put forth His hand, touched him, and said, "I will" (Matt. 8:3).

Jesus never said, "I won't." Of all the people who ever came to Jesus for healing, Jesus never said, "It's not My will to heal you. God's trying to teach you a lesson. You just be patient in this, and let patience have her perfect work." Not one single time did Jesus ever say that. And no man has any right to say it to others in His Name, because Jesus Himself never said it.

Settle on God's willingness to heal you. He not only *can*, but He *will*! So don't just believe that He can; believe that He will!

Confession:

God desires to heal me. I believe that He is not only ABLE to do it, but He is also WILLING to do it.

August 19

And Jesus put forth his hand, and touched him, saying, I will; be thou clean. And immediately his leprosy was cleansed.

— MATTHEW 8:3

God's Willingness To Heal Is Unchanging

When I was sick as a teenage boy, I believed that God *could* heal me. I believed that God was *able* to do anything. But I was taught that He wasn't willing today. I heard people say, "Now God can do it. He has the power to do anything — *if* it is His will."

I remember one particular pastor I heard on the radio who said just that. He talked about a nine-year-old boy whose parents were members of his church. This little boy was their only child. He was desperately ill and under the care of a doctor. The parents called this pastor, weeping, and said, "The doctor just left and said, 'I've done everything I know to do. There isn't anything anyone can do. I'm just going to tell you the truth about it. The child is not going to live. In fact, he's dying now.'"

I heard the pastor say on the radio, "I knew James 5:14 was in the Bible, but I had never done anything about it." James 5:14 and 15 says, *"Is any sick among you? let him call for the elders of the church; and let them pray over him, anointing him with oil in the name of the Lord: And the prayer of faith shall save the sick, and the Lord shall raise him up. . . ."*

Confession:

I believe what the Bible says. As others pray for me, anointing me with oil in the Name of the Lord, I am healed, because the Bible says that the prayer of faith shall save the sick.

Is any sick among you? let him call for the elders of the church; and let them pray over him, anointing him with oil in the name of the Lord.

— JAMES 5:14

'I Want You To Pray'

The pastor continued, "When I got there, the boy had lapsed into unconsciousness. The doctor said he would never regain consciousness. He said that he would die. So I asked the mother, 'What do you want me to do?'

"She said, 'I want you to pray. I just don't believe it's the will of God for us to lose the only child we've got. It's not the will of God that he die at nine years of age. I just can't accept that. I don't believe that. I want you to pray.'"

So the pastor asked the mother if she had any olive oil. She went into the kitchen and brought some back. He prayed and anointed the child. The boy opened his eyes and said, "Mama, Mama." And he was all right.

Then the pastor said to his listening audience, "I've been doing that for some of my church folks. Now don't get your hopes up, because if it is the will of God, He will heal. But if it's not, He won't."

When I heard that, the devil immediately put the light out. He said, "You're one of those who it's not God's will to heal." And, of course, at that time, I believed what the devil said.

Confession:

It is always the will of God to heal. I refuse to believe what the devil says. I believe what God says, and I receive the healing Jesus bought and paid for me to have.

August 21

Verily, verily, I say unto you, He that believeth on me hath everlasting life.

— JOHN 6:47

Believing Is Having

The same Greek word translated *everlasting* is also translated *eternal*. Here it's describing the God-kind of life, which never ends. In other words, Jesus was saying, "He that believeth on Me has the God-kind of life."

Notice the phrase: "He that believeth *hath*." You see, believing is having. That's the way you have whatever God has made available to you in His Word — by believing it. Believing is possessing.

Many times, people substitute mental assent, or mental agreement, for believing. They agree that the Bible is true and even admire the Word of God. They confess that every word of the Bible is true. But they don't possess anything, because they're just mentally agreeing to it. But real believing is possessing; it's having.

Someone once said, "Believing ends in the glad confession, 'It's mine. I have it now.'"

Remember, Mark 11:24 says, *"Therefore I say unto you, What things soever ye desire, when ye pray, believe that ye receive them, and ye shall have them."* He that believes *has*. Believing is having.

When you pray, believe that you receive it and you'll have it. When are you going to have what you desire? *After* you believe you receive it. Believing is having. If you believe you receive something, you're going to say, "It's mine. I have it now." You're saying that by faith.

Confession:

Believing is having. I believe I receive healing. I believe I receive whatever I need. It's mine. I have it now.

What doth it profit, my brethren, though a man say he hath faith, and have not works? can faith save him?

— JAMES 2:14

Faith Has Corresponding Actions

Real believing is acting on God's Word. I've used that phrase for many, many years, because it's very simple to understand. So act on the Word. That's what believing the Bible is. It's acting on the Word.

In Mark chapter 2, a man is brought into the presence of Jesus by four of his friends. Because of the crowd, they couldn't get into the house where Jesus was teaching. So they let the man down through the roof! This account illustrates some important things about faith that I want you to notice.

Mark 2:5 says, *"When Jesus saw their faith, he said unto the sick of the palsy, Son, thy sins be forgiven thee."* Well, can you see faith with your physical eyes? No, because it's of the spirit. You can't see spiritual things with the physical eye. Think about this in the natural for a moment. For example, can you see the wind? No, but you can see the *results* of the wind. So what did Jesus see when He saw their faith? He saw their *actions*.

James 2:20 says, *"But wilt thou know, O vain man, that faith without works is dead?"* The New Testament in Modern Speech says, "Faith without corresponding actions is dead."

In other words, you show me your faith without your actions, and I'll show you my faith *by* my actions. Jesus saw the actions of the four men and their lame friend. They were determined. They believed.

Confession:

My faith must have corresponding actions. Otherwise, it is dead faith. I believe the Word, and I act on the Word.

And immediately he arose, took up the bed, and went forth before them all; insomuch that they were all amazed, and glorified God, saying, We never saw it on this fashion.

— MARK 2:12

Act on What Jesus Said

Was the man who was lowered through the roof healed on the faith of his four friends alone? No, the man had to have faith too. How do we know that he had faith?

Well, how many bedfast people would let someone carry them to the roof of a house? Most bedfast people would say, "Wait a minute. Maybe we'll see Jesus when the service is over. I'm already bedfast, and if you happened to drop me, I'll surely break some bones. I'd be in a mess then." But this man who was lowered through the roof permitted himself to be carried up to the roof by four men. He believed that something was going to happen, or he wouldn't have let them take him up there.

Jesus said to the bedfast man, *"...Arise, and take up thy bed, and go thy way into thine house"* (Mark 2:11). I want you to notice something. When Jesus said to the man, "Arise, take up your bed and walk," the man was just as helpless as he ever was. What if the man had said, "Lord, didn't You see them bring me in here and let me down through the roof"? He wouldn't have been healed. But when Jesus spoke to him, he made an effort to do what Jesus said. He made an effort to get up.

When he acted on what Jesus said, the healing was consummated. What if he hadn't acted on what Jesus said? It wouldn't have been consummated; the healing would not have come. It's when he acted in faith on what Jesus said that the healing was manifested.

Confession:

I act in faith on what Jesus said. And as a result, my healing is consummated. It is manifested.

But without faith it is impossible to please him: for he that cometh to God must believe that he is, and that he is a rewarder of them that diligently seek him.

— HEBREWS 11:6

God Honors Faith

A number of years ago during the early days of the Pentecostal movement, I read about an outstanding healing evangelist. At one particular meeting, there were four people in wheelchairs who had been pushed down to the front. After the evangelist preached and gave the invitation, he walked off the platform and spoke to those in the wheelchairs.

He said to the first one, "I command you to rise and walk in Jesus' Name." He just got up and walked out of that chair. The evangelist said to the second one, "I command you to rise and walk in the Name of the Lord Jesus Christ." He rose up and walked right out of the chair. Then he said to the third one, "I command you to rise and walk in the Name of the Lord Jesus Christ." He got up and walked right out of the chair. The evangelist said to the fourth one, "I command you to rise and walk in the Name of the Lord Jesus Christ." And he said, "I can't. Didn't you see them push me in here?" The evangelist had to walk off and leave him there.

Some people might say, "If that evangelist healed three of them, why didn't he heal the fourth one?" The evangelist didn't heal any of them. The Lord healed three of them. Why didn't the Lord heal the other one? Because the fourth one didn't act on what was said.

God honors faith. God is a faith God. He operates on principles of faith. Find out how God works and work with Him. Then you'll get results.

Confession:

I act on what God said in His Word. God honors faith. He is a faith God. I choose to cooperate with Him and act on principles of faith. Then I see results.

August 25

Jesus saith unto him, Rise, take up thy bed, and walk.

— JOHN 5:8

Rise and Walk

In 1950, I was preaching at a meeting in Oklahoma, and at the close of my sermon, the word of the Lord came to me saying, "Minister to those who have anything wrong with them from their hips down." So I just spoke that out.

Well, twelve people came. The first man looked like he was sitting down, but he was scooting his feet along because his legs were drawn up. I asked him what was wrong, and he explained that he had been burned. In fact, that was the first day he had been out of bed in a whole year. He had spent six months in the hospital and six months in the bed at home. His legs were burned so deeply that the muscles and ligaments had left his legs drawn up.

When the Lord said to *minister* to these people, I thought He meant to lay hands on them. But as the people were coming down to the front, the word of the Lord came to me again saying, "Don't touch a single one of them. Don't pray for them. Deal with each one of them individually, not as a group. Say to them, 'The Lord told me to tell you to run down that aisle and back up this aisle, and you'll be healed.'"

I said to the man who had been burned, "Can you run?" It so startled him that he just said, "No, I can't walk, much less run."

I said, "Well, the Lord told me to tell you to run down that aisle and back up this one, and you'll be healed." That man never doubted for a minute. He started scooting as fast as he could. He scooted down one aisle and back up the other one. And he was no better. Well, when God speaks to you, don't give in to the devil.

I said, "Do it again." He did it again. When he came by me, the Spirit of God came on me, and before I knew what I was doing, I leaped off the platform and took him by the arm and ran down that aisle with him. When we ran up the other aisle, he was running as well as I was! His legs were straight!

Confession:

I obey God. Whatever He tells me to do, I do. I act in faith, and I back up my faith with works, with corresponding actions. Then I see what I have believed was mine. I see the manifestation of my healing.

And all these blessings shall come on thee, and over-take thee, if thou shalt hearken unto the voice of the Lord thy God.

August 26

— DEUTERONOMY 28:2

Obey the Voice of the Lord

After the man who had been burned was healed, I took the next one aside and dealt with him individually. I asked him what was wrong with him. Then I said to him, "The Lord said, 'Run!'" He whirled around and started running. Eleven out of the twelve were instantly healed as they obeyed God.

When I got to the twelfth one, I said, "Are you ready to run?" I thought she would be just as thrilled as the rest of them were and take off running. Instead, she said, "Oh, Brother Hagin, I can't run. I have arthritis."

I said to her, "Didn't you hear as I talked to the other people? In fact, a woman who couldn't even walk down to the front by herself was healed. Three men had to hold her up. She had arthritis, too, but as she started to run, her body straightened out and was all right. Did you see her?"

She said, "Yes, but I know I can't do it."

I answered, "All I know to do is tell you what the Lord told me. And you saw that eleven people have already been healed."

She turned around and made one or two feeble steps. I said, "You got down here by yourself. Some of the rest of them had canes and crutches. You don't even need a cane or a crutch."

Then, without thinking, I said to her, "Turn around and look at me. You don't want to run, do you? Something on the inside of you rose up against it, didn't it?"

She said, "Yes, it sure did."

I said, "You just go sit down and do without it. You're not going to get it as long as you're thinking like that."

Confession:

I obey the voice of the Lord. I hearken unto His voice, and unto His Word, to do all of His commandments. Then I am blessed. Then I am healed.

239

But be ye doers of the word, and not hearers only, deceiving your own selves.

— JAMES 1:22

Make an Effort

Even when God speaks to you, you can choose not to act on it. The bedfast man who was let down through the roof didn't have to act when Jesus said, "Rise, take up your bed, and walk" (Mark 2:11). He could have refused. But he came for results, so he made an effort to do what Jesus said.

When I was bedfast as a seventeen-year-old boy, the doctors said I had to die. My body was almost totally paralyzed. I couldn't walk. I wasted away until I weighed only eighty-nine pounds.

When I began to act upon the Scriptures, I heard these words on the inside of me, "Now you believe you're well. Get up then." So I pushed my paralyzed body off the bed. I made an effort, just like the man in the Bible who was bedfast.

Well, Jesus still speaks to us today, because He is here in Spirit. He still speaks, just as He spoke to the man and said, "Rise, take up your bed, and walk." And when He does, if you'll act upon His Words, you'll get results, because the written Word is given to us by the Holy Spirit. It's inspired by the Spirit of God.

Confession:

When God speaks to me, I make an effort. I do what He tells me to do. He speaks to me through His Word, and I obey His Word. Then I receive the blessings that come as a result of obedience.

You Can Depend on God's Word

Are you ready to act on the Word? What does it mean to "act on the Word"? It means to act like the Word of God is so, because it is.

Did you ever borrow money from a bank? Did you ever act on what the banker said? Well, I have.

I remember one time I wanted to buy an air conditioner for a travel trailer I had. I was holding a meeting in a certain place, and a man came up to me and said, "I'll sell you one." I had already priced them, and I knew I would be saving almost two hundred dollars if I purchased it from this man. Besides that, he said that he would install it. I was only at the meeting a few days, and I didn't have that much money on me. And I didn't have that much money in my bank account. So I made a long distance call to Mr. Mitchell, my banker.

I said, "Mr. Mitchell, I'm buying an air conditioner for my trailer, and I have to give this man a check. When I get home on Monday, I'll come to the bank and sign a note. I don't want to write the check without the money in my account."

He said, "That's all right, Brother Hagin. You just go ahead and write the check. We'll put the money into your account."

Well, I took his word for it. I knew him. And when I got home on Monday, I went to the bank and signed the note. Sure enough, the money was there just as Mr. Mitchell promised.

Confession:

I depend on God's Word. If God said it, it's true. If He said it's mine, I believe it's mine. According to the Word of God, healing is mine.

Then said the Lord unto me, Thou hast well seen: for I will hasten my word to perform it.

— JEREMIAH 1:12

God's Word Is Good

I remember another situation in which I had to act on what the banker said. I needed a car that could pull my trailer up mountainous roads. So I bought a 1955 V8 Chevrolet. Well, I didn't have the money to buy it. I found a salesman who would let me have it at cost. However, instead of letting me have it at cost, it cost him one hundred and fifty dollars to sell it to me.

So I called from California to Garland, Texas, to speak to my banker. I said, "Mr. Mitchell, I am buying a three-quarter ton pick-up truck." Then I told him the price.

He said, "Wow! There's got to be some mistake here."

So the salesman got on the phone with Mr. Mitchell and said, "I'm staying with the figure I gave him. We made a mistake. We figured it wrong. He's getting the truck at one hundred and fifty dollars less than what we put in it. But I'm a man of my word. I'm going to stay with what I said. He can have it for that price."

Mr. Mitchell said, "All right. Just give the pick-up truck to him, and I'll put the check in the mail for you." Well, I drove that truck away in fifteen minutes. All the salesman and I had was the banker's word. And all the banker had was my word. But we just acted on one another's word and enjoyed the benefits thereof!

I wonder if God's Word is as good as Mr. Mitchell's word! I wonder if God's Word is as good as the car dealer's word! I wonder if God will back His Word up! I wonder if you can depend on what He said! You have to know that God stands by His Word. Then you won't be afraid to trust Him.

Confession:

I know that God stands by His Word. His Word says that I'm healed, that I'm not sick anymore. So I believe Him. I know that God's Word works for me.

And Simon answering said unto him, Master, we have toiled all the night, and have taken nothing: nevertheless at thy word I will let down the net.

— LUKE 5:5

'At Thy Word, I Will'

In Luke chapter 5, we see an example of a person who acted on the Word and got results. Peter and John had been fishing. They had fished all night and had caught nothing. Then Jesus told Peter, *". . . Launch out into the deep, and let down your nets for a draught"* (Luke 5:4).

Peter said, *". . . Master, we have toiled all the night, and have taken nothing: nevertheless at thy word I will let down the net"* (Luke 5:5).

What change would come in our lives if we said, "At Your Word, I will!" What change would come if we would just do it because the Word said so, whether we felt like it or not.

You see, we've clung to the theories of men and have ignored the living Word of God. Healing and victory belong to you and to me. The Bible tells us so. So adopt as your motto: "At Your Word, I will."

Confession:

Instead of following the traditions of men, I follow the Word of God. At God's Word, I let down my net, so to speak. I reach out and receive all that He has for me.

His mother saith unto the servants, Whatsoever he saith unto you, do it.

— JOHN 2:5

Don't Wait for Evidence To Believe

In John chapter 2, we see the account of Jesus attending the wedding in Cana with his mother. His mother told Him that they had run out of wine. Jesus said to the servants, *". . . Fill the waterpots with water. . . ."* (John 2:7).

Let's continue reading in John.

JOHN 2:7-10
7   . . . And they filled them up to the brim.
8   And he saith unto them, Draw out now, and bear unto the governor of the feast. And they bare it.
9   When the ruler of the feast had tasted the water that was made wine, and knew not whence it was: (but the servants which drew the water knew;) the governor of the feast called the bridegroom,
10   And saith unto him, Every man at the beginning doth set forth good wine; and when men have well drunk, then that which is worse: but thou hast kept the good wine until now.

The water became wine. Now what if the servants had stood there and said, "We're going to stand right here and wait until the water becomes wine and *then* we'll start filling these pots"? Nothing would have happened.

You see, that's the thing that defeats many Christians. They want to stand around and wait until they can see it done — until they have the sense evidence that things have happened. In the case of healing, they want to start believing when all the symptoms have disappeared. No, you must believe ahead of time what God says. Act on God's Word, and then what He has said will become a reality. Because the servants acted on the words of Jesus, a miracle was wrought.

Confession:

I believe what God says before I ever see anything in the natural. I act on God's Word, and as I do, I see miracles wrought in my life.

Let the word of Christ dwell in you richly in all wisdom . . .

— COLOSSIANS 3:16

Let the Word Dwell in You Richly

I knew a Baptist woman who was only thirty-six years old and had cancer. She was bedfast and wasn't supposed to live very long. A Baptist pastor who had seen the light on divine healing visited her each day and read scriptures to her and prayed. However, she remained bedfast. This pastor would walk to her house because she didn't live far from the parsonage where he lived.

As he was walking home one day, he said, "Lord, I don't understand. I mean, we're believing You for healing. This woman says that she believes the scriptures I'm reading to her."

As soon as he said that, the Spirit of God spoke to him and said, "No, she doesn't believe them. She's just mentally agreeing to them. If she believed them, she would be out of bed and doing her housework."

The next day he went back to her house and began reading scriptures to her. She said, "Yes, I believe that." And he said, "No, you don't. If you believed it, you'd be out of bed doing your housework."

Well, she looked at him sort of startled, as if he had slapped her! But she got it. She said to him, "You go in the next room, and I'll get up." She got up, put her housecoat on, and he left. And when her husband came home, he found her up well, cooking the evening meal.

That Baptist pastor said to me, "Nineteen years have come and gone, and she's still well and healed. She's still doing her housework."

Someone might say, "Well, I believe I'll try that." It won't work by trying it. She didn't *try* it; she *did* it. She got the Word down into her spirit. She didn't just mentally act on what God said. There is a difference. Don't act presumptuously or foolishly. Let the Word get down on the inside of you — then you can act in faith. And when you do, results will be forthcoming.

Confession:

I am not just a HEARER of the Word. I am a DOER of the Word. I act on what God's Word says. I let His Word get down on the inside of me, and then I act in faith.

September 2   *Therefore let no man glory in men. For all things are yours.*

— 1 CORINTHIANS 3:21

Rights of Sonship

In this passage of Scripture, Paul is writing to the Church at Corinth. But it applies to the whole Body of Christ. How many things does he say are ours? *All things*! All things that God has provided belong to us.

Do you remember the story of the prodigal son in Luke chapter 15? The elder brother got upset that the father was throwing a party for the younger son. The elder brother was so angry that he wouldn't even go into the house. Some of the servants evidently told his father about it, so his father went out and entreated him.

The elder son said to his father, "I've served you faithfully all these years, and you never threw a party for me. You never killed any fattened calf or had a feast for me. And this, thy son [he didn't even call him brother], who spent your living in riotous living, has come home and you've killed the fattened calf" (Luke 15:29).

"Well," the father said, "my son who was lost is found." But notice what else he said to the elder brother: "Son, all that I have is thine." All the while that the elder son was complaining, he had a right to everything his father had — including a fattened calf. Glory to God! If God has it, it belongs to us! All He has is ours.

Confession:

If God has it, it belongs to me. Health and healing belong to God, so they belong to me also. I thank God for my health and healing!

*And he said unto him, Son, thou art ever with me,
and all that I have is thine.*

September 3

— LUKE 15:31

All That God Has Is Yours

Are the resources of God yours? Yes! That being true, you need to find out what He has. When you find out what He has, you know what belongs to you, and you will be closer to enjoying the blessings of God. Does He have forgiveness? Yes! That's yours. Does He have healing? Yes! And it's yours too. Does He have poverty or wealth? *Wealth!* Is He a poor God or a rich God? He's rich! What does He have? Does He have grace? Yes. Then those things are yours.

All that God has is yours. Who is to blame if you don't have it? Him? No, He has already told you that it's yours. How are you going to get it? How are you going to have it in reality? By acting on what He said. In other words, by acting like it's yours.

The Bible says that we are heirs of God and joint-heirs (equal heirs) with Jesus Christ (Rom. 8:17). Some people say, "Jesus has it all, and God has it all, but we're just left without anything. We'll have it after awhile, when we get to Heaven." The Bible didn't say that we're *going to be* heirs of God. The Bible says that we *are* heirs of God. All that God has is ours *now!*

Confession:

I am an heir of God and a joint-heir with Jesus Christ. All that belongs to the Father and all that belongs to Jesus belongs to me now!

247

September 4

For by grace are ye saved through faith; and that not of yourselves: it is the gift of God.

— EPHESIANS 2:8

How To Enjoy the Reality of God's Word

It took faith for you to become a child of God. By grace you were saved through faith. And the children of God own all that Christ has wrought for them. They own it all!

Now can you understand why Peter said, *". . . by whose stripes ye were healed."*? As far as God is concerned, healing is already yours. You can be certain that if you accept First Peter 2:24 and Isaiah 53:3-5, healing is bound to be manifested in your body.

It's been a while since we've looked at Isaiah 53. Let's look at that passage again.

ISAIAH 53:3-5
3   He is despised and rejected of men; a man of sorrows, and acquainted with grief: and we hid as it were our faces from him; he was despised, and we esteemed him not.
4   Surely he hath borne our griefs, and carried our sorrows: yet we did esteem him stricken, smitten of God, and afflicted.
5   But he was wounded for our transgressions, he was bruised for our iniquities: the chastisement of our peace was upon him; and WITH HIS STRIPES WE ARE HEALED.

You may read verse 5 and say, "Yes, but it doesn't seem real to me." How is the reality of salvation effected or manifested in your life? By acting on it. All you need to do is meditate and act on the Word.

Confession:

As I act on the Word — as I simply do what the Word says — it becomes a reality in my life. Healing becomes a reality in my life when I act on the words, "BY HIS stripes, we were healed."

Obedience: An Important Key in Receiving From God

It is deeply important that you learn this simple truth: It's not struggling, praying, or crying that brings results; it's acting on what God has spoken that gets the job done.

Because we've been religious-minded rather than Bible-minded, we want to *do* something to get God to move on our behalf. We think, *If I could pray enough, cry enough, get enough people praying, or do enough of something myself, things would change.* No, God has already done it. He has already planned the great plan of redemption and sent Jesus to consummate that plan. All that the Father has is ours.

Some people say, "Well, maybe I'm not doing enough." Religious thinking can trip you up. You can keep falling over it.

Let me say it again, because it is so important, and I don't want you to forget it. Even if you don't agree with it, think on it, because the time will come that you'll see it's so. Spiritual growth is similar to natural growth. So don't stop growing and just throw something away because you don't see and understand it right then. It will be a real gem that could bless you one day if you're open and you don't throw it away.

Confession:

It's not crying and praying that bring results in my life. It's not struggling that brings results in my life. It is acting on the Word that brings results.

And the prayer of faith shall save the sick, and the Lord shall raise him up; and if he have committed sins, they shall be forgiven him.

— JAMES 5:15

Faith and Believing

Let's look at two words: faith and believing. They have something to do with healing, because the Bible says, "The prayer of faith shall save the sick." The word "faith" is a noun. The word "believe" is a verb. It's an active verb. And that's what we've been talking about — believing God and acting on the Word

Just as you act on the word of a physician or the word of a lawyer or the word of a loved one, you are to act on the Word of God. If you have the word of your mother for something, you don't ask yourself the question, *Do I believe what she said?* Or, *Do I have faith in her word?* You just simply say, "That's what Mama said. And that's it."

If you are a child of God, it took faith to get in the family of God. But you're in the family now, and all that God has is yours. It's not a matter of having faith. It's a matter of finding out what is yours and then acting on it. Don't ask yourself the question, *Do I believe?* or *Do I have faith?* You just simply say, "That's what God said," and then act accordingly.

Didn't God say that by Jesus' stripes you were healed? Yes! And since God said it, then you must be healed. Act on what God has spoken.

Confession:

If I am a Christian, I don't have to try and get faith. I already have faith. I simply act on what God says in His Word. I believe that by Jesus' stripes, I am healed and made whole.

Blessed be the God and Father of our Lord Jesus Christ, who hath blessed us with all spiritual blessings in heavenly places in Christ.

— EPHESIANS 1:3

You Have Already Been Blessed

It is a remarkable fact that nowhere in the Epistles — the letters that are written to the Church — do Paul, James, John, Jude, or any of the other writers urge Christians to believe or have faith. Our urging Christians to believe is the result of the Word having lost its reality to them. That's what the problem is.

Since Paul never encouraged the Church to believe, what *did* he tell them? According to Ephesians 1:3, he tells us that God *has already blessed us* with all there is. There isn't any more. He has blessed us with every spiritual blessing. If you're blessed with every spiritual blessing, then you're blessed!

You don't need to ask for spiritual blessings. All you need to do is thank God that you have them. All you have to say is, "Father, I thank You for my healing. I thank You for my deliverance."

Confession:

I am blessed. I don't need to ask for spiritual blessings, because they already belong to me. I thank God for healing. I thank God for health.

251

September 8

For they that are after the flesh do mind the things of the flesh; but they that are after the Spirit the things of the Spirit.

— ROMANS 8:5

Become Spirit-Conscious

It helped my faith immeasurably when I was able to say, "I am a spirit being. I have a soul. And I live in a body" (*see* First Thessalonians 5:23). You see, my spirit is my heart. It is with the heart, with the spirit, that I believe. When I learned this, I stopped paying attention to my body. I stopped paying attention to my feelings. Instead of being body-conscious, I became spirit-conscious.

Now if you're more body-conscious, you're concerned about the body. And you'll see someone and say, "How are you feeling?" And the person will respond by saying, "I've got a sore throat [or some other ailment]."

People are more conscious of the body than they are of the spirit. The body dominates them. The body rules them. All they can ever talk about is the physical man. Well, the spirit man ought to be first. And if they'll stop being so conscious of their body and become spirit-conscious, their body will get in line and will start acting and feeling better.

If someone asks me how I'm feeling, I don't tell him or her how I feel. I don't pay any attention to my feelings. I say, "I'm well. Thank you." Then I begin to tell them what the Bible says. And I have learned by experience that the more I say what the Bible says, the better I feel. I believe in health and healing, so I talk health and healing. And my body responds to those words.

Confession:

I am a spirit. I have a soul. And I live in a body. Instead of being so concerned about my body — instead of allowing my body to rule me — I let my spirit man, my heart, rule me. As a result, my body lines up with my spirit.

But I keep under my body, and bring it into subjection: lest that by any means, when I have preached to others, I myself should be a castaway.

— 1 CORINTHIANS 9:27

September 9

Keep Your Body Under

Notice that this scripture says, "I keep under my body." If your body were the real you, Paul would have said, "I keep *myself* under. I bring *myself* into subjection." But he didn't say that. He said, "I keep my body under."

Well, what did he bring his body into subjection *to*? His spirit. He didn't let his body dominate him. Rather, his spirit dominated his body. He didn't let his body dictate to his spirit. His spirit dictated to his body.

This principle has to do with divine healing. Speak to your body and tell it to obey the Word. Say to your body, "The Word says that you're healed now, so quit acting up." That's keeping your body under. Don't let your body dominate you in any way, shape, form, or fashion. Don't let your body tell you what to do. You tell your body what it can and can't do. And if your spirit is dominating your body and the life of God is in your spirit, that life is going to be flowing into your body. That's divine healing.

Confession:

I keep my body under. I don't let it dominate me. I don't let it tell me what to do. Instead, I tell my body what to do. I dictate what it can and can't do.

I beseech you therefore, brethren, by the mercies of God, that ye present your bodies a living sacrifice, holy, acceptable unto God, which is your reasonable service.

— ROMANS 12:1

Present Your Body to God

Present your body to God. You can do it, because the inward man, or the spirit man, has the life and nature of God in him. In addition to that, you can be filled with the Holy Ghost and have the power of God in him.

Let's look at the next verse in Romans chapter 12. Verse 2 says, *"And be not conformed to this world: but be ye transformed by the renewing of your mind, that ye may prove what is that good, and acceptable, and perfect, will of God."*

It astounded me in 1949 when I really saw what these verses said. It dawned on me one day when I was reading these scriptures that Paul was writing to born-again, Spirit-filled believers. He told them that they needed to do something with their bodies and minds. You see, they were born again and filled with the Holy Ghost, but their bodies and minds had not yet been affected.

The New Birth is not a physical or a mental experience. It's a spiritual experience. Jesus said, *"That which is born of the flesh is flesh; and that which is born of the Spirit is spirit"* (John 3:6). And being filled with the Holy Ghost is not a physical or mental experience. It's a spiritual experience. And after that experience, *we* must then do something with our mind and body. We must present our body to God and renew our mind with His Word.

Confession:

I present my body to God as a living sacrifice. And I renew my mind with the Word of God. I do something with my body and my mind. I bring them into subjection to my spirit.

Therefore if any man be in Christ, he is a new creature: old things are passed away; behold, all things are become new.

— 2 CORINTHIANS 5:17

September 11

Transfigured Bodies and Transformed Minds

God does something with your spirit. You do something with your body and mind. God is not going to do anything with your body; He *can't*. God is not going to do anything with your mind; He *can't*. *You* have to do it. Now He will *help* you *do* something with your body and mind, but He won't just do it on His own.

God does something with your spirit. What does He do? He recreates it. He makes it a new creature. Old things pass away and all things become new.

But you are to do something with your body and your mind. Remember, Romans 12:1 says, *"I beseech you therefore, brethren, by the mercies of God, that YE present your bodies a living sacrifice, holy, acceptable unto God, which is your reasonable service."* You present *your* body as a living sacrifice, wholly acceptable to God. And then, *you* renew *your* mind (Rom. 12:2). You get your mind renewed with the Word of God.

God wants transfigured bodies and transformed minds. Many Christians let their bodies dominate them. That's the reason they are sick. Disease and sickness can come in when you aren't doing what you are supposed to do. Many Christians don't take the time to renew their minds with the Word of God. They are still thinking like the world thinks. You see, your mind is trained to think negatively. From the time you were a child, your mind is trained that way. It takes effort on your part to retrain it by renewing it with the Word of God.

Confession:

God does something with my spirit. He recreates it. But I am supposed to do something with my body and my mind. I present my body to God. And I renew my mind with the Word of God.

255

For verily I say unto you, That whosoever shall say unto this mountain, Be thou removed, and be thou cast into the sea; and shall not doubt in his heart, but shall believe that those things which he saith shall come to pass; he shall have whatsoever he saith.

— MARK 11:23

Believe With the Inward Man

Notice that this scripture says, "shall not doubt *in his heart.*" It never said a word about doubting in his head. You see, faith will work in your heart with doubt in your head. You can have doubt in your head, because the devil has access to our physical senses. He is the god of this world, and he can bring doubt to you. If you see that things are not working out right — maybe your body doesn't feel well — your mind will begin to doubt that you're healed. What must you do? Hold yourself in the arena of faith by casting down negative thoughts and by believing with the inward man.

Proverbs 3:5 says, *"Trust in the Lord with all thine heart; and lean not unto thine own understanding."* Don't lean on what your head tells you. Faith will work in your heart with doubt in your head.

I know from my own personal experience that my head fought me all the way concerning some of the greatest things that have ever happened to me in life. My head said, "It won't work. It's not so. You don't have it." But I refused to entertain those thoughts. I refused to listen to my head. On the inside of me, I held steady. All kinds of thoughts were flying through my head — faster than machine gun bullets can fly! Thoughts went through my head, such as, "You've messed up this time. You've made a fool of yourself. That's not going to work."

Yes, I had doubt in my head, but I didn't lean to my own understanding. I trusted the Lord with all my heart, and He brought it to pass. Now if I had given in to those thoughts and listened to my head, I would have been defeated.

Confession:

I can have doubt in my head, but still have faith in my heart. I follow my heart. I don't lean unto my own understanding. I trust the Lord with all my heart to bring His Word to pass in my life.

For we walk by faith, not by sight.

— 2 CORINTHIANS 5:7

Listen to Your Spirit

Sight is one of the five physical senses. We could say, "We walk by faith, not by our physical senses."

I'm not preaching something to you that I don't do myself. I mean, I've been in some alarming situations. I had a severe heart condition and an incurable blood disease as a boy. The doctor told me that I was going to die. He said, "Your white corpuscles eat up the red corpuscles faster than you can build them up or medically do anything about them. If you didn't have the heart condition, if you didn't have the paralysis, this incurable blood disease would prove to be fatal to you."

Doctors said that to me when I was a teenager. Well, I learned a lesson as I lay on that bed. And years later after I was healed, when death came and fastened itself upon my body again, I started laughing. Why? I had learned to listen to my spirit. I had learned to let my inward man dominate me. I just started laughing out loud. Right in the face of death, I laughed. I knew death was upon me, but I started laughing in the face of death. And the Holy Spirit, who is in my spirit, rose up in me. I could feel Him rise up in me. He just drove death out of me. And my body began to respond.

Confession:

I walk by faith and not by sight. I listen to my spirit. In the face of seemingly insurmountable obstacles, I laugh. I know that my God is greater than any circumstance!

September 14

While we look not at the things which are seen, but at the things which are not seen: for the things which are seen are temporal; but the things which are not seen are eternal.

— 2 CORINTHIANS 4:18

Look at What Is Unseen

How can you look at something unseen? You're certainly not looking at it with your physical eyes. No, you're looking at it with your spiritual eyes, or the eyes of your spirit. You're looking at it through the eyes of faith. A person who does not look at what is seen is not motivated by what is seen. Rather, he or she is motivated by the unseen.

People who are sick and are prayed for again and again do not get healed because they are motivated by their sight or by their feelings. The same people, if they feel well, say they're well. And if they feel sick, they say they're sick. They're motivated entirely by their feelings. I pay no attention to my feelings whatsoever. I couldn't care less about them. I'm moved only by what I believe.

I adopted a motto from Smith Wigglesworth many years ago: "I'm not moved by what I see. I'm not moved by what I feel. I'm moved only by what I believe." That has helped me through many a hard place. I mean, I have looked around me in times past when everything seemed to indicate defeat. But I just kept looking the situation right in the face, saying, "I'm not moved by what I see." I stood my ground calmly and deliberately, saying, "I'm not moved by what I see. I'm not moved by what I feel. I am moved only by what I believe." That's faith. It has brought me through many a hard place, and it will do the same for you.

Confession:

I am not moved by what I see. I am not moved by what I feel. I am moved only by what I believe. And I believe that God is working everything out for good, according to His Word.

Look to the Word of God

I was holding a meeting in Oklahoma, and several churches were cooperating. The associate pastor of the church where we were holding the meeting said to me one day, "Brother Hagin, why doesn't Sister _____ receive her healing?"

"Well," I said, "I don't know. I don't even know who Sister _____ is." He went on to explain to me that Sister _____ was a pastor from one of the churches that was cooperating with this meeting. When he described her, I remembered seeing her.

He said, "She's been in every healing line and hasn't received her healing. So some of the folks from our church who need healing have said, 'If Sister _____ can't get healed, there is no use in us getting in the healing line.'

"I've known her all my life. She used to be Presbyterian before she was baptized with the Holy Ghost. One time, she was voted the most outstanding Christian among the Presbyterians in her part of the state. After being filled with the Holy Ghost, she built a church and pastored it very successfully. She is such a holy person, a separated person, and an outstanding minister of the Gospel. People are concluding that if she's in the healing line every night and can't get healed, they're not going to get healed either."

Well, that was wrong thinking. And that kind of thinking will defeat you.

Confession:

I think in line with God's Word. I look to God's Word as the authority in my life. I don't look at other people, or the experiences of other people, to determine what is true. I look to the Word of God.

Then said Jesus unto him, Except ye see signs and wonders, ye will not believe.

— JOHN 4:48

Don't Let Your Physical Senses Dictate What You Believe

That night I went to the service, and after I had preached, people got in the prayer line to be healed and to be filled with the Holy Ghost. I began to lay hands on them, and when I came to this woman pastor, I was very conscious of her, because it hadn't been more than three hours or so since the associate pastor and I had been talking about her case.

I spent a little extra time with her and put up my spiritual antenna. I checked to see if the Lord would say anything to me. I asked her what she came for, and she told me she came for healing. Then she described some of the things that were wrong with her. I laid hands on her and prayed. She said, "No, no, I didn't get it. I don't have it."

I said, "I'll pray for you again." So I laid hands on her and prayed again.

She began to press around on her body and said, "No, it's still sore right there. I didn't get it."

I said, "I'll pray for you again." I thought three times ought to be enough for anybody. I knew she wasn't going to get anything, but on the other hand, I didn't want to slight her.

So I prayed for her the third time. By the time I said, "Amen," she was already feeling around on her body. Then she said, "It's still sore right here. No, I didn't get it." I passed her, and the next person stepped up in place.

Confession:

Instead of listening to my body — the physical symptoms of my body — I listen to my spirit man, my heart. I live and walk by faith, not by sight.

Therefore I say unto you, What things soever ye desire, when ye pray, believe that ye receive them, and ye shall have them.

— MARK 11:24

September 17

You Have To Believe Before You Receive

I remember saying to the Lord in my spirit, "Lord, this woman is the pastor of a church, and she's standing in the way of some people here that need to be healed. Can I help her?" Sometimes God will speak to you in an inward voice. But sometimes the revelation of the word of knowledge comes to you as a picture on the inside. That's what happened in this case. On the inside of me, I saw the whole thing. I knew she wouldn't be helped, but the Lord showed me exactly what to do to help the crowd.

I said to the woman, "Come back up here."

She retraced her steps up the aisle and stood in front of me again. I said to her, "When are you going to start believing that you are healed?"

She said, "When I get healed."

"Well," I said, "why in the world would you want to believe it then? You would *know* it then!"

She said, "Say that again." So I said it again. I never will forget it. The dear woman looked up at me, batted her eyes like a toad frog in a west Texas hail storm, and said, "Now listen, I'm not going to believe that I have something that my physical senses don't tell me I have." Well, what was her faith based on? Her physical senses! She was not believing with her heart.

I said, "Well, sister, you go sit down and do without it, because you'll never get it." She went and sat down, and did without it.

Now, the other people who were sitting there got what I was saying. So they came and received healing. A man from her church who was in the most desperate condition (he couldn't walk by himself) was instantly healed. And not only that — but was also deaf and was instantly healed of the deafness.

Confession:

I believe that I receive my healing before I see the manifestation of it, because Mark 11:24 says to believe I receive WHEN I PRAY. I believe I receive healing now!

> For with the heart man believeth unto righteousness.
> . . . For the scripture saith, Whosoever believeth on
> him shall not be ashamed.
>
> — ROMANS 10:10,11

Heart Faith Versus Head Faith

Five years later, I was preaching in that same area, and the man who was healed of deafness and lameness was still well. He walked perfectly without a cane and didn't need any hearing aids. He was seventy-seven years old. But this woman pastor was still in every healing line I had, trying to get healed.

Five more years went by and I visited the same area. The man, now eighty-two years old, was still healed from all the serious problems he'd had. He was still well and strong. And the woman pastor was still in every healing line I had.

She finally said, "I'm resigning my church. My health has gotten so bad that I can't carry on."

My heart went out to her, but I couldn't help her because she refused to believe that she had something that her physical senses told her she didn't have. That's not Bible faith. The Bible says, *"For with the HEART man believeth . . ."* (Rom. 10:10).

Proverbs 3:5 says, *"Trust in the Lord with all thine heart; and lean not unto thine own understanding."* This woman pastor was not trusting in the Lord with all her heart. Instead, she was trying to trust the Lord with all of her senses. She was leaning unto her own understanding.

Many people practice Proverbs 3:5, but they practice it in reverse. They trust in their understanding and lean not to their heart. We are told to trust in the Lord with all our heart and lean not unto our own understanding. What does it mean to believe with the heart? To believe with the heart is to believe independently of human reasoning or sense knowledge.

Confession:

I believe with my heart. I listen to my heart. I don't listen to my physical senses. I believe that I am healed no matter what my physical senses tell me.

*But sanctify the Lord God in your hearts: and be
ready always to give an answer to every man that
asketh you a reason of the hope that is in you with
meekness and fear.*

— 1 PETER 3:15

The Lordship of Jesus

Our spirit responds when we yield to the lordship of Jesus. The key to
biblical faith is the recognition in our own heart of the lordship of Jesus.
Sanctify the Lord God in your heart. The word "sanctify" means *to separate*
or *to set apart.*

The Amplified Bible says, "But in your hearts set Christ apart as holy
[and acknowledge Him] as Lord. Always be ready to give a logical defense
to anyone who asks you to account for the hope that is in you, but do it
courteously and respectfully."

We set Christ apart in our heart when we crown Jesus as the Lord of
our life. We crown His Word as the Lord of our lives. This gives the Word
its proper place. When we give the Word its place, faith becomes perfectly
natural.

Confession:

*I set Christ apart as holy in my heart. I acknowledge Him as my Lord and
Savior. I crown God's Word as the Lord of my life. And faith comes as a
natural result.*

September 20

In all thy ways acknowledge him, and he shall direct thy paths. Be not wise in thine own eyes: fear the Lord, and depart from evil.

— PROVERBS 3:6,7

The Word of God Is Supreme

The New Testament counterpart to this scripture is Second Corinthians 10:4 and 5.

2 CORINTHIANS 10:4,5
4   For the weapons of our warfare are not carnal, but mighty through God to the pulling down of [Satan's] strong holds;
5   Casting down imaginations, and every high thing that exalteth itself against the knowledge of God, and bringing into captivity every thought to the obedience of Christ.

Verse 4 says "weapons," *plural.* What are some of these weapons? Verse 5 lists one of them as casting down imaginations or reasonings. We are told to cast down imaginations or reasonings that exalt themselves against the knowledge of God.

If you want to walk by faith, the Word of God must be superior to natural human knowledge, whether that knowledge is yours, mine, or someone else's. Remember, Proverbs 3:7 says, *"Be not wise in thine own eyes. . . ."* One translation says, "Be not wise with thine own conceit." This is talking about your own natural human thinking or reasoning.

You see, if the Word is to work for you, it must be to you as superior to all human reasonings, because human knowledge — sense knowledge — is always limited. The mind learns through the physical senses; it's trained that way. Therefore, no one has perfect human knowledge. But the Word of God is perfect. If you're going to walk by faith, you're going to have to settle on the integrity of the Word of God.

Confession:

I cast down everything that exalts itself against the knowledge of God. Instead of following my own natural human reasonings, I follow the Word of God. And I continue to walk on in faith.

264

Believing Is Resting

The Word of God is perfect, and it can meet every crisis of our lives. It holds the answer to every problem or need of our lives. If we trust that Word with all of our hearts, a quietness, or a rest, comes into our spirits.

Hebrews 4:3 says, *"For we which have believed do enter into rest. . . ."* Believing is knowing that God's Word is true and can be depended upon. We know that the Word of God is true. Philippians 4:19 says, *"But my God shall supply all your need according to his riches in glory by Christ Jesus."* So we know in our spirits that every need will be supplied. We don't have to worry or have anxiety. If we are worrying or anxious, then we're not believing.

Smith Wigglesworth said, "If what some people claim to be believing doesn't happen overnight, they're ready to give up on it. That proves that they never did believe God to begin with. If you're really believing God, you'll trust Him until the end. And sometimes God will permit you to be tempted, or tested, right up to the hilt."

Confession:

The Word of God meets every need and every crisis of my life. And as I trust the Word, there is a rest on the inside of me, in my spirit man. I know that according to the Word of God, I'm healed. So I rest in that fact.

Ye are of God, little children, and have overcome them: because greater is he that is in you, than he that is in the world.

— 1 JOHN 4:4

The Greater One Within

We know that spiritual things are superior to physical things. God, a Spirit, created physical things. We know that spiritual forces are stronger than physical forces. And we know that greater is He that is in us, than he that is in the world. The Greater One within us is Master of disease and weakness. And we trust in Him with all of our hearts. He rises up in us and gives illumination which we can get from no other source. We know that we cannot be conquered!

So what exactly is the Greater One doing in you? Is He in you as extra baggage for you to carry through life? No, there's a divine Personality in you. And He is greater than the personality that's in the world — Satan, the god of this world.

The Greater One in you is greater than sickness and disease, and He is greater than the devil and demons. He is greater than any force or power that can come against you. He is greater than any test or temptation you face. And He will put you over. He will make you a success.

Confession:

The Greater One in me will put me over in life. He is greater than sickness and disease. And He always causes me to triumph in Christ Jesus.

September 23

Attend to God's Word

God tells us to attend to His Word. Let me give you an illustration. Let's say I meet someone on the street who says, "Brother Hagin, I want to talk to you." And I respond, "Well, I can't talk right now. I've got some business to attend to." What does that mean? It means I have to put that other business first.

God said to listen to His sayings. Some people are listening to what others are saying instead of to what God is saying. Donald Gee, a pioneer of the Pentecostal movement, said that every man in his family died before the age of forty. Well, when he got up around that age, fear came on him. Some of the symptoms his relatives experienced started showing up. And the devil said, "The same thing is happening to you. You're going to die. You'll not live past forty. It's incurable. The doctors can't cure it."

As he was driving down the road one day, he dealt with that fear and threw it out of the car. He said, "I'll not be afraid, because the Bible said, 'Fear thou not'" (Isa. 41:10). Then he said, "God is with me. God is in me. The Greater One is in me."

Did he die at forty? No, he was nearly ninety when he went home to be with the Lord. He was the first male in his family to live past the age of forty. Why? He began to attend to God's words. He began to incline his ears unto what God said.

Confession:

I attend to God's sayings. I put them first place in my life. I listen to what God says, rather than the words of people. I believe that God is WITH me. I believe that God is IN me. He puts me over in life.

He shall not be afraid of evil tidings: his heart is
fixed, trusting in the Lord.

— PSALM 112:7

Fear Thou Not

After one of my morning services, a woman came up to me crying and
said, "Brother Hagin, I'm afraid. There is a hereditary condition that is
passed down in my family. It is going to happen to me."

I said, "Open your Bible to Isaiah 41:10. God said, *'Fear thou not; for I
am with thee. . . .'* God is with you, sister!" I asked her if she was born again.
And she said that she was. I asked her if she was filled with the Spirit and she
said that she was. I said, "Then greater is He that is in you than he that is in
the world" (1 John 4:4).

I said to her, "Can you really believe that God is with you and be afraid?
No, you're afraid when you think that He is not with you."

Then she said, "You don't understand how weak and helpless I am."

I read her the rest of Isaiah 41:10, *". . . be not dismayed; for I am thy
God: I will strengthen thee; yea, I will help thee; yea, I will uphold thee with
the right hand of my righteousness."* The God of the universe is with us! He
who spoke the worlds into existence is with us! We don't have to be weak,
or helpless, or afraid!

Confession:

*I know that God is with me. He is in me. So I don't have to be afraid. God
will strengthen me. He will help me. He will uphold me with the right hand
of His righteousness.*

September 25

— PSALM 118:17

'He Will Live and Not Die'

Several years ago, a woman came to one of my crusades. When she saw what the Bible said about healing, she started shouting. I didn't pray for her. She just jumped up and started shouting. I stepped back and let her holler and shout. I noticed that others seemed to be quite blessed by it. The pastor said to me, "Brother Hagin, that woman and her husband are some of the wealthiest people in this area. They're worth billions! Now they're not Pentecostal; they belong to the First Presbyterian Church."

After awhile, the woman ran down to the front, and we all praised God with her. When I dismissed the service, she came and thanked me. I said, "There's no use in thanking me. Thank the Lord."

"Yes," she said, "but you brought the truth to me. My son is in the UCLA hospital. He's only twenty-one years old. He'll be twenty-two in a few days. The doctors say he'll never live to see his twenty-second birthday. He has an incurable blood disease. They've changed the entire blood in his system several different times. He's under an oxygen tent and he's hooked up to machines to keep him alive.

"But, bless God," she said, "God is on my side. He is with me. And I'm going over to that hospital right now. I want you to know that my son will live and not die."

I said, "That's right. He won't die." And she marched right over to that hospital.

Confession:

God is on my side. He is with me. I will live and not die. I will declare the works of the Lord.

September 26

Fear thou not; for I am with thee: be not dismayed; for I am thy God: I will strengthen thee; yea, I will help thee; yea, I will uphold thee with the right hand of my righteousness.

— ISAIAH 41:10

Get Thrilled About the Truth

On the last Sunday night of the meeting, eleven days after I last saw this Presbyterian woman, I was sitting on the platform with the pastor. I saw her walk in with a young man by her side. The pastor whispered to me, "That's her son."

As the pastor was making an announcement, this woman jumped up and said, "I can't wait! I've got to testify!" She ran down the aisle and said to me, "This is my son, Brother Hagin. Remember, I was telling you about him just eleven days ago? We've taken him in our private jet to one healing meeting after another. But when you read and quoted Isaiah 41:10 several days ago, I began to realize my authority. I began to realize that God is with me and there's no use in me being afraid. After the service, I rushed to the hospital and laid hands on my son. The doctors said, 'We don't understand it. The disease has gone into remission.'"

Now isn't it strange that an incurable blood disease suddenly went into remission? No, it's perfectly normal if you believe the Bible. This woman said, "The doctors wanted to keep my son in the hospital for a little while. So I said it would be all right. They ran all kinds of tests, and every test came back negative. So they turned him loose." This boy looked the very picture of health.

This woman said, "I'm so glad for the truth."

You know, that's when the truth works for you — when you get thrilled about it!

Confession:

I love the Word. I love the truth. I get thrilled about the truth. I get excited about the truth. And I see it working for me.

270

For with the heart man believeth unto righteousness;
and with the mouth confession is made unto salvation.
— ROMANS 10:10

September 27

The Power of a Right Confession

Notice this scripture says that we are not only to believe with our heart, but we are also to confess with our mouth. It says that confession brings about salvation.

Actually, all that we receive from God is received that way — through faith. It's always with the heart that we believe and with the mouth that we confess. With the heart we believe for healing, and with the mouth confession is made unto healing. Everything we receive from God comes this way.

Now the same thought appears in another text that we've looked at: *"For verily I say unto you, That whosoever shall say unto this mountain, Be thou removed, and be thou cast into the sea; and shall not doubt in his heart, but shall believe that those things which he saith shall come to pass; he shall have whatsoever he saith"* (Mark 11:23). Both Romans 10:10 and Mark 11:23 talk about believing in your heart and saying with your mouth.

Then Romans 10:8 says, *"But what saith it? The word is nigh thee, even in thy mouth, and in thy heart: that is, the word of faith, which we preach."* You see, the word of faith must be in your mouth and in your heart for it to work for you. That's the thing that defeats many people. They believe God's Word in their heart, but their mouth is always talking something else.

Set a watch on your mouth. See to it that it only speaks what is in line with the Word of God. Stop saying what doesn't line up with God's Word. If you keep saying anything long enough, those words will eventually register on your heart. And when they do, they'll control your life.

Confession:

I set a watch on my mouth. I only speak what I believe in my heart that lines up with God's Word. I believe that I am healed. I believe that I am well. I believe it in my heart and I speak it out of my mouth.

Death and life are in the power of the tongue: and they that love it shall eat the fruit thereof.

— PROVERBS 18:21

The Importance of Your Words

In 1951, I was holding a meeting in a town in Texas. We had day and night teaching services. Between the services, I would walk up and down the aisles of the church, praying and reading my Bible.

One day, I was reading the Book of Mark as I was on my knees near the altar. I got tired, so I sat down on the floor and finished reading the Book of Mark. Now I wasn't even thinking about Mark 11:23. I was thinking about the sixteenth chapter of Mark, where Jesus said, "Go into all the world, and preach the Gospel to every creature." Then I got tired of sitting, so I just lay down on my back. As I was lying there on my back with my hands under my head, staring at the ceiling, I came to the place my mind got quiet. Then I heard these words on the inside of me: "Did you notice in Mark 11:23 that the word 'say' in some form is in that verse three times, and the word 'believe' is in there only once?"

I answered out loud, "No! No! I never did notice that." And I had read that verse thousands of times. I turned the pages in my Bible back to the eleventh chapter and read that verse again. I counted three times that some form of the word 'say' was in there.

Then I heard these words on the inside of me, "My people are not missing it primarily in their *believing* because they have been taught to believe and to have faith. My people are missing it in what they *say*." Many times, that's what happens when it comes to healing.

Confession:

I know that death and life are in the power of my tongue. I line my words up with what God says about me. I believe that I am healed, so I constantly speak words of health and healing out of my mouth.

That if thou shalt confess with thy mouth the Lord Jesus, and shalt believe in thine heart that God hath raised him from the dead, thou shalt be saved.

— ROMANS 10:9

What Is Confession?

What is confession? First, it's *affirming something that we believe.* Second, it's *testifying to something that we know.* And third, it's *witnessing for a truth that we've embraced.*

What are we to confess? Well, our confession should center around five things: (1) What God in Christ has wrought for us in His great plan of redemption; (2) what God through the Word and the Holy Spirit has wrought in us in the New Birth and the baptism in the Holy Ghost; (3) what we are to God the Father in Christ Jesus; (4) what Jesus is doing for us now at the right hand of the Father in His present-day ministry; and (5) what the Word of God will do through our lips.

Now you cannot confess or witness about things you do not know about. It's what you personally know about the Lord Jesus Christ and what you are in Him that counts.

If you were called to be a witness in court, it's not what you have heard about that counts. It's what you've seen and what you know for yourself that counts. Hearsay isn't accepted. And your opinion isn't accepted. They want to know what you know!

Confession:

I read and study the Word to find out what belongs to me in Christ — what I have as a result of Jesus' death, burial, and resurrection. Then I walk in the light of that knowledge. I confess what belongs to me.

September 30

Therefore if any man be in Christ, he is a new creature: old things are passed away; behold, all things are become new.

— 2 CORINTHIANS 5:17

You Have Rights and Privileges

So many people may know the Lord Jesus as their personal Savior and yet not know a thing in the world about their rights and privileges in Him. They don't know who they are in Christ, because you'll still hear them saying, "I'm so weak and unworthy." No, they're not!

If your spirit has been born again, you've become a new man in Christ Jesus (2 Cor. 5:17). And God doesn't make any unworthy creatures. You're a new creature in Christ Jesus. You have the life and nature of God in you. Greater is He that is in you than he that is in the world (1 John 4:4). You are the righteousness of God in Christ (2 Cor. 5:21).

You have been redeemed from the hand of the enemy. Colossians 1:13 says, *"Who hath delivered us from the power of darkness, and hath translated us into the kingdom of his dear Son."* You're not in the kingdom of darkness. You're in the Kingdom of light. Satan is not your lord or master. Jesus is your Lord and Master.

Therefore, sin and sickness and disease can no longer lord it over you, because they are not your lord. Jesus is your Lord. And He doesn't have sickness and disease. He has health and healing.

Confession:

I am a new creature in Christ Jesus. I have the life and nature of God in me. I have been redeemed from the hand of the enemy. I'm no longer in the kingdom of darkness. I'm in the Kingdom of light. Jesus is Lord of my life — and He has health and healing, not sickness and disease.

*Behold, I give unto you power to tread on serpents
and scorpions, and over all the power of the enemy:
and nothing shall by any means hurt you.*

— LUKE 10:19

'No Trespassing!'

Satan and sickness and disease are not your masters. I found that out
many years ago. In 1937, I read an excerpt in *Reader's Digest* that got me
thinking along this line. It stated that in front of one of the government office
buildings in Washington, D.C., there was a little patch of grass about fourteen feet by twenty-eight feet. Instead of people walking on the sidewalk,
they would cut right across that little patch of green grass. They had worn
out that grass, so the caretaker put stakes and a string up. It wasn't very
high. And people just stepped over the string and kept walking on the grass.

To fix this problem, the caretaker painted a crude sign and put it up
right in the middle of the grass. The sign said, "Gentlemen *will* not and
others *must* not trespass on this property." And that stopped it.

When I read this, I decided to put a sign up on my body, so to speak,
in my spirit. Now you can't see it, but the devil can. It's written with spirit
language and spirit ink, and it reads, "Gentlemen *will* not and others *must*
not trespass on this property." Then in parentheses it says, "Devil, this
means you!" That sign has been on my body since 1937.

The devil has no right to trespass on your body. He has no right to put
sickness and disease on you. Sickness and disease are of the devil; they're not
of God. They do not come from Heaven. There isn't any sickness or disease
up there. God is not the author of sickness and disease, so you can boldly tell
the devil, "No trespassing!"

Confession:

*The devil shall not trespass on my property. He has no right to trespass on
my body. He has no right to put sickness and disease on me. I resist him in
Jesus' Name.*

October 2

This book of the law shall not depart out of thy mouth; but thou shalt meditate therein day and night, that thou mayest observe to do according to all that is written therein: for then thou shalt make thy way prosperous, and then thou shalt have good success.

— JOSHUA 1:8

Meditating and Speaking Bring the Blessings

The following is a word from the Lord that I received many years ago, but its truth is eternal; it applies to all of us everywhere, even today.

Take heed; listen very carefully.

For right here is where man primarily fails.

All failure in the Christian life can be found in what is being said at this very moment.

Listen carefully; listen with an open mind.

Receive it with a receptive heart.

Meditate upon it, until the truth of it you'll find.

And then, speaking [it] forth out of your heart will cause all that's Mine to become thine.

For many of My own children who are very sincere and honest, and even seeking to find, do not find, because they do not meditate in My Word and listen attentively to that which is said, nor [do they] continue to read My Word.

But meditating upon My Word — receiving it into your spirit and confessing, "It's mine!" — shall surely bring the blessings every single time.

Confession:

I take heed to the Word of God. I attend to the Word of God. I receive it with an open mind and an open heart. I meditate on the Word and speak forth out of my heart, "It's mine!"

Receive What God Has for You

I received a letter some time ago that I'd like to share with you because it will inspire you and be a blessing to you.

Dear Brother Hagin,

My husband received healing through your ministry. My husband and I had begged God for years to no avail. But when we realized that healing was something we already had, and we decided to stand on the Word, it was only a matter of a few months until the manifestation of my husband's healing began to appear. We not only stood on the Word by saying it to ourselves, we also said it to others.

My husband first became ill in 1970 at the age of forty. The diagnosis was a non-crippling, but extremely painful form of arthritis. During the last five years, my husband had to stay in bed. The only time he got up was to go to the bathroom, see the doctor, or go to the hospital when the pain got so bad that he had to have some relief. For the past two or three years, an additional nerve problem in his legs and feet caused so much pain that sleep was next to impossible. I would be awakened by his sobbing from the relentless pain that constantly wracked his body.

A couple of years ago, we turned to Jesus and got born again, but there was still no change in my husband's body. I began reading your books, but I didn't understand how to *activate* God's power by faith and receive. Finally, about three months ago, as I was studying the *Spring Faith Food* book, the revelation hit me. We began to confess our victory through Jesus. Then we joined a Spirit-filled church in our area. The elders came and anointed my husband with oil and prayed. Even though there was no manifestation of healing, we continued our faith confessions.

Two weeks ago, the pain suddenly left. A few days later, his feet began to lose their numbness. And a week ago, he trimmed a tree in our backyard. Today he took our car to be serviced. I can't remember the last time he drove a car! He has no pain! Thank God! And thank you for teaching us how to receive what God has for us.

Confession:

I receive what God has for me by faith. By believing in my heart and speaking with my mouth, I receive salvation, healing, and all the blessings of God.

October 4

Confession Precedes Actual Possession

Notice that even after the man with arthritis was anointed with oil and prayed for by the elders, there was still no manifestation. But they continued to confess that he was healed. You see, confession *precedes* possession. Or we could say, "Possession *follows* confession." Another way to put it is, "Faith's confessions create realities."

The man's pain was gone. He was out of bed trimming a tree in his backyard. Then he drove his car. The reality of his healing was there. Well, that's what most people want; that's what they're seeking. They want the reality of their healing. How do they get it? By confessing that they have it before they ever see it.

I encourage you to read through the New Testament, underlining the expressions "in Him," "in Christ," and "in whom." These scriptures tell you what belongs to you in Christ. You may have read some of these scriptures before and said, "I know it says that, but it doesn't seem real in my life. I'm going to pray that it will become real to me." No, it won't become real by praying! How does it become real? By confessing it.

You can read in the Bible about who you are and what you have as a Christian. But the only way it will ever become real to you is by your confession. Confession is the key that unlocks faith.

Confession:

I am a new creature in Christ Jesus. I am the righteousness of God in Christ. Greater is He that is in me than he that is in the world. I confess these things from my heart. And as a result, I have what the Bible says I can have.

For my thoughts are not your thoughts, neither are
your ways my ways, saith the Lord.
For as the heavens are higher than the earth, so are
my ways higher than your ways, and my thoughts
than your thoughts.

October 5

— ISAIAH 55:8,9

God's Way of Thinking

You can read what the Bible says, and from the natural standpoint, it doesn't sound reasonable sometimes. But these verses in Isaiah have helped me greatly. Isaiah is contrasting our thoughts (man's thoughts) with God's thoughts. He says that God's thoughts, or God's way of thinking, is higher than man's way of thinking.

The Bible contains God's thoughts. If you want to know God's thinking on any subject, see what the Bible says on that subject. Now if your mind has not been renewed with the Word of God, it's difficult for you to think in line with God's way of thinking. (You get your mind renewed with the Word of God by meditating on it.) And even if your mind has been renewed, you still may not understand with your natural mind everything the Bible says. But if you'll act on the Word from your spirit, or your heart, it will work for you.

Keeping these verses in Isaiah in mind, let's read Mark 11:23 again: *"For verily I say unto you, That whosoever shall say unto this mountain, Be thou removed, and be thou cast into the sea; and shall not doubt in his heart, but shall believe that those things which he saith shall come to pass; he shall have whatsoever he saith."* To the natural mind, this verse doesn't sound reasonable. It's a different kind of thinking — it's *God's* way of thinking!

Good Christians who are dedicated and consecrated to God have said to me, "I'm not going to believe I have something I can't see. If I say I have something and I don't have it in reality, I'm lying." They missed the whole thing! God's thoughts are not our thoughts.

Confession:

God's thoughts and ways are higher than my thoughts and ways. I renew my mind with the Word of God so that I can think God's thoughts and know His ways.

279

October 6

For we walk by faith, not by sight.

— 2 CORINTHIANS 5:7

Go Ahead – Brag About Who You Are *in Christ*!

Years ago, a dear preacher friend of mine said to me, "I don't believe like you believe." At the time he said that, I'd been well for the past forty-five years, and he'd been sickly off and on for forty-five years. Well, I liked my way of believing a whole lot better than his way.

This preacher would say, "If God ever heals me, I'll start believing in healing." He meant that if all his symptoms disappeared, he would believe. I started believing I was healed while I was bedfast and still paralyzed. I couldn't walk or move a bit when I began believing I was healed.

Some people have said, "You're just bragging on yourself. You're stuck on yourself. You think you're something." No, I'm stuck on God's Word! I'm bragging on *Him*!

Anyone who knows Jesus — anyone who knows what God has done for him — has plenty to brag about. And he *ought* to brag about it! I'm bragging because I'm a new creature (*2 Cor.* 5:17). I didn't make myself a new creature; *God* made me one. I'm bragging about who I am in Christ. I didn't put myself in Christ; *He* did it. I'm bragging about who God said I am, not who *I* said I am.

Confession:

I walk by faith in God's Word, rather than what I can see with my physical eyes. I believe I am who God says I am and that I can do what God says I can do. I brag about who I am in Christ and what God has done for me.

280

According as his divine power hath given unto us all things that pertain unto life and godliness, through the knowledge of him that hath called us to glory and virtue.

— 2 PETER 1:3

Speak Out What the Word Declares Is Yours

The following is another word of instruction and exhortation that I received from the Lord:

Healing and health, life and peace,
Joy and rest, all belong to the saints of God.
Defeat and failure, shortcomings, sickness, disease, and all that's worse
Belong to Adam's race, because of the Fall.
But remember that He [Jesus] came to redeem us all.
So rejoice and be glad and let your mouth do its duty.
Speak forth that which the Word has said
And be ready to believe all that you have read.
Yea, speak out that which the Word declares is yours,
And your faith will create the reality of the same in your heart, and life, and body too.
So you'll have cause to rejoice and be glad while others are so sad.
Yea, you will be filled with joy and gladness and rejoicing and health and healing,
While others are filled with remorse and sadness, dominated by failure.
Because, you see, the light did shine, and they turned the light off.
But you opened your heart and said,
"Light shine! Shine in, light! Shine upon my spirit, and I'll rise and walk in the light of life.
For the Lord has redeemed me and I walk above all strife."

Confession:

God has given me all things that pertain to life and godliness. I speak out what belongs to me in Christ. I thank God for all of His many blessings!

October 8

. . . The word is nigh thee, even in thy mouth, and in thy heart: that is, the word of faith, which we preach.

— ROMANS 10:8

The Realm of Faith

The greatest thing that will ever happen to you is when you move into this realm of faith that I'm talking about. Your intellect, or your mind, will fight you. And your physical senses will fight you every step of the way. They will fight to keep you from moving into this realm. If the natural mind is not renewed with the Word, or if it is just partially renewed with the Word, it will try to hold you in the natural realm.

But there is a spiritual realm to enter into, where you think differently than you used to think. You talk differently than you used to talk. When you get right down to it, wrong thinking, wrong believing, and wrong confessing are the things that defeat us. Right thinking, right believing, and right confessing are the things that put us over.

Now if what you *say* is wrong, it's because your *believing* is wrong. If your *believing* is wrong, it's because your *thinking* is wrong. They all three go together. If your confession is right, it's because your *believing* is right. If your *believing* is right, it's because your *thinking* is right. And if your thinking is right, it's because you are thinking in line with God's Word. If your thinking is wrong, it's because you are thinking out of line with God's Word. Dare to think God's thoughts!

Confession:

I choose to think God's thoughts. I search the Word of God to find out what God says about me and my situation. Then I apply the Word to my life. I think on it, believe it, and speak it out of my mouth!

For with the heart man believeth unto righteousness;
and with the mouth confession is made unto salvation.

— ROMANS 10:10

A Wrong Confession

A wrong confession is a confession of defeat — and, really, a confession of Satan's supremacy. Talking about how the devil is hindering you, how he's keeping you sick, is a confession of defeat. When you talk about God, you are glorifying God. Well, in the same way, when you talk about the devil, you are glorifying the devil.

Most Christians spend more time glorifying the devil than they do God. They spend more time making a wrong confession. And that kind of confession saps the very life out of them. It destroys their faith.

Our confession should be in line with what God said. Remember, confession is *affirming something that we believe, testifying to something that we know,* and *witnessing for a truth that we have embraced.* Our confession should be a witness for a truth that we have embraced. It should affirm that we believe the Word. Then what we are confessing comes into being.

Most people want to wait and see if it ever comes into being before they will start confessing it. No, it doesn't work that way. You see, a wrong confession destroys your faith and holds you in bondage. But the confession of your lips that has grown out of faith in your heart will absolutely defeat the devil in every combat!

Confession:

I keep my confession in line with what God says in His Word. I glorify God with a right confession. I speak forth what has grown out of the faith in my heart. And I enforce the devil's defeat in every situation of life.

Set a watch, O Lord, before my mouth; keep the door of my lips.

— PSALM 141:3

Don't Give the Devil Permission

Here is an important scriptural principle that many dear Christians have never seen or realized yet: With your mouth, you're either going to give God dominion over you or you're going to give Satan dominion over you.

To be saved, you must confess the Lordship of Jesus. Romans 10:9 says, *"That if thou shalt CONFESS WITH THY MOUTH THE LORD JESUS, and shalt believe in thine heart that God hath raised him from the dead, thou shalt be saved."* You give Jesus dominion over you by confessing Him as your Lord. Then He begins to rule in your life.

However, when you confess Satan's ability to hinder you, to keep you from success, to hold you in bondage, or to keep you sick, you are giving Satan dominion over you. He is the god of this world, and he'll move right in, because you've permitted him to do so.

Many dear saints of God have opened the door to the devil ignorantly; they didn't even realize they were doing it. But it's still permission. Whether they're knowledgeable or ignorant of what they're doing, it's still permission. Those who always talk sickness find that sickness dominates them.

Confession:

I keep the door closed on the devil. I don't allow him into any part of my life. I keep a watch on the words of my mouth, only speaking those things that bring glory and honor to God.

Don't Talk Sickness

I remember one dear person who was certain that she had cancer. For ten years, every time I saw her, she was sure that she had cancer. I'd say to her, "Well, you don't." Every six months, she would go to the doctor for a check up. The doctor never found a trace of cancer. But she would say, "I'm just sure I've got it." Now she was a born-again, Spirit-filled Christian.

I said to her, "Don't talk sickness. You'll never hear me talking sickness, because I don't want sickness to dominate me and have a place in me." But she would go right back to talking sickness.

Then I just said outright, "Quit talking sickness! If you keep talking sickness, sickness will develop in your system. I don't ever talk sickness. I talk healing and health. I don't believe in sickness. I believe in healing and health. And, you see, what I confess I have. What I confess dominates me!"

Well, she wouldn't listen. She wouldn't talk in line with God's Word. Instead, she spoke sickness. And after ten years of telling me she had cancer, the doctor finally found cancer in her body. She talked herself into cancer. She talked herself into dying. I'm glad she went to Heaven, but she could have still been here.

Let me say it again: When you confess Satan's ability to hinder you, to keep you sick, to keep you from success or from any of the blessings of God, you're giving him dominion in your life.

Confession:

I don't talk sickness. I talk health and healing. I talk in line with God's Word. And I see the fruit of my words manifest in my own life.

October 12
    Fear thou not; for I am with thee: be not dismayed;
for I am thy God . . .

— ISAIAH 41:10

Don't Talk Fear

Don't confess fear. Some people might say, "But what if I'm afraid?" Well, you're not really afraid if you look at it the way God looks at it. Dare to think like God thinks. Second Timothy 1:7 says, *"For God hath not given us the spirit of fear; but of power, and of love, and of a sound mind."* God has not given you a spirit of fear. So begin to confess only what God has given you.

Confess, "I have a spirit of power that drives away fear. I have a spirit of love. I have a spirit of a sound mind." Fear will tell you, "You're losing your mind." And if you listen to it, you will become fearful, nervous, and distracted. The devil will tell you that you're losing your mind. But don't confess that. Start confessing, "I don't have a spirit of fear. God didn't give it to me, and I won't accept it. I have a spirit of power, love, and a sound mind."

Fear comes from the outside to take hold of you. It's not in you if you're a Christian. So don't open the door to the devil. Don't invite him in.

Your confession of something creates the reality of it. That's what I want you to get. If you're going to wait for something to become real before you start believing and confessing it, it will never happen. But when you confess it, then it begins to dominate you.

Now there will be battles, because the devil is the god of this world. He'll put every kind of obstacle he can in your way. But every time you win a victory, it gets easier and easier. And after awhile, you'll come to the place where every time the devil sticks his head up, you'll just start laughing, because you know the way of victory.

Confession:

I don't talk fear. God has not given me a spirit of fear. God has given me the spirit of power, love, and a sound mind. Therefore, I confess that I have a spirit of power, love, and a sound mind. And that's what I have! That's what becomes a reality in my life.

Jesus answered and said unto them, Verily I say unto you, If ye have faith, and doubt not, ye shall not only do this which is done to the fig tree, but also if ye shall say unto this mountain, Be thou removed, and be thou cast into the sea; it shall be done.

— MATTHEW 21:21

Don't Talk Doubt

Spiritual growth is similar to physical growth. You didn't grow up physically overnight. So don't get discouraged when you don't grow up spiritually overnight. Begin to practice the Word of God, and you will grow spiritually.

Don't confess your doubts. Doubt will hinder your spiritual growth. Many people think they are being honest when they confess their doubts. Now if you're saved, you're not full of doubt. There has to be some faith in your heart or you couldn't have been saved. The Bible says, *"For by grace are ye saved through faith; and that not of yourselves: it is the gift of God"* (Eph. 2:8).

Instead of talking doubt, why not just say, "I'm a believer and I do have faith"? If you're saved, you know you are. Confess who you are in Christ. Don't confess your doubts. Rev. F. F. Bosworth said, "Doubt your doubts, and believe your beliefs." The trouble with most Christians is that they are *believing* their doubts and *doubting* their beliefs. Doubting your doubts and believing your beliefs will put you over if you'll just practice it.

Confession:

I'm a believer and I do have faith. I doubt my doubts and believe my beliefs. And doing this will put me over in every area of life.

October 14

Doubt and Fear

The following is a psalm given to me by the Lord:

Doubt and fear: the two tormenting twins of the enemy,
Sent to torment you down here.
Doubt and fear will rob you of faith,
Health and healing, and all spirituality too.
Doubt and fear will dog your tracks as you walk down here.
But doubt and fear do not belong to the child of God.
For, you see, you're a child of the Father — a child of faith and love.
Faith and love come down from the Father above —
Faith and love to abide in your spirit and heart
For you to walk in love and to act by faith.
And so, you'll not, when the enemy shows his head, run away and hide,
But, rather, you in the Word of God shall abide
And will speak forth by faith in love.
And all of God's blessings shall be showered on you from above.

Confession:

I'm a believer. I don't doubt the Word of God. I BELIEVE the Word of God. I resist doubt and fear, for they come from the enemy. And I receive faith and love, because they come from the Father up above.

. . . for thou hast magnified thy word above all thy name.

— PSALM 138:2

What Does God's Word Say?

So much of the time, we accept the testimony of our physical senses instead of accepting the testimony of God's Word. What does God's Word say? Instead of stopping to ask ourselves that question, we let our physical senses dominate us.

Now you can ask that question on any subject. For instance, what does God's Word say about sickness? Does God's Word have anything to say about sickness? Certainly it does! Don't spend all your time talking about how sick you are and what your symptoms are and what the doctor said about it. If you keep talking like that, you'll die.

In the face of sickness, stop and ask yourself, "What does God's Word say about this disease?" Matthew 8:17 says, *"That it might be fulfilled which was spoken by Esaias the prophet, saying, Himself took our infirmities, and bare our sicknesses."* What are you going to do with that? Believe it and confess it! And if you really believe it in your heart and confess it with your mouth, the reality of it will be created in your life.

It doesn't happen overnight. You have to continually practice God's Word for it to work. You may have to confess some scriptures for a while, but if you continue and don't give up, you'll see the reality of it.

Confession:

What does God's Word say about my situation? I search and find out. Then I believe it and confess it. I continually practice God's Word. I continually give it first place in my life.

289

October 16

. . . and thou wilt cast all their sins into the depths of the sea.

— MICAH 7:19

Don't Let Your Past Mistakes Hinder You

Something that hinders many people's faith from working is their past mistakes, their failures, and their faults. Well, what does God's Word have to say about it? What does God's Word have to say about your mistakes? What does God's Word have to say about your failures? God's Word says, *"If we confess our sins, he is faithful and just to forgive us our sins, and to cleanse us from all unrighteousness"* (1 John 1:9).

Every time the devil brings a picture of your past mistakes, confess what God says instead of confessing how you feel about it. Confess that God has forgiven you and cleansed you. Say, "I'm forgetting it, because *He* has forgotten it." Even though the devil may bring a picture of it to your mind, don't entertain it, because God has forgiven you and has forgotten it. You can stand in the Presence of God as though you had never done anything wrong. As you confess God's Word, the reality of it will be developed in your life until you'll feel so clean and pure.

When the devil brings a picture of a past wrong you did, don't deny it. Just say, "Yes, I did that. I was wrong. I missed it. But First John 1:9 says that if I confess my sins, God is faithful and just to forgive me and cleanse me of all unrighteousness." God has forgiven you. Thank Him for it and your faith will start working again.

Confession:

God is not holding my past mistakes against me. He has forgiven me and forgotten it. I can stand in the Presence of God as though I had never done anything wrong.

So then faith cometh by hearing, and hearing by the word of God.

— ROMANS 10:17

Faith To Be Healed

Healing is in God's plan of redemption, so it belongs to all of us. And faith for obtaining healing comes the same way that faith for obtaining salvation comes — by hearing the Gospel (the Word of God) preached.

Acts chapter 14 tells us about the first missionary journey of Barnabas and Paul. It tells us where they went and what they did. Verse 7 says, *"And there they preached the gospel."*

Let's continue reading.

ACTS 14:8-10
8   And there sat a certain man at Lystra, impotent in his feet, being a cripple from his mother's womb, who never had walked:
9   The same heard Paul speak: who stedfastly beholding him, and perceiving that he had faith to be healed,
10   Said with a loud voice, Stand upright on thy feet. And he leaped and walked.

This man was definitely healed on his own faith. He was not healed because Paul was an apostle, or by any special manifestation of the Spirit. He was healed because he had faith. Where did he get the faith to be healed? Did he have faith to be healed because God just sort of flew over him like a bird and dropped faith down in his heart? No! He heard Paul speak.

There is a connection between hearing the Word preached or taught and having faith to be healed. He got faith to be healed from what he heard Paul speak. What did Paul speak? According to verse 7, he preached the Gospel or the Word of God.

Confession:

I receive faith to be healed by hearing the Gospel, the Word of God. And then I act on my faith!

With long life will I satisfy him, and shew him my salvation.

— PSALM 91:16

Set Your Goals High

In going from church to church preaching, I would try to get it over to people that it is the perfect plan of God that they live out their full length of time down here below without sickness or disease, and then fall asleep in Jesus. I've preached it for more than sixty-five years and I'm still preaching it. I haven't changed my message.

The pastor would usually say to me, "Brother Hagin, I know all this is in the Bible, but you have just set it too high. Nobody can attain to it. A person can't live without sickness."

I would respond, "Well, I am. I'd rather set my goals high and reach half of them, than to set them at nothing and get all of it." He agreed to that. That's our problem many times in life — both naturally and spiritually. We set our goals too low.

I don't know about you, but I want everything God has for me. I want the best. I don't want to get into Heaven by the skin of my teeth, so to speak.

I enjoy reading the following verse in Douglas Mallock's lesson "Is Healing for All?"

Death comes, and then, we blame our God and weakly say,
"Thy will be done."
But never underneath the sod has God imprisoned anyone.
God does not send disease, or crime, or carelessness, or fighting clans.
And when we die before our time, the fault is man's.
He is a God of light, not death.
He is one God that gives us birth.
He has not shortened by breath any on the earth.
And He would have us dwell within the world our full allotted years.
So blame not God, for our sin makes our tears.

Confession:

It is God's will that I live out my full length of time down here on the earth. It is God's plan that I live without sickness and disease and eventually just fall asleep in Jesus.

He brought them forth also with silver and gold: and there was not one feeble person among their tribes.

— PSALM 105:37

October 19

Is Healing for All?

To answer the question, "Is healing for all?" let's look in Exodus 15. Just after the Israelites passed through the Red Sea (which typifies our redemption), God gave His first promise to heal. And this promise was for all. It was here that God gave the covenant of healing. God named the conditions, and the conditions were met. Revealed by and sealed by God in His first covenant redemptive Name, Jehovah Rapha, He said, "*. . . I am the Lord that healeth thee*" (Exod. 15:26).

I'm glad that God is the same yesterday, today, and forever (Heb. 13:8). If He wasn't, then we would have to say, "He *was* the Lord that healeth thee." But He *is* the Lord that healeth thee. This is a never-changing fact, because God's Word is forever settled in Heaven (Ps. 119:89).

To say that this privilege of health is not for God's people today is to change God's "I Am" to "I was." But God is the same God now that He was then (Mal. 3:6). I don't believe that He is the great God that *was* or the great God that's *going to be*. He is the great *I AM* — present tense!

Confession:

God is the same yesterday, today, and forever. Since He was Jehovah Rapha, "the Lord that healeth thee," in the Old Testament, He is Jehovah Rapha, "the Lord that healeth thee," today!

October 20

For I came down from heaven, not to do mine own will, but the will of him that sent me.

— JOHN 6:38

Jesus: The Will of God in Action

Remember, the Lord Jesus Christ came on the scene to unveil the Father to us. Everything that Jesus did was the will of God. Well, what did He do? Among other things, He went about doing good and healing all that were oppressed of the devil (Acts 10:38). Not one single time did someone come to Jesus for healing and Jesus say to them, "It's not your Father's will to heal you."

In John chapter 14, Philip said to Jesus, "Show us the Father." And Jesus said, "Philip, have I been so long with you and have you not known Me? He that has seen Me has seen the Father." If you want to see God at work, look at Jesus. If you want to hear God talking, listen to Jesus. He is the express will and purpose of God. And in His earthly ministry, Jesus went about doing good and healing all that were oppressed of the devil.

Hebrews 13:8 says, *"Jesus Christ the same yesterday, and to day, and for ever."* He was the Healer yesterday. Has He abandoned His office of the Healer today? No! Thank God, He hasn't, because He is the same yesterday, today, and forever!

Confession:

Jesus is the same yesterday, today, and forever. Jesus is the Healer today. I believe that in my heart. Because I believe that in my heart, I accept Him as my Healer. I acknowledge Him as my Healer.

But thou, O Lord, art a God full of compassion, and gracious, longsuffering, and plenteous in mercy and truth.

— PSALM 86:15

God's Mercy

In F. F. Bosworth's book *Christ the Healer*, he brings out the following point:

"The psalmist David understood healing to be a universal privilege. In Psalm 86:5, he said, *'For thou, Lord, art good, and ready to forgive; and plenteous in mercy unto all them that call upon thee.'*"

In his book, Bosworth has a chapter called "The Lord's Compassion" that goes into detail about this and brings out this point: "Throughout the Scriptures, when the sick came for healing, they asked for mercy. You see, God's mercy covers man physically as well as spiritually."

Again and again, we read in the four Gospels that Jesus had compassion on the sick (*see* Matthew 9:36; 14:14; Mark 6:34; and Luke 7:13). The same Greek word for "compassion" is also translated "mercy."

Blind Bartimaeus, who sat by the wayside begging and crying, said, "Jesus of Nazareth, have mercy on me." And Jesus stopped and asked him what he wanted. He said, "That I might receive my sight." Jesus had mercy on him and healed him. (*See* Mark chapter 10.)

When you read through the four Gospels, every time it says, "Jesus had compassion," it means He had mercy. Therefore, Jesus, according to the Old Testament promise, showed that He was plenteous in mercy by healing not some, but all who came to Him!

Confession:

God is good, ready to forgive, and plenteous in mercy. He is compassionate and gracious to me, healing all my sicknesses and diseases.

October 22

The Lord is merciful and gracious, slow to anger, and plenteous in mercy.

— PSALM 103:8

The Mercy of Healing

In Psalm 103, we see again that David believed that the mercy of healing was as universal a privilege as the mercy of forgiveness. He calls upon his soul to bless God. He said, *"Bless the Lord, O my soul: and all that is within me, bless his holy name. Bless the Lord, O my soul, and forget not all his benefits: Who FORGIVETH all thine iniquities; who HEALETH all thy diseases"* (Ps. 103:1-3). The phrase "who healeth all" is just as permanent as the phrase "who forgiveth all."

When we talk about healing, some people will say, "But healing was just for those people back then." But those same people believe that God still forgives all that come to Him today! Most people understand that truth.

Well, if people believe that God still forgives all iniquities, they ought to believe that He still heals all diseases. And if they don't believe that He heals all diseases, I can't say that they have any right to believe that He forgives all iniquities. I want you to notice this: God puts forgiving sins and healing sickness on the same level.

Confession:

God still forgives sins today. Therefore, God still heals sick bodies today. Thank You, God, for Your mercy and compassion to heal all my diseases.

He that dwelleth in the secret place of the most High shall abide under the shadow of the Almighty. . . . With long life will I satisfy him, and shew him my salvation.

— PSALM 91:1,16

God Satisfies Us With Long Life

In Psalm 91, God said that the man who dwells in the secret place of the Most High would be satisfied with long life. God did not say that he would be full of sickness, disease, pain, and misery all the days of his life.

Is the privilege of dwelling in the secret place only for a few, or is it for all? God's promise is for all — to satisfy all with long life! You need to get this settled in your heart. You need to find out what the Bible says and then refuse to be moved from it. I settled this issue of healing years ago, and it has worked for me ever since.

Sometimes good people who know some spiritual things in some areas don't know some things in other areas. They just sit around like a young bird with its eyes shut and its mouth wide open, swallowing everything that comes along. Don't believe everything you hear preached, no matter who is preaching or teaching it. Examine it for yourself in the light of the Word.

Confession:

I dwell in the secret place of the Most High. I abide under the shadow of the Almighty, and God satisfies me with long life. I am satisfied with a life free of sickness and disease.

Beloved, I wish above all things that thou mayest prosper and be in health, even as thy soul prospereth.

— 3 JOHN 2

'Well Days' on the Earth

I was reading after an internationally known Full Gospel Bible teacher. He was someone whom I esteemed highly. Now I didn't agree with everything he said. But, you know, you can disagree on some things without being disagreeable. In many different areas, he blessed me. For example, he was an excellent Bible teacher in the area of the Holy Spirit.

In a particular article he wrote, he said, "'With long life' is not a New Testament blessing. God only promised long life to those in the Old Testament."

I thought to myself, *I'd rather follow Paul than follow him.* I mean, if long life isn't a blessing that you get under the New Testament, why did Paul say, *"Honour thy father and mother; (which is the first commandment with promise;) That it may be well with thee, and thou mayest live long on the earth"* (Eph. 6:2,3)? Paul was writing to the Church at Ephesus, a New Testament church.

God wants you to be well and to live long on the earth. If you're always sick and in doctors' offices and hospitals, are those "well days" on the earth? No! Why would the Spirit of God instruct Paul to tell people to get something they couldn't get? He didn't. Long life is promised to all!

If you haven't believed that long life belongs to you, repent. Turn around and get back in the truth so that you can stand in the Presence of God and walk on in the light.

Confession:

God wants me to be well and live long on the earth. I change my thinking to line up with the Word of God. I believe that long life is promised to me!

Honour thy father and mother; (which is the first commandment with promise;)
That it may be well with thee, and thou mayest live long on the earth.

— EPHESIANS 6:2,3

Honor Your Father and Mother

After I was healed as a teenage boy, the thought never entered my mind that I might die prematurely. Now since then, I almost died a time or two because I got into disobedience. But I got back into that secret place of the Most High just as fast as I could.

I taught my children that if they honored their father and mother, they would experience well days on earth and live a long time. When they were little, I read the Bible to them. And if I had to (I didn't have to do it very much), I would give them a spanking, because, like any other child, they disobeyed me at times. I would say to them, "I'm not doing this because I want to. I'm doing it for your benefit. I want it to be well with you. I want you to live a long time on the earth. I don't want you to be in the hospital. And I know you want to live a long time on the earth."

Neither one of our children ever had to go to the hospital. (Pat went there to have her babies, but that was it.) Very seldom was either one of our children even sick, in any way. When Ken was twelve years old, my mother-in-law called me and Oretha while we were on the road holding a meeting. He had the mumps. Ken said, "Daddy, I told Grandma to call and have you pray. There's no use in me missing school. God will heal me." So I prayed. And within forty-five minutes, the mumps disappeared, and he went back to school the next day. He never did miss a day of school. God's Word works!

Confession:

I want to live long on the earth. I want to enjoy my time down here without sickness and disease. Therefore, I obey the Word of God. I stay in obedience and enjoy the blessings of God, such as health and healing.

And the Word [Jesus] *was made flesh, and dwelt among us . . .*

— JOHN 1:14

Jesus Gave Up His Divine Privileges

When talking about the ministry of Jesus, most people, including those in the Church, will say, "He was the Son of God." Well, of course, He was. That's true. He was and is the Son of God.

But they also infer something that is not true — something that has robbed us of blessings that God intended we should have. You see, they infer that Jesus healed the sick in His earthly ministry by some kind of power inherent in Him. In other words, they believe that He healed people just because He was the Son of God. They infer that this power isn't available today, because it was inherent in Him. Now that is not true. It's false!

Yet the devil has used that false statement to rob the Church of God's blessings. Philippians 2:7 says, *"But* [Jesus] *made himself of no reputation, and took upon him the form of a servant, and was made in the likeness of men."* Paul was talking about Jesus coming into the world. *The Modern Language New Testament* says, "But emptied Himself as He took on the form of a slave and became like human beings."

What did He empty Himself of when He came into this world? *The Amplified Bible* says, "But stripped Himself [of all privileges and rightful dignity], so as to assume the guise of a servant (slave), in that He became like men and was born a human being."

Though He was the Son of God, He emptied Himself and laid aside His mighty power and glory and became just like a man. When it came to the power to heal or work miracles, he was just like other men. He didn't have any more power to heal than any other man did. He was born a human being. Then how did He heal people? Through the anointing. Jesus had to be anointed to heal.

Confession:

Jesus emptied Himself of all divine privileges in order to become a man. And He went about doing good, healing all those who were sick. The healing anointing that flowed through Jesus to minister healing to people is still available today.

How God anointed Jesus of Nazareth with the Holy
Ghost and with power: who went about doing good,
and healing all that were oppressed of the devil; for
God was with him.

— ACTS 10:38

Jesus Had To Be Anointed To Heal

Because Jesus emptied Himself of His privileges and became a man, He
had to be anointed to heal. I mean, if He already had the power in Him to
heal people, wouldn't God have known that? Why would God have to anoint
Him? Couldn't God have just said to Him, "Go ahead and use what you've
got"? But, you see, Jesus didn't have the power.

Now I am not belittling Jesus or what He did for us. He is the Son of
God. Divine blood runs through His veins. But He laid aside His mighty
power and glory when He came to the earth to be our Savior. He emptied
Himself and became like men. He became like human beings.

Jesus was just as much the Son of God when He was 21 years old as
when He was 30 years old. And at age 21, He didn't heal anyone. He was
just as much the Son of God when He was 25, 26, and 27 years old too. Yet
in none of those years do we read that He healed one single person or
worked one single miracle. Why? Wasn't He concerned about the sick?
Didn't He have just as much compassion then as He did later on when He
healed the sick? Yes, of course!

You see, if Jesus already had healing power — the ability to heal people —
just because He was the Son of God, He wouldn't have needed to be
anointed by God at 30 years of age. He would have been healing people all
along. But because He laid aside His mighty power and glory and took
upon Himself the form of a man, He needed to be anointed. Without the
anointing, God's healing power, He was just as helpless as any other man.

Confession:

*Healing has not been done away with. The power of God is still present
today to heal, deliver, and set people free. I tap into the power of God, the
healing anointing, by faith, and I draw out what I need.*

The Working of Miracles

After John baptized Jesus in the Jordan River, the Holy Ghost descended upon Him in bodily form (Luke 3:22). Full of the Holy Ghost, He was led by the Spirit of God into the wilderness. After the temptation in the wilderness, Jesus returned in the power of the Spirit to Galilee. He came to Nazareth, His hometown, went to the synagogue on the sabbath, and stood up to read. Let's pick up the scriptural account there.

LUKE 4:17-18,20-26

17   And there was delivered unto him the book of the prophet Esaias. And when he had opened the book, he found the place where it was written,

18 The Spirit of the Lord is upon me, because he hath anointed me. . . .

20   And he closed the book, and he gave it again to the minister, and sat down. And the eyes of all them that were in the synagogue were fastened on him.

21   And he began to say unto them, This day is this scripture fulfilled in your ears.

22   And all bare him witness, and wondered at the gracious words which proceeded out of his mouth. And they said, Is not this Joseph's son?

23   And he said unto them, Ye will surely say unto me this proverb, Physician, heal thyself: whatsoever we have heard done in Capernaum, do also here in thy country.

24   And he said, Verily I say unto you, No prophet is accepted in his own country.

25   But I tell you of a truth, MANY WIDOWS WERE IN ISRAEL IN THE DAYS OF ELIAS, when the heaven was shut up three years and six months, when great famine was throughout all the land;

26   BUT UNTO NONE OF THEM WAS ELIAS SENT, SAVE UNTO SAREPTA, a city of Sidon, UNTO A WOMAN THAT WAS A WIDOW.

Jesus was saying here that Elijah couldn't go into just any widow's house and have the working of miracles manifest as it did in this case (*see* 1 Kings 17). Elijah was just a man anointed by the Spirit, and he had to obey the Spirit of God. And the Spirit of God told him to go only to that particular house.

When Elijah got to the widow's house, there was just enough meal and oil left to make one cake. After that, the widow and her son were going to starve to death. But by the working of miracles, for three-and-a-half years, the oil and meal kept coming. That's the working of miracles — one of the manifestations of the Spirit of God (1 Cor. 12:4,10,11).

Confession:

I don't have to wait for a manifestation of the Spirit of God to receive my healing. By faith in God's Word, I can receive healing now!

Don't Wait for Healing – Receive It by Faith *Now!*

If you need healing and there isn't a manifestation of the Spirit, such as gifts of healings (1 Cor. 12:9), what are you going to do? Get the Word of God in you! Feed on the Word. Feed your faith, because you can receive healing by faith anytime.

Continuing in Luke 4, we read, *"And many lepers were in Israel in the time of Eliseus the prophet; and none of them was cleansed, saving Naaman the Syrian"* (v. 27). Now all of the lepers in Israel could have been cleansed if they had believed in their covenant of healing (Exod. 34:10). Yet under the ministry of Elisha, not one single leper was healed in Israel except Naaman.

Naaman wasn't even an Israelite, and he didn't have a covenant of healing with Jehovah Rapha. But because Elisha was well known for getting people healed, Naaman went to him. Naaman was an outsider in Israel, but he got healed.

So what was Jesus talking about in Luke 4:27? He was talking about the manifestations of the Holy Spirit. The Holy Spirit will manifest Himself as He wills, not as man wills (1 Cor. 12:11). And what Jesus was saying was, "I'm ministering just as a prophet would minister. I don't tell the Holy Spirit what to do; the Holy Spirit tells Me what to do." So if the Holy Spirit didn't manifest Himself, what was Jesus going to do?

Well, if He was going to help the people, there was only one way to do it. Mark 6:6 says, *"And he marvelled because of their unbelief. AND HE WENT ROUND ABOUT THE VILLAGES, TEACHING."* Jesus had to do something about the people's unbelief to get them healed, because faith works anytime — and every time — whether there's a special manifestation of the Holy Spirit or not. So Jesus went about their villages teaching, because faith comes by hearing, and hearing by the Word of God (Rom. 10:17).

Confession:

I don't have to wait for a manifestation of the Spirit to be healed. I can be healed by faith right now. Unbelief can hinder my faith, so I get rid of any unbelief by feeding on the Word of God and by hearing teaching from the Word of God concerning healing.

October 30

Jesus saith unto him, Go thy way; thy son liveth. And the man believed the word that Jesus had spoken unto him, and he went his way.

— JOHN 4:50

Have Faith in Jesus' Words

In John chapter 4, we find the account of the nobleman's son.

JOHN 4:46-50

46 So Jesus came again into Cana of Galilee, where he made the water wine. And there was a certain nobleman, whose son was sick at Capernaum.

47 When he heard that Jesus was come out of Judea into Galilee, he went unto him, and besought him that he would come down, and heal his son: for he was at the point of death.

48 Then said Jesus unto him, Except ye see signs and wonders, ye will not believe.

49 The nobleman saith unto him, Sir, come down ere my child die.

50 Jesus saith unto him, Go thy way; thy son liveth. And the man believed the word that Jesus had spoken unto him, and he went his way.

Notice that it was by simple faith in Jesus' words that this nobleman's son was healed. Jesus simply said to him, "Go your way; your son lives" (v. 50). And the nobleman believed the words that Jesus had spoken unto him.

Now this man had no physical evidence that his son was healed. And evidently, he had some distance to travel, because it wasn't until the next day that he arrived home. Some people met him and said, "Your son lives." He asked them when his son began to amend, and they said that the fever left the day before at the seventh hour. So all night long, the nobleman had no physical evidence that his child was any better. He simply believed the words that Jesus had spoken.

Many people think that if they could see something, they would start believing. But that's not the Bible kind of faith. Jesus is endeavoring to move this man away from what he sees and feels to simple faith in His Word. And He was successful in doing it. The nobleman showed his faith by quietly going back home with no evidence — with nothing that he could see or feel to base his faith on except what Jesus said. And it was his faith in what Jesus said that brought the healing of his son to pass.

Confession:

I believe the words of Jesus. If He said it, I believe it. And my faith in what God has said in His Word concerning healing is what brings it to pass in my life.

304

And Jesus went about all the cities and villages,
teaching in their synagogues, and preaching the
gospel of the kingdom, and healing every sickness
and every disease among the people.

October 31

MATTHEW 9:35

Teaching Should Come First

When Jesus encountered unbelief, He went about teaching (*see* Mark 6:5 and 6). Notice that the ministry of Jesus consisted of three aspects in this order: *teaching, preaching,* and *healing.* Many people want to reverse that order. They want healing first, then preaching, and no teaching. But if you want to get the results Jesus had, follow His example.

Let's continue reading.

MATTHEW 9:36-38
36   But when he saw the multitudes, he was moved with compassion [or mercy] on them, because they fainted, and were scattered abroad, as sheep having no shepherd.
37   Then saith he unto his disciples, The harvest truly is plenteous, but the labourers are few;
38   Pray ye therefore the Lord of the harvest, that he will send forth labourers into his harvest.

Now these laborers that are to be sent into the harvest should have the same kind of ministry that Jesus had: teaching, preaching, and healing. Teaching should come first.

Confession:

I follow the ministry of Jesus. And if He emphasized teaching, then I emphasize teaching in my own life. I make sure that I receive good teaching from the Word of God to help build my faith.

And [they in the synagogue] *rose up, and thrust him* [Jesus] *out of the city, and led him unto the brow of the hill whereon their city was built, that they might cast him down headlong.*

— LUKE 4:29

Teaching, Preaching, and Healing

Jesus once said something to me that astounded me. He said, "If I ministered like people thought I did, then when I came to Nazareth, instead of just getting a few healed and getting run out of town [That's exactly what happened. In fact, they would have killed Him if they could have, and thrown Him off a cliff.], I would have gotten all the people together — including the leaders of the city of Nazareth — and said to them, 'Get six totally blind people and line them up here. We'll have the doctors examine them to certify the fact that they're totally blind.'"

Jesus continued, "Then I would have gotten six deaf and mute people and had the doctors examine them to certify the fact that they were totally deaf and mute. I would have found six people with the palsy and creeping paralysis and had the doctors examine them to prove that they had the disease. Then I would have healed them right in front of everyone to prove who I am.

"But," He said to me, "I didn't minister that way, and I don't expect *you* to minister that way. My ministry consisted of teaching, preaching, and healing. And those who didn't accept the teaching and preaching didn't get the healing." We've imagined that they did.

Most people want to go to meetings and be healed, but they don't want to pay any attention to the preaching or teaching of God's Word. God doesn't work that way. God works in line with His Word. God works through faith in His Word, and faith comes by hearing, and hearing by the Word of God (Rom. 10:17).

Confession:

I pay attention to the Word of God. I take heed to the Word that I hear. And I line myself up with the Word. For it is then that I will see results.

And Jesus, immediately knowing in himself that virtue had gone out of him, turned him about in the press, and said, Who touched my clothes?

— MARK 5:30

God's Power Is Tangible

Is God available to men today? Yes, He is available to men today. Is God's power any less available to us today? No, God has not deprived us of His power. His power is available to us today.

John G. Lake said, "It's one of the most difficult things in all the world for people who are not familiar with the ministry of healing to comprehend that the power of God is tangible, actual, and a living quantity. It is just as real as electricity or any other native force. Yes, and a great deal more so. It is the life principle that stands behind all manifestations of life everywhere."

Dr. Lake went on to say, "If we could make the world understand the pregnant vitality of the Spirit of God, or the healing power of God, men would discover that healing is not only a matter of faith and a matter of the grace of God, but a perfectly scientific application of God's power to man's needs.

"The power of God is just as tangible as electricity is. You handle it. You minister it to one another. You receive it from God through faith and prayer, and your person becomes supercharged with it."

Confession:

I receive the healing power of God through faith and prayer. And I can minister that healing power to others.

And God wrought special miracles by the hands of
Paul.

— ACTS 19:11

Anointed With Power

We can learn something from the Lord Jesus Christ's ministry and from
the apostle Paul's ministry. Notice the similarity between Acts 19:11 and Acts
10:38. Acts 19:11 and 12 says, *"And God wrought special miracles by the
hands of Paul: So that from his body were brought unto the sick handkerchiefs or aprons, and the diseases departed from them, and the evil spirits
went out of them."* Acts 10:38 says, *"How God anointed Jesus of Nazareth
with the Holy Ghost and with power: who went about doing good, and healing
all that were oppressed of the devil; for God was with him."*

Many people read these verses without really looking at them and say,
"Yes, but that was Jesus and Paul. Jesus was the Son of God, and Paul was an
apostle." They miss the whole thing. They say, "That couldn't happen today,
because I'm not Jesus, and I'm not an apostle."

But notice that these verses do not tell you something that Jesus did or
Paul did; they tell you something that *God* did. *God* anointed Jesus of
Nazareth. And then Jesus did something with that anointing.

God wrought special miracles by the hands of Paul. How do you suppose
God wrought those special miracles by the hands of Paul? It must have been
the same way — by anointing him with power. When Paul laid hands on
those cloths, they became storage batteries, so to speak, of God's power.
Then, when those cloths were laid on the people's bodies, that power was
transmitted to their bodies, the diseases departed from them, and the evil
spirits went out of them.

God anoints men and women with healing power today. And anyone
may receive of that anointing by faith.

Confession:

*God anointed Jesus. And then Jesus did something with that anointing. God
anointed Paul. And then he did something with that anointing. The anointing,
the healing power of God, is available to all. It is available to me!*

Now he which stablisheth us with you in Christ, and hath anointed us, is God.

— 2 CORINTHIANS 1:21

A Handkerchief Full of the Power of God

I remember a woman who attended one of Smith Wigglesworth's meetings the last time he was in the United States. She knew that he was a man of God. It was quite obvious that he was anointed by the power of God. After the meeting, he returned to England, his native country.

Over a year later, it was discovered that this woman had cancer. By the time the cancer was found, it was too late, from a natural standpoint. Medically speaking, nothing could be done about it. She had become bedfast in her sister's home.

She decided to contact the headquarters of the Assemblies of God in Springfield, Missouri, to find the address of Wigglesworth in England. She wrote him a letter, sent him a handkerchief, and asked him to lay his hands on the handkerchief. When he received the letter, he laid his hands on the handkerchief and sent it back to America.

When the postman delivered the letter with the handkerchief in it, this woman's sister rushed it into her sister's room, laid the handkerchief on the chest at the side of the bed, and read the instructions, which said, "Get all the believers in the household together, those who believe in divine healing and the power of God. After you lay the handkerchief on the woman, everyone together should claim her healing. Then begin to praise God for the healing of the bedridden, cancer-stricken patient."

Confession:

The healing power of God drives out all sickness and disease. As I apply the healing power of God to my body, every sickness and disease must go!

November 5

And they were all amazed at the mighty power of God.

— LUKE 9:43

The Power of God in Manifestation

The sick woman's sister picked up the handkerchief, laid it on the pillow next to her sister's head, and went to get her husband, who was the only other believer in the house.

She called for her husband who was outside working on his car. His hands were greasy, so he had to take a little extra time to get cleaned up. While he was washing his hands, they heard someone jumping and shouting in another part of the house. Well, they knew it couldn't be the sister, because she was bedfast. She couldn't get out of bed. She was totally helpless.

They rushed toward the sound of the noise, and the sister was jumping, leaping, and praising God all over the bedroom! She was yelling, "I'm healed! I'm healed! I'm healed!" And she was healed. Two years later, she was still healed.

Her sister asked her, "What happened?"

She said, "You were hardly out of the room when I felt something coming out of that handkerchief into the side of my head. It felt just like a warm glow. It kept coming out of that handkerchief into my head. Then it went down all over me and out the end of my feet. And every pain and symptom disappeared."

Confession:

I believe the Word of God, which says, "Handkerchiefs and aprons were laid on the sick, and the diseases departed from them."

> *So that from his [Paul's] body were brought unto the sick handkerchiefs or aprons, and the diseases departed from them, and the evil spirits went out of them.*
>
> — ACTS 19:12

Five Handkerchiefs Charged With the Power of God

One year, a Lutheran pastor from Omaha, Nebraska, attended our annual Campmeeting. He and his wife had received the baptism of the Holy Ghost, and several people in his church had become charismatic, so they all came to Campmeeting. The pastor brought five handkerchiefs and laid them on the platform. He had five people in his congregation who were ill. I laid hands on them with the anointing of God's healing power.

When the meeting was over, the Lutheran pastor's wife came down to retrieve the five handkerchiefs. She had them pinned together with each person's name on each handkerchief. She reached down to pick up the handkerchiefs and felt something come out of them. It scared her, and she jumped back. (She later said it felt like electricity.)

Her husband was standing close by and said, "What's the matter?" She had turned white. She said, "I don't know. I don't understand it. I started to pick those handkerchiefs up, and something came out of them. It went up my arm like electricity."

The Lutheran pastor said, "Didn't you hear what Brother Hagin said? That's the healing power of God." He grabbed the handkerchiefs and took them home. He gave one handkerchief to each of the five sick members in his church. And all five of them were healed.

We ought to expect the same thing to happen today that happened in Bible days. God's power is the same today! You see, the Church has relegated the healing anointing to Jesus and to the Early Church. They've said, "Well, Jesus could; He is the Son of God. Paul could; he was an apostle." But what about God? Is He the same God? Yes, He is! He never changes. He is still a healing God.

Confession:

God never changes. The same healing power that was available in Bible days is available today. And that power drives out sickness and disease.

So that from his body were brought unto the sick handkerchiefs or aprons, and the diseases departed from them, and the evil spirits went out of them.

— ACTS 19:12

Two Minds Restored by the Power of God

During Campmeeting 1978, two women brought handkerchiefs and laid them down on the altar. One brought a handkerchief for her uncle who was sixty years old and had been in a mental institution for thirty-eight years. The doctor said he would die in that institution because he wasn't responding to any of the treatments they were giving him.

She took that handkerchief from Campmeeting and gave it to her uncle. She didn't tell him what it was. He wore that handkerchief for ten days. On the tenth day, suddenly — as quick as you could snap your fingers — his mind was perfectly all right!

In fact, when she wrote me the letter, she said, "He's home. They've pronounced him normal and have dismissed him."

Now the other woman brought a handkerchief for her brother who was only twenty-eight years old. He had a similar condition. The doctor said his condition was incurable. So she gave the handkerchief to him, and within three days, his mind was perfectly all right!

The Bible says that God wrought special miracles by the *hands* of Paul (Acts 19:11). Well, your hands are part of your body. Paul laid his hands on those cloths. And the anointing flowed into them and saturated them with God's power. Those cloths became storage batteries, so to speak, of God's power.

When the handkerchiefs were taken to the sick and laid on them, that power was transmitted to their bodies. The diseases departed from them, and the evil spirits went out of them.

Confession:

The power of God is greater than the power of the devil. The power of God is greater than sickness and disease. The power of God drives out any sickness and disease in my body.

For as many as are led by the Spirit of God, they are the sons of God.

— ROMANS 8:14

Be Led by the Spirit of God

At a meeting I was conducting in Oklahoma in September 1950, a woman came up to me and said, "Brother Hagin, I've never been to one of these kinds of meetings before in my life. I've never been to a Full Gospel church. I'm Methodist. But when I read the advertisement in the newspaper about the meeting, the Spirit of God witnessed to me that I should come."

She continued, "I've been wondering why the Lord wanted me to come. But tonight, when you were relating how the Lord appeared to you and so on, the Lord spoke to my heart and said, 'That's why I wanted you to come. I want you to take a handkerchief to your sister.'"

You see, this woman had a sister who had spent several years in a mental institution in Oklahoma. And after four years, the state authorities contacted her relatives and said, "If one of you can keep your sister in your home, the state will pay you for it. She does not respond to institutional care. She cannot be helped. It will make room in the institution for someone who will respond to institutional care."

The youngest sister of the woman who attended my meeting took the mentally handicapped sister into her home. The state put a metal door on her bedroom and iron bars on her bedroom window. The state also put a ten-foot privacy fence around the backyard with barbed wire on top of it. When the weather was nice and sunny, she could go outside and get some exercise.

Confession:

I am led by the Spirit of God. I follow the inward witness on the inside of me. I know what to do and when to do it.

> *So that from his [Paul's] body were brought unto the sick handkerchiefs or aprons, and the diseases departed from them, and the evil spirits went out of them.*
>
> — ACTS 19:12

A Mind Made Whole

The mentally handicapped sister spent four years in the mental institution in Oklahoma and another three years either shut up in her bedroom or outside when the weather was good.

This woman at my meeting shared with me, "Before my sister lost her mind, she and I seemed closer than any of our other sisters. But after she lost her mind, I couldn't even visit her at my youngest sister's house. If she saw me, she would jump on me like a wild animal and start tearing my clothes off. The only time I could ever see her was from the other side of the fence when she was in the backyard."

Then she said, "Brother Hagin, I want you to lay hands on this handkerchief."

I said, "Okay, I'll lay hands on it tomorrow night when I begin ministering to the sick." After I laid hands on the handkerchief, she came and got it, thanked me, and left.

A few weeks later, this Methodist woman stood up in the congregation and asked if she could testify.

She said, "I took that handkerchief to my youngest sister's house. I said to her, 'I want you to pin this handkerchief to our sister's clothes every day and let her wear it.' She wore it for ten days, and, suddenly, her mind was all right! My sister called me and I rushed over there. When I went into the living room, instead of jumping on me like a wild animal, she hugged me and told me how much she loved me. She was just as normal as the rest of us."

Confession:

There is nothing too difficult for God. No matter how long it has been or how impossible it may seem, God can turn the situation around!

And it shall come to pass in that day, that his burden shall be taken away from off thy shoulder, and his yoke from off thy neck, and the yoke shall be destroyed because of the anointing.

— ISAIAH 10:27

The Anointing of God's Spirit

One time while I was preaching in east Texas in one of the Assembly of God churches, the pastor said to me, "Brother Hagin, do you remember my son?"

I said, "Yes, I remember."

He continued, "He's away at college now. He goes to Texas Tech in Lubbock. You know, ever since he was twelve years of age, he has had asthma and related respiratory conditions. I've prayed and fasted. Many people have laid hands on him and prayed for him. Well, he just called us. He's had another terrible attack."

The pastor said, "Here's one of his handkerchiefs. I want you to lay hands on it, and I'll send it to him." So I laid hands on it, and he sent it to him.

Several years later, I was preaching a meeting for that same pastor. His son was out of college and in the business world by this time. He was a great success. The pastor said, "Brother Hagin, he's never had another attack of asthma from the time that handkerchief touched him."

There had to be some connection. From the time this boy was little, he'd had this condition. But it disappeared instantly. There *was* a connection. It's the anointing of God's Spirit!

Confession:

The yoke is destroyed because of the anointing. Any yokes in my life are destroyed because of the anointing of God.

November 11   *. . . Not by might, nor by power, but by my spirit, saith the Lord of hosts.*

— ZECHARIAH 4:6

By the Spirit of God

When I was in Louisville, Kentucky, a woman came up to me at a church service and said, "There is a woman in my prayer group who has cancer of both lungs. She has lapsed into a coma and is in the hospital under an oxygen tent. The doctors say that she'll not live past midnight. Will you come and pray for her?"

I said, "No, I can't go, but do you have a handkerchief?"

She said, "Just a regular lady's handkerchief? I have a clean one right here in my purse."

I said, "All right. I'll lay my hands on it when we are ministering under the anointing, and you take it and lay it on her."

She said, "Will that work?"

I said, "Just as good as if I'd laid hands on her in person."

So I laid hands on the handkerchief. She took the handkerchief and went to the hospital. At 9:30 p.m., she lifted up the oxygen tent and laid the handkerchief on the woman. Two hours later, the woman suddenly revived and said, "I'm healed."

A doctor said, "They get better sometimes before they die." The doctors kept her there for three days and then dismissed her. They said, "We don't understand it. Both lungs have cleared up. We can't find a thing in the world wrong with her. Every test we run comes back negative."

You see, there has to be a connection. And that connection is the anointing of God's Spirit!

Confession:

I am healed, not by my might or by my power. I am healed by God's Spirit. The anointing of God heals me.

But if the Spirit of him that raised up Jesus from the dead dwell in you, he that raised up Christ from the dead shall also quicken your mortal bodies by his Spirit that dwelleth in you.

— ROMANS 8:11

Stay Open to God

Don't try to dictate to God the way in which you'll receive healing. I've had the Lord say to me sometimes in the area of healing, "Now this is the only way you're going to get it this time. And if you don't get it this way, then you just won't get it. You'll do without it." Well, I got lined up with Him in a hurry and got my healing.

We need to stay open to the Spirit of God and let Him guide us and direct us. We need to realize that the healing power of God is just as real today as it ever was. It didn't cease to exist when Jesus died on the Cross. I've heard people say, "Yes, but Jesus was anointed with healing power." But that healing power didn't come from Him; it came from God.

Acts 10:38 says, *"How GOD ANOINTED JESUS OF NAZARETH with the Holy Ghost and with power: who went about doing good, and healing all that were oppressed of the devil; for God was with him."*

Also, the healing power of God didn't cease to exist when Paul died. I've heard people say, "Yes, but Paul was an apostle." Look at Acts 19:11 again. It doesn't tell you what *Paul* did. It tells you what *God* did. *"And GOD wrought special miracles by the hands of Paul."* God is not dead. The healing power of God is just as real today as it ever was.

Confession:

Healing power comes from God. I follow the leading of the Holy Spirit in receiving my healing from God. However God wants to heal me is fine with me. As I follow His direction, my mortal body is quickened with healing power.

November 13

> And it came to pass, as they were burying a man, that, behold, they spied a band of men; and they cast the man into the sepulchre of Elisha: and when the man was let down, and touched the bones of Elisha, he revived, and stood up on his feet.
>
> — 2 KINGS 13:21

Raised From the Dead

Sometime after the prophet Elisha was buried, a certain man died. As some Israelites took him out to bury him, they spotted a Moabite raiding party. The Israelites quickly looked around for a place to put this man. They saw Elisha's sepulchre and threw him in the tomb with Elisha! When the dead man touched Elisha's bones, the man revived. He was raised from the dead!

You see, even though Elisha's flesh had already rotted off his bones, there was enough power left in his bones — enough residue of anointing — to raise that man from the dead.

Some people say, "Well, why didn't that power raise Elisha?" Did you ever notice in the Bible that elderly people were never raised from the dead? It was always children, young people, or middle-aged people. Why? Because they hadn't lived out their life. Elisha had lived out his life, but this particular man wasn't old. He had died prematurely. God didn't promise us that we would live down here forever. He said, "... *the number of thy days I will fulfill*" (Exod. 23:26)

Confession:

God promised that I can live my life out down here on this earth without sickness and disease. I thank God for His healing power and for health and healing on this earth.

I shall not die, but live, and declare the works of the Lord.

November 14

— PSALM 118:17

There Was Nothing the Doctors Could Do

In 1943, God sent my wife and I back to Farmersville, Texas — a little farming town in the blackland of northcentral Texas. One of the women in our church lived fifteen miles away in Greenville, Texas, but her mother lived right behind the church in Farmersville. When the mother learned that my wife and I were going to Greenville to do a little shopping, she said, "Brother Hagin, I don't want to impose on you, but could I ride over there with you and visit my daughter? She only lives two blocks from the highway. Just let me off there and I'll walk to her house."

"Well," I said, "sure, you can go." We took her right to her daughter's house and then went on and did our shopping.

Later in the afternoon, at about six o'clock in the evening, we went by to pick up the mother. The daughter said, "Brother Hagin, there's a woman right down the street here who is bedfast. Could you pray for her? Her husband took her to the clinic here, and the doctors said, 'There's nothing we can do. She's very weak. She'll just grow weaker and weaker and, eventually, die.'

"She has several things wrong with her. One of those things is a blood disease in the last stages. Her husband, who isn't a Christian, wasn't satisfied with what the doctors said. So he put her in an ambulance and took her to a clinic in another city. They kept her there several days, and ran all kinds of tests. Then they said the same thing: 'She's not many days from death right now. She could die before you get her back home.'"

Confession:

God is bigger than a doctor's report. God is bigger than any negative report. No matter what the doctors have told me, I believe that God can turn the situation around.

November 15　　*Then touched he their eyes, saying, According to your faith be it unto you.*

— MATTHEW 9:29

The Ability To Believe

The daughter continued to share, "The second clinic's results didn't satisfy the husband, either. So he put his wife in an ambulance and took her to another clinic in another city, even farther away from home. They said the same thing: 'You might as well take her back home. She has a blood disease in the last stages. She'll not live many more days.' So he brought her back home."

The daughter found out about this woman's situation and went to visit. She discovered that the woman was saved and filled with the Holy Ghost. Her pastor had already anointed her with oil and prayed. I don't know why she hadn't received. The daughter began to tell this woman what was going on in our church. Every weekend, people were getting saved, healed, and filled with the Holy Ghost. Miracles were happening constantly.

Well, it was almost six o'clock and we had a night service to conduct. We had to get back home.

She insisted, "Brother Hagin, ever since I told this woman about you and your church, she's been saying that she believes if you'll come and pray for her, she'll be healed."

Now the ability to believe was there all the time. I don't know why she hadn't believed when her pastor prayed for her. But when this woman had heard what God was doing in our church, she said, "I believe that if Brother Hagin comes and prays for me, I will be healed." I couldn't refuse her.

Confession:

I receive according to MY faith, not someone else's faith. I believe God's Word and act on God's Word in faith.

Again I say unto you, That if two of you shall agree on earth as touching any thing that they shall ask, it shall be done for them of my Father which is in heaven.

— MATTHEW 18:19

Two People in Agreement

The daughter, her mother, my wife, and I walked down the street to the woman's house. We went in, and the daughter introduced us. I couldn't hear what the woman said. I had to get on my knees and put my ear close to her mouth. Even talking in a whisper took so much of her strength. She didn't have enough strength to lift her hand to shake hands with us. She was lying on the bed, wasting away. She was skin and bones, so to speak.

When I put my ear close to her mouth, I heard her say, "Ever since Sister _____ told me about you, I told her that if you'd come and pray for me, I know I'll be healed." Well, was I going to say, "No, you won't"? No, I said, "Yes, you will!" If two people are agreeing on something, they'll get it.

My wife and I knelt by the bed. I laid my hand on the woman's forehead and started praying. Then the Word of the Lord came unto me, saying, "Don't pray. Just get up and say to her, 'You're healed. Get out of bed and walk.'" Well, to make a long story short, I did, she did, and God did!

That happened on Thursday. On Sunday, she was in our church services jumping, shouting, and testifying about being raised up from the deathbed.

Confession:

When two people are in agreement, things happen! When we agree with the Word of God, we see results!

Jesus saith unto him, Rise, take up thy bed, and walk.
— JOHN 5:8

He Can Walk!

A pastor friend of mine asked me to come by his Assembly of God church and preach Sunday through Wednesday night. In that church, there was a man there who was forty-eight years old who had never walked one step in his life. He had been a member of that church most of his life. Now I knew when I laid hands on him on Monday night that the healing power of God went into him. And I told him it did.

As I went on to others in the healing line, some of the men of the church got him up and tried to get him to walk, but he couldn't. When they turned him loose, he fell in a heap on the floor. They finally gave up on him, sat him back in his chair, and left him alone. They carried him home.

The next night they carried him to church. The pastor and I drove to the side of the church to park. We were sitting there talking about a particular verse of Scripture. Now his church building was very old. It had high steps leading to the entrance. The pastor said, "Look! Look!" Well, I looked and saw a man running up the steps into the church. But I quietly turned back to the pastor because I wanted to see what he had to say about this particular verse we were discussing.

He said to me, "That didn't register on you, did it?"

I said, "What do you mean?"

He said, "That was Brother _____." I still didn't know the man's name. It didn't mean a thing in the world to me.

I said, "What do you mean, Brother _____?"

"Oh," he said, "that's the man who has never walked. He has been in this church for nearly forty years, and he has never walked in his life. That was him running up those steps!"

Then I got excited.

Confession:

I know that the healing power of God works. I cooperate with the healing power of God in my own life. And what I couldn't do before, I can now do!

He giveth power to the faint; and to them that have no might he increaseth strength . . . . they shall run, and not be weary; and they shall walk, and not faint.

November 18

— ISAIAH 40:29,31

A Surge of Strength

The pastor had this man who had never walked before testify. He said, "I knew the power went into me. I felt it go all over me, like a warm glow. Yet I still couldn't walk. I wasn't any better. They took me home, and my youngest brother put me to bed." You see, this young man was helpless enough that he couldn't get dressed and undressed by himself.

He continued, "The last thing I said before I went to sleep was, 'The healing power of God was ministered to my body and is working in me to heal me.' When I woke up the next morning, my family got me out of bed, dressed me, and put me in my chair. Then at several different times in the day, I said, 'That power was ministered to my body. That healing power is working in my body to heal me.' At times, when I would say that, I could feel it in my body. It was just like a warmth all over me.

"Suddenly, I felt a surge of strength go through me. I had never stood on my feet in my life. But I had an urge to stand, so I pushed myself up. I was standing for the first time in my life. I stood there for a few moments, and it seemed like I was going to fall, so I sat back down. I sat there praising God, because the healing power of God was ministered to me. Before I knew what I was doing, I stood up on my feet again and began to walk. I've been walking ever since!"

Now this man could have missed it after I ministered to him. He could have said, "I felt that power go through me, but it didn't work." Thousands have done that. They've said, "I felt the power, but I'm no better." But this man didn't say that. He said, "The healing power of God was ministered to me. It is working. It's working in my body to effect a healing and a cure." Thank God, it did. We all saw it.

Confession:

The healing power of God is working in my body to effect a healing and a cure. It is working in my body now!

323

November 19
And he said unto her, Daughter, thy faith hath made thee whole; go in peace, and be whole of thy plague.
— MARK 5:34

Add Faith to the Power

Over the years, I've noticed that many people think that just because they feel the power of God go into them, they are automatically healed. Again and again, I've had people get tripped up by this and say to me, "Brother Hagin, can you help me?"

I always say, "Well, I will if I can."

They respond, "When you prayed for me, I felt the power of God go through me. I felt a warm glow go all over me, and every symptom I had disappeared. For several days, I never felt better in my life. But now, every symptom has come back on me. I'm worse than I ever was. Can you help me?"

I say, "Yes, I sure can. Now you thought that just because you felt the power, you were healed. Is that right?"

"Yes, I sure did," they say.

"Well," I said, "that's fine. But you didn't add any faith to it. You just thought that the power was going to do it by itself. But you're going to have to add faith to that power. Jesus said in Mark 5:34, '. . . Daughter, THY FAITH hath made thee whole. . . .' What did it? Her faith!"

I've had those same people come back to have hands laid on them again. And this time, they received their healing and held on to it. Even years afterwards, they were completely well.

We need to realize this: Sometimes the healing power of God is ministered to a sick person to the degree that the person is manifestly supercharged with the power of God, yet no real or final healing takes place until something happens that releases the faith of the individual.

Confession:

I mix faith with the power of God in order to receive and keep my healing.

*Then enquired he [the father] of them the hour when
he [his son] began to amend. And they said unto him,
Yesterday at the seventh hour the fever left him.
So the father knew that it was at the same hour, in
the which Jesus said unto him, Thy son liveth. . . .*
— JOHN 4:52,53

You Can Begin To Amend

I want you to remember the woman I told you about who came by ambulance to a meeting I held in California. As I said before, she had a special nurse with her. I never saw so much medical equipment at a church service! I mean, she had a machine that was breathing for her, and it made a lot of noise. Without that machine, she would die.

As I was laying hands on people, I went over to this woman. I asked the nurse, "Can she hear and understand what someone says?"

She said, "Yes, she can understand. She can't respond much, but she can understand you."

I bent down close to her ear because the machine was making so much noise. I said to her, "I'm going to lay hands on you. Did you hear what I said in the service?"

She didn't say anything, but she nodded her head.

I said, "When I lay hands on you, the power of God is going to go into you." As I laid hands on her, I could feel that power go into her. I could feel that warmth go out of my hands and into her body.

I asked her if she felt it, and she muttered, "Yes, I feel it."

I said, "That's it then." Now she didn't look any better. She wasn't the least bit improved. The machine had to keep breathing for her, and she was as helpless as she ever was. But I knew I had done what God said to do, and she said that she believed.

The woman was put back in the ambulance and taken home. The next day, she came back and seemed to be a bit more alert and slightly improved. The third day, she was taken off the machine and was sitting up in bed. In a few days, she was up and about!

When did the woman receive her healing and begin to amend? On the third day? No, she began to amend "from that hour" — from the time I laid hands on her and she received God's healing power by faith.

Confession:

From the moment the healing power of God goes into my body, I begin to amend. And each day, no matter what it looks or feels like, I get better and better until I see the full manifestation of my healing.

November 21

Confess your faults one to another, and pray one for another, that ye may be healed. The effectual fervent prayer of a righteous man availeth much.

— JAMES 5:16

Don't Stop Praying!

In the spring of 1953, I was preaching in Dallas, Texas, and two gentlemen came up to me and said, "Brother Hagin, I don't know whether you heard about it or not, but about two years ago, some of our young people were in an automobile accident. A young woman's back was broken in two places and her neck was also broken."

All across town, people prayed for this young woman. One doctor said, "You should just leave her alone and let her die. [He realized that the people's prayers were holding her here.] We don't think she will ever regain consciousness. And even if she does, she won't know anything. Her mind will not function right, and she will be like a vegetable."

But the people just couldn't give up on her. They kept praying. Eventually, she revived and her mind was clear. She spent a year in the hospital and then went to therapy. She finally regained some use of the upper part of her body. And for another year, she had been at home in a hospital bed. She couldn't rise up. Someone had to crank her bed to a sitting position. She couldn't lift her body up on her own. She could use her hands a little, but not much.

Confession:

The effectual, fervent prayer of a righteous man avails much. I continue to pray for my loved ones and for those I know who need healing. God is faithful to answer my prayers!

And the whole multitude sought to touch him [Jesus]:
for there went virtue out of him, and healed them all.

— LUKE 6:19

A Warm Glow

The young woman had recovered some, but she still didn't have use of the lower part of her body. Her brother said to me, "We're going to bring her to the church service one night."

I said, "Before she comes [she hadn't heard any of my messages on faith or healing], I would like to give her a message to read. Can she hold her New Testament?"

"Yes," he said, "she can hold her little New Testament."

I gave him a printed sermon of mine. I said, "I want her to read all these scriptures." You see, I wanted to get the Word into her. Romans 10:17 says, *"So then faith cometh by hearing, and hearing by the word of God."* I wanted her to begin to confess the Word.

They brought her in an ambulance. I knelt at the foot of the stretcher and laid my hands on her feet and ankles. I felt the power of God flowing out of my hands and into her feet and ankles. I knew she didn't have any feeling in the lower part of her body, but I said to her, "Can you feel?"

She said, "I do feel something warm. A warm glow is coming out of your hands and spreading up my legs."

I said, "I'm going to kneel here and keep my hands on your feet and ankles a little while."

Then she said, "It seems like my legs are burning."

I stood up and said to her, "Move your feet." And she began to move them. You could see her feet moving under the sheets.

Then I said, "Pull your knees up." She pulled her left leg up and said, "I can't make my right one move, but I can wiggle my toes and foot."

"Well," I said, "I don't know everything, but I do know this. You'll walk! The power of God was ministered to you."

Confession:

I spend time meditating on healing scriptures. I get the Word of God in me, because faith comes by hearing the Word of God. Then I release my faith and receive healing.

November 23

For unto us was the gospel preached, as well as unto them: but the word preached did not profit them, not being mixed with faith in them that heard it.

— HEBREWS 4:2

Mix Faith With the Power

Some time later, I was preaching in what was then my home church in Garland, Texas. After the service, the pastor and his wife along with my wife and I decided to go to Dallas to eat lunch. We were sitting at a restaurant and a young woman walked into the restaurant with her mother and father. It was this young woman I had prayed for! She was walking just as well as anyone. She came over to the table and talked to us.

She said, "Brother Hagin, do you remember telling me that I would walk?"

I said, "I sure do. I knew that you would if you mixed *your* faith with God's power. I knew that the power of God was ministered to you."

It was the next morning when her faith gave action to the power that had already been ministered to her body. If her faith wasn't there to give action to that power, there wouldn't have been a final manifestation of healing.

I am sure of this: Healing is by degree based on two conditions: (1) the degree of healing power administered; and (2) the degree of faith that gives action to the power administered. Hebrews 4:2 says, *"For unto us was the gospel preached, as well as unto them: but the word preached did not profit them, not being mixed with faith in them that heard it."* You'll not receive any healing from Heaven if you do not believe there is any for you. You'll never get it applied to your body, soul, or spirit so that it will do you any good — until you lay hold of it intelligently and receive it.

Confession:

Faith and power are an unbeatable combination! I mix my faith with the power of God to receive healing for my entire being.

And Caleb stilled the people before Moses, and said, Let us go up at once, and possess it; for we are well able to overcome it.

— NUMBERS 13:30

No Comparison!

In Numbers chapter 13, we read that twelve spies were sent to spy out the land of Canaan. Ten of them brought back an evil report; they came back talking doubt. They said, "We can't take the land. We aren't able to do it."

But two of the spies, Joshua and Caleb, said, "Let us go up at once and possess it. For we are well able to overcome it." That means, "We can do it!"

You know, the crises of life come to all of us. Don't think you are just going to float through life on flowery beds of ease. But my faith has been buoyed up and my confidence strengthened by just simply looking that problem, test, or trial in the face and saying, "Greater is he that is in me than he that is in the world" (1 John 4:4). Then I begin shouting about it. While I'm shouting, I look around and the problems are all gone.

If you measure the disease or sickness — or test or trial — you're going through against God and *His* ability rather than against you and *your* ability, there will be no comparison! There would be no more comparison than there would be between an elephant and an ant!

Confession:

Sickness and disease are no match for God. He is greater than sickness. He is greater than disease. And I am well able to overcome, because greater is He who is in me than he who is in the world!

November 25

It was meet that we should make merry, and be glad: for this thy brother was dead, and is alive again; and was lost, and is found.

— LUKE 15:32

The Prodigal Son

In the 1950s, I read a testimony in *Reader's Digest* which was endorsed by the Secretary of the Navy. He stated, "All of these facts are true, and we endorse this article to show what faith and prayer will do."

One of the youngest officers ever in the United States Navy — an admiral — got cancer. Ninety percent of his liver was gone. He was functioning on ten percent of his liver when the cancer was discovered. They put him in the "terminal ward" at the hospital. Everyone who was placed there was given up to die. The doctors said that he would be dead in ten days.

The young officer shared, "The fear in that death ward was so much in manifestation that it seemed you could cut it with a knife. The very atmosphere was filled with fear. I was too! But as I lay there in the night, I remembered that I knew the Lord as a youngster. I was raised in a Lutheran church, and at the age of thirteen, I had a personal experience with Jesus. But at nineteen, I got away from Him, and had been away from Him all those years.

"I remembered the story of the prodigal son and said, 'Lord, I'm that prodigal son. I'm coming home.' I lay there on that bed in the night with tears — not tears of sadness, but tears of joy. If it wasn't for disturbing the other fellows, I think I would have shouted. The peace of God came into my heart."

Confession:

I ask You, Jesus, to take me in, as You said in Your Word that those who come to You will in no wise be cast out (John 6:37). I come to You with all my heart, and I thank You that my burden of sin is rolled away. Old things have passed away, and all things have become new!

I shall not die, but live, and declare the works of the Lord.

— PSALM 118:17

Live and Declare the Works of the Lord

In this *Reader's Digest* article, it also stated that a person couldn't be an officer in the United States Navy if he'd ever had a deadly disease. So after he was healed, this admiral couldn't go back to being an officer.

He appeared before Congress. I was impressed by the speech that he made. He told them about his healing and then he said, "Since being out of the hospital and reading the Bible daily, I've found that God has promised us at least seventy or eighty years, and I'm not even half that old. I could get a pension and sit down the rest of my life. But I want you gentlemen to know that I'm going to live my life out. I'm going to live for God first and my country second. Serving my country is all I've ever been trained for, and I want to serve my country. But I'm going to serve God first."

By a unanimous vote, they voted to reinstate him to his former position.

I thought this was one of the greatest testimonies of someone who had never heard healing taught, but listened to his spirit as he got back in fellowship with God. We serve a mighty God, and the point I want to emphasize is this: That liver cancer wasn't any bigger to God than a headache!

Confession:

The Greater One that is in me is the Healer. Christ dwells in me through the Person and power of the Holy Spirit. The Healer is in me. And He is working in my body now to bring forth healing and health. I've claimed healing and health. Sickness and disease, you have to go!

> *The spirit of man is the candle of the Lord, searching all the inward parts of the belly.*
>
> — PROVERBS 20:27

Listen to Your Spirit

This young admiral who was dying of liver cancer then said to the Lord, "I know the doctor said that ninety percent of my liver is already eaten up with cancer and that I'm operating on ten percent of it. I know the doctor said that I'll be dead in ten days. I'm not afraid to die now. But I just can't believe that it is Your will for me to die at my age and leave my wife and two children. I can't believe that. I know that You can do anything. I know that if I had a headache, You could heal a headache. I'm sure You have that much power. But it would be just as easy for You to heal cancer of the liver as it would be to heal a headache. I'm going to ask You to heal me, and believe that You'll do it."

Scriptures began to come back to him that he learned as a child in Sunday school. He began to quote them.

The next day, his wife came in and broke down in tears. She thought she was about to lose a husband. He said to her, "Honey, don't cry. I've been away from the Lord, but I've come back to Him. And I want you to know that I'm not going to die."

She said, "Yes, but the doctor said you're going to die."

"I don't care what the doctor said," he replied.

Think about this. He had no teaching about faith and healing. But just by following his spirit, he knew that God would heal him. He was so much improved the third day that the doctors ran some special tests and said, "We don't understand it. Instead of your liver operating at ten percent, it's operating at fifty percent." A few days later, his liver was operating at one hundred percent.

Confession:

Greater is He that is in me than he that is in the world. The Greater One is in me. He is greater than sickness and disease. He is greater than pain. He is greater than distress. He is greater than the enemy. He is greater than any test, trial, or anything I face!

— LUKE 5:17

The Power Has a Purpose

I remember an Assembly of God traveling minister who received a thrilling revelation concerning the power of God.

One Saturday night, he was ministering in a certain church. As the congregation was singing, he was sitting on the platform. Suddenly, a surge of power came into the little church room and went through his body. He could have jumped up and started shouting, but he didn't. He just held steady. They kept on singing, and a surge of power swept over the whole crowd.

"The third time, that power swept over me again," he said, "I could have shouted, jumped, run, or done all three at one time! I literally had to hold on to the pew to keep myself down. It seemed like I was going to float away."

He said to the Lord, "I know You must have some purpose for this other than for me to just shout and have a good time in the Lord. I believe in shouting, but no one else is shouting right now. They're all singing. What is the purpose?"

About that time, the front doors of the church opened, and a woman in a wheelchair was pushed in. He watched as they pushed her down the aisle and set her almost in front of him.

He shared, "The Spirit of God said, 'That's what I want you to use that power for.' And I found myself rising up right in the middle of the song service, pointing to her, and saying, 'Sister, arise and walk in Jesus' Name.' As God is my witness, she got up and walked out of that chair!"

He learned later that she had been in that chair for several years. She'd had two strokes and was paralyzed. Doctors said that she would be that way until her dying day. But there she was walking up and down the aisle!

Confession: ✗

I believe that the power of God is present to heal me. I release my faith in God and receive healing.

November 29

'They Jerked the Power of God Out of Me!'

I've laid hands on people for healing, ministering to them by faith the healing power of God. And I knew it when that healing power went into them. I felt it in my hands as it went into them. But somehow, many weren't even conscious of it. It was like I had laid my hands on a doorknob. There was no response.

I've seen those same people come back with their faith active and say, "Just put your hand on me. I'll receive right now." I'd reach out to touch them, and it seemed like they jerked the power of God out of me!

I remember one woman in particular. I didn't know it was going to happen. I didn't even know what had happened afterward until I started getting up! You see, when I laid hands on her, the power of God came out of me so strong that she fell, and I fell on top of her! I didn't even know I had fallen; I didn't have a consciousness of falling. It was just like someone suddenly knocked us both down. But, you see, she had come in faith. It's completely different when I lay hands on people and they've come in faith. I've had them jerk the power of God out of me so strong that it startled me!

Confession:

I come to God in faith. God responds to faith because faith pleases God. And when my faith is coupled with the power of God, there is a supernatural explosion that meets my every need!

Wherefore also we pray always for you, that our God would count you worthy of this calling, and fulfil all the good pleasure of his goodness, and the work of faith with power.

— 2 THESSALONIANS 1:11

Faith and Power

I remember one gentleman whom I laid hands on fifteen or sixteen times during the course of an extended meeting we held. I thought to myself, *That poor fellow! Dear Lord, I've laid hands on him, and every time, it's like laying hands on a doorknob.* But somehow, he eventually got his faith into action.

I was standing on the platform and laying hands on people as they walked by. Usually, I lay hands on people and pray, but since I had already laid hands on this man many times, I intended to just touch him and send him on his way. I thought, *He is not going to get anything, anyway.*

But when I touched the man's forehead, he jerked the power of God out of me until all I could see in my eyes was what looked like lightning. I felt as if I had gotten hold of an electric wire. (The power of God in the spirit realm is a lot like electricity in the natural realm.) I mean, I saw fire! With my eyes wide open, I saw fire shooting like lightning.

Confession:

Faith gives action to God's power. Faith puts it to work. The power is inactive, inoperative, and inert until faith is exercised.

And the whole multitude sought to touch him [Jesus]: for there went virtue out of him, and healed them all.

— LUKE 6:19

The Tangibility of the Power of God

There is a parallel between electricity in the natural realm and the anointing, or power of God, in the spiritual realm. There are spiritual laws that govern the power of God, just as there are natural laws that govern the operation of electricity. The Lord Jesus Christ and the apostle Paul revealed and applied the laws of the Spirit of God and the power of God.

The power of God is a tangible substance. It is a heavenly materiality. The word "tangible" means *capable of being touched* and *perceptible to the touch*. It has to be tangible, because Jesus knew *immediately* when that power went out of him into the woman with the issue of blood (Mark 5:30). If it weren't tangible, how would He have known? Not only was He aware of the outflow, the woman with the issue of blood was aware of the reception (vv. 29,33).

The healing power of God is a tangible substance. It is a heavenly materiality. It is capable of being stored in a material such as a handkerchief, as demonstrated by the handkerchiefs of Paul and the garments of Jesus. For example, the woman with the issue of blood did not touch Jesus' person; she touched His *garment*. She touched His clothes.

The power of God can be transmitted from handkerchiefs to a person. We see in the Bible that its action on the sick was so powerful that diseases left. The demonized also were delivered. Both the physically sick and the insane were healed by this method.

Confession:

The power of God is just the same today as it was in the ministry of Jesus. And I receive that power and benefit from it the same way people received it under Jesus' ministry — by faith.

They shall take up serpents; and if they drink any deadly thing, it shall not hurt them; they shall lay hands on the sick, and they shall recover.

— MARK 16:18

A Desperate Situation

At a meeting one time, a woman whose husband was a senator said to me, "I want one of those instant treatments." She was talking about receiving an instant manifestation of healing.

I said, "Well, I'm not giving out treatments."

The senator said to his wife, "Honey, the *Lord* is the one who does it, not the minister."

"Yes," she said, "but I've suffered for so long, and I'm tired of suffering. I want one of those instant treatments."

I said, "All I can tell you is that the Bible says, *'. . . They shall lay hands on the sick, and they shall recover'* [Mark 16:18]. I can lay hands on you and expect you to recover." So I laid hands on her and prayed.

About ten days later, I saw the senator and his wife again. He stood up in the meeting and asked the associate pastor if he could testify.

He said, "You know, we're not Full Gospel; we're Baptist. I brought my wife to be prayed for because the doctors had given up on her."

He told everyone what medications his wife had been taking and continued, "She hadn't been able to do anything. We have a housekeeper, but my wife has always liked to cook. Yet she hadn't been able to cook in thirteen years. But I want you to know something. My wife is not only cooking now, she has dismissed the housekeeper and is doing all the housework and cooking! She gets up and cooks my breakfast every morning before I go to work. And she sleeps well at night now. Before, she couldn't sleep without taking all kinds of medications. Now she just sleeps like a baby!

"I wanted to come here and testify. I'm Baptist, but I wanted to thank you Full Gospel people. I guess we wouldn't have come if we hadn't been so desperate. We felt that if there was help in God, we were going to find it. And we did. Thank you."

Confession:

I know that the help I need is found in God. He is my Healer!

337

December 3

> *And he is the propitiation for our sins: and not for*
> *ours only, but also for the sins of the whole world.*
>
> — 1 JOHN 2:2

God Is on Your Side

God is on your side. He is not against you; God is *for* you. Your Heavenly Father loves you. I've heard people say, "But what if I miss it?"

He's still not against you. If He was against you, He wouldn't have made provision for you to get back in right standing when you miss it. He would have just said, "Let him go." But, no, He made provision. First John 1:9 says, *"If we confess our sins, he is faithful and just to forgive us our sins, and to cleanse us from all unrighteousness."* God said in the second chapter of First John, *"My little children, these things write I unto you, that ye sin not. . . ."* (v. 1). You see, God is a holy God and cannot encourage or condone sin. But He went on to say, *". . . if any man sin, we have an advocate with the Father, Jesus Christ the righteous"* (v. 1).

Even if you've missed it, you still have help. An *advocate* means *a lawyer or someone who pleads your case.* First John 2:2 says, *"And he is the propitiation for our sins: and not for ours only, but also for the sins of the whole world."* He's talking about our sins and the sins of the whole world. Jesus is the propitiation or atonement for our sins!

When you miss it, there's a way back. But, you see, if He wasn't on your side, He wouldn't have provided a way back for you. He would have just left you alone, condemned, helpless, and undone. But, no, He provided a way. Aren't you glad He did? Your Father loves you. He's on your side.

Confession:

My Father loves me. He's on my side, and I'm on His side. My Father is for me; He's not against me. He has made provision for me. I receive forgiveness and healing now.

Study to shew thyself approved unto God, a work-man that needeth not to be ashamed, rightly dividing the word of truth.

— 2 TIMOTHY 2:15

December 4

Three Attitudes Toward Divine Healing

There are at least three different attitudes toward healing among Christians that I want to explore.

One attitude is held by the group that teaches that healing is not for us today. They base this on the theory that healing is a miracle, and miracles do not belong to us today; they only belonged to the apostolic age. And when the last apostle died, divine healing ceased.

A second attitude holds that God heals today in answer to special prayer or a special act of faith, but it is according to God's own will in the matter.

A third attitude teaches that healing for the body is the legal right of every child of God and that the child of God receives healing for his physical body on the same grounds that he receives the remission of sin for his spirit.

Confession:

I base my attitude toward divine healing on the Word of God. Matthew 8:17 says, "Himself took my infirmities and bare my sicknesses." And First Peter 2:24 says, "By Jesus' stripes, I was healed!"

December 5   *Jesus Christ the same yesterday, and to day, and for ever.*

— HEBREWS 13:8

The First Attitude

Those with this first attitude believe that healing is not for us today. They believe that healing is a miracle, and that miracles do not belong to us today. I think this first attitude can easily be shown to be erroneous by the simple definition of a miracle. According to the dictionary, a miracle is *an act or happening in the material or physical sphere that apparently departs from the laws of nature or goes beyond what is concerning these laws.* A miracle is an intervention of God into the realm of natural laws or human activity. In other words, it's God coming on the scene. And whenever God comes into immediate contact with man, a miracle is performed.

Every answer to prayer, regardless of how small or how big, is a miracle. Every New Birth is a miracle. In fact, you can ask God for no greater miracle than the New Birth. Think about it. In the New Birth, man becomes a new person. He is not just revamped or worked over. He is *born again* and becomes a new man, a new creature in Christ Jesus (2 Cor. 5:17).

Therefore, an act of healing whereby God comes into immediate contact with man's physical body is no more a miracle than the New Birth in which God comes into contact with the spirit of man. It takes a miracle to change the nature of an individual.

So to say that miracles belong only to the apostolic age would be to say that the New Birth is not for us today and that from the apostolic age until now, God is only a mere specter in the world that He created.

It's easy to see the fallacy of this teaching. If miracles have passed away, then the New Birth has passed away, and no one can be saved in this day. We know this is not true.

Confession:

I know that the New Birth has not passed away, because I am saved. I am a new creature in Christ Jesus. Therefore, miracles have not passed away. I receive my miracle — my answer to prayer — now!

*And he said unto her, Daughter, thy faith hath made
thee whole; go in peace, and be whole of thy plague.*

— MARK 5:34

A Settled Fact

While on the bed of sickness as a sixteen-year-old boy, I struggled with
the subject of miracles. And every time I would have a good scripture about
healing, the devil would come to my mind and say, "Healing is not for us
today." And sometimes he would say, "Now that's not for the Church; that's
just for the Jews." Well, I'd listen to those words and put the light out. What
little light I had on the subject of healing would be gone.

I didn't know how to follow my spirit. I didn't know that I *could* follow my
spirit. I now know that it was my spirit that knew about healing and miracles,
because my spirit received the life and nature of God in it when I got born
again. And my spirit was picking up things from God and trying to pass them
on to my mind. My spirit told me that there was help for me.

I had been bedfast for six months. As I was reading one day from the
Gospel of Mark, I read about the woman with the issue of blood. I heard
these words on the inside of me, in my spirit, "Did you notice that the
woman's faith made her whole?" I said out loud, "No, I didn't notice that."

Then I heard on the inside of me, "Did you ever hear anyone say that
faith has been done away with?" You see, her faith made her whole. After
thinking a little bit, I said, "No, I never heard a preacher say that." Then I
heard that inward voice say, "No, and you never will. For if faith has been
done away with, then there are no Christians and there's no Church.
Ephesians 2:8 says, '*For by grace are ye saved through faith. . . .*'"

Finally, I heard these words, "If faith hasn't been done away with and her
faith made her whole, then *your* faith can make *you* whole." From that
moment on, no one could talk me out of the fact that healing is for us today!

Confession:

*Faith hasn't been done away with. If faith made the woman with the issue of
blood whole, then MY faith can make ME whole!*

341

For by grace are ye saved through faith; and that not of yourselves: it is the gift of God.

— EPHESIANS 2:8

The Second Attitude

Remember, the people who have the second attitude toward healing believe that God heals today, but only according to a special act of faith.

I had people say to me after I was healed and raised from the bed of sickness, "Well, God just gave you a special faith so you could be healed." No, He didn't!

These people believe in healing, but they believe that God only heals in answer to a special act of faith — and only when He wills to. They believe that healing doesn't belong to the child of God and that it's not included in God's redemptive plan.

They will say, "If God gives you faith to be healed, you will, and if He doesn't, you won't. You just have to do the best you can." I've heard them say it. I don't believe them, though. I believe that healing is a part of man's redemption in Christ and that it belongs to every child of God.

No special act of faith is required to obtain healing. Remember, the Lord said to me, "Her faith made *her* whole; your faith will make *you* whole." Well, what kind of faith is required to obtain it? Just the faith you are saved by.

Confession:

I don't have to have a special kind of faith to receive healing. I can use the same faith that I was saved by. I can receive healing according to my redemptive rights in Christ.

December 8

Whom God hath set forth to be a propitiation through faith in his blood, to declare his righteousness for the remission of sins that are past, through the forbearance of God.

— ROMANS 3:25

The Third Attitude

Those who adhere to the third belief or attitude believe that healing for the body is the legal right of every child of God. The child of God receives healing for his physical body on the same grounds that he receives remission of sin for his spirit.

Healing is part of redemption — it's found in God's plan of redemption. And we receive healing just as we receive the remission of sin — by the same act of faith. *We're not saved by some special act of faith!*

Everyone gets saved the same way. God doesn't just single someone out and say, "Well, I'm going to save him. I'm going to drop faith in his heart so that he can be saved." No, Mark 16:15 and 16 says, *"And he* [Jesus] *said unto them, Go ye into all the world, and preach the gospel to every creature. He that believeth and is baptized shall be saved; but he that believeth not shall be damned."*

There should be no question at all as to whether it's God's will to heal. It is in His redemptive plan; therefore, it is His will.

Confession:

In the same way that I receive remission of sin for my spirit, I receive healing and health for my physical body. God's plan of redemption provides for forgiveness and healing.

343

In whom the god of this world hath blinded the minds of them which believe not, lest the light of the glorious gospel of Christ, who is the image of God, should shine unto them.

— 2 CORINTHIANS 4:4

The Source of Pain and Sin

The fact cannot be denied that evil exists in this world. And the existence of evil has caused many earnest people to reject the belief in a God of love. They've not understood that evil was the result of Satan's reign over humanity as the prince and god of this world. They thought that God was ruling over everything. But, no, Second Corinthians 4:4 says that Satan is the god of this world. The Bible does not say that God is the God of this world. Satan is the god of this world. He is also called the prince of the power of the air (Eph. 2:2).

There are philosophers who have been so affected and impacted by the reign of evil that they have concluded that the "central principal" of the universe is evil. But they're wrong. It is not the Creator, but the usurper, Satan, who is the source of evil.

The two divisions of evil are pain and sin. Now pain may have several subdivisions, but the major body of pain known and expressed by humanity is the pain caused by disease. Sin and disease are both the work of Satan. Sin is a disease of the spirit, and sickness is a disease of the physical body.

Settle in your spirit once and for all that Satan is the author of sickness and disease. And when you know where it came from, you are not afraid of it anymore.

Confession:

Satan is the god of this world; he is the author of sickness and disease. Therefore, I resist sickness and disease in Jesus' Name.

Every good gift and every perfect gift is from above, *December 10*
and cometh down from the Father of lights, with
whom is no variableness, neither shadow of turning.
— JAMES 1:17

God's Attitude Toward Sickness

What is God's attitude toward sickness and disease? We know what His attitude is toward sin. We've heard that preached all our lives. But have we ever heard someone talk about what God thinks about sickness? What's His attitude toward sickness and disease? Well, the Word of God is clear on that subject. God looks upon disease as He looks upon sin; it is the work of Satan in the life of His creation, man.

Christ came to reveal the Father God, to make known His attitude, toward man. By carefully following the life of Christ, we can learn God's attitude toward sickness. Christ was the will of God the Father. He said, *"For I came down from heaven, not to do mine own will, but the will of him that sent me"* (John 6:38). Christ's ministry from the beginning to the end was a twofold ministry: He brought peace to the spirits and souls of men, and He brought healing to their bodies.

Healing had a major place in the ministry of Jesus. Some people say that healing was just a side issue with Jesus and the apostles. Well, if it was, Jesus spent a great deal of His time on a side issue. If you read the four Gospels, you'll see that Jesus spent more time teaching and healing the sick than He did anything else.

Confession:

Jesus was the will of God in action on the earth. Jesus went about doing good and healing all that were oppressed by the devil. So I know that it is God's will to heal me.

December 11

How God anointed Jesus of Nazareth with the Holy Ghost and with power: who went about doing good, and healing all that were oppressed of the devil; for God was with him.

— ACTS 10:38

The Twofold Ministry of Jesus

Almost everyone believes that Jesus healed the sick when He was here on earth. Almost everyone believes that the apostles ministered to the sick. But many also believe that when the last apostle died, all of that ceased.

Well, when Jesus was here on earth, His ministry was twofold: (1) to affect the spirits of men and (2) to affect the bodies of men. When He died on the Cross, His death was twofold: (1) bearing our sins and (2) bearing our diseases. It is written, *". . . Himself took our infirmities, and bare our sicknesses"* (Matt. 8:17). The same is true today. The twofold ministry of blessing for our spirit and body has continued from the earthly ministry of Christ unto this present day in which you and I live.

Christ bore man's spiritual death that man might have life. And Christ bore man's diseases that he might have health. God has made provision for man's salvation and his health. And He has revealed it to us in His Word.

Confession:

God has made provision for me to be saved and to be healed. I believe His Word and receive salvation and healing.

I [Jesus] can of mine own self do nothing: as I hear, I judge: and my judgment is just; because I seek not mine own will, but the will of the Father which hath sent me.

— JOHN 5:30

Christ Is the Will of God in Action

Christ is the expression of God's will. People sometimes say, "I don't know what God's will is." Well, Jesus is the will of God. I like to say it this way: *Christ is the will of God in action. If you want to see God at work, look at Jesus. If you want to hear God talk, listen to Jesus.* There's no better way of ascertaining the proper answer to, "Is it God's will to heal me?" than by reading the Gospels. They record the teachings and works of Christ.

You see, when Jesus healed the multitudes that thronged Him day after day, we see the Father revealing His will. We see God at work. When Jesus laid hands on everyone and healed them, He was doing and revealing the will of God for our bodies.

One time I was reading a report by some theologians of the Episcopal Church. They had appointed a commission to study the subject of divine healing and to report back to them. After three years of study and research in both the Bible and history, their report concluded, in effect, "The healing of the sick by Jesus was done as a revelation of God's will for man. No longer should the Church pray for the sick with the faith-destroying qualification, 'If it be Thy will.'"

The message taught throughout the Gospels is one of complete healing for the spirit, soul, and body of men.

Confession:

To discover healing as the will of God for me, I look at Jesus in the Gospels. He revealed the Father's will. He healed those who were sick. Therefore, I know that it is God's will that I be healthy and whole.

For I came down from heaven, not to do mine own will, but the will of him that sent me.

— JOHN 6:38

Jesus Revealed the Will of God

Throughout His ministry, Jesus delivered those who were oppressed by Satan. Acts 10:38 says, *"How God anointed Jesus of Nazareth with the Holy Ghost and with power: who went about doing good, and healing all that were oppressed of the devil; for God was with him."* Who was it that Jesus healed? He healed *all*. Where did their sickness come from? It was the oppression of the devil.

Matthew 8:16 and 17 says, *"When the even was come, they brought unto him many that were possessed with devils: and he cast out the spirits with his word, and healed all that were sick: That it might be fulfilled which was spoken by Esaias the prophet, saying, Himself took our infirmities, and bare our sicknesses."*

Mark 1:32-34 says, *"And at even, when the sun did set, they brought unto him all that were diseased, and them that were possessed with devils. And all the city was gathered together at the door. And he healed many that were sick of divers diseases, and cast out many devils; and suffered not the devils to speak, because they knew him."*

Jesus was the will of God revealed to man. And He revealed that it was God's will to break the power of sickness and disease over man's body and to set him free from pain and suffering. Christ's ministry proclaimed healing and blessing to the physical side of man's nature as well as to the spiritual side.

Confession:

Jesus is the will of God revealed to man. Jesus healed all those who were oppressed by the devil. Therefore, it is God's will that I be healed, whole, and well.

And when Jesus saw her, he called her to him, and said unto her, Woman, thou art loosed from thine infirmity.

— LUKE 13:12

'Thou Art Loosed'

There are several scriptural references in which Christ's attitude toward disease is clearly shown. I think one of the best is in Luke chapter 13. Jesus loosed a woman from a spirit of infirmity on the Sabbath day. She'd had the disease for eighteen years. The rulers of the synagogue criticized Jesus for healing the woman on the Sabbath. He answered, *"And ought not this woman, being a daughter of Abraham, WHOM SATAN HATH BOUND, lo, these eighteen years, be loosed from this bond on the sabbath day?"* (v. 16). Jesus clearly stated that Satan was the cause of the infirmity that had bound her physical body.

Another instance is found in Mark chapter 2. A man with the palsy was brought to Jesus, and Jesus said, *". . . Son, thy sins be forgiven thee"* (v. 5).

When the scribes questioned the statement Jesus made, He answered them with this: *"Whether is it easier to say to the sick of the palsy, Thy sins be forgiven thee; or to say, Arise, and take up thy bed, and walk?"* (v. 9). In other words, Jesus was saying, "Which is easier? To forgive sins, which are the result of spiritual death in man's spirit, or to heal the disease of his physical body, which is the result of the same spiritual death?" In either case, Jesus was dealing with the bondage of man to Satan. Sickness is bondage; it's oppression. Jesus Christ came to set man free.

Confession:

I know that sickness is bondage. It comes from Satan. It doesn't come from God. Healing comes from God.

But not as the offence, so also is the free gift. For if through the offence of one many be dead, much more the grace of God, and the gift by grace, which is by one man, Jesus Christ, hath abounded unto many.

— ROMANS 5:15

You Can Rule and Reign

Romans 5:17 says, *"For if by one man's offence death reigned by one; much more they which receive abundance of grace and of the gift of righteousness shall reign in life by one, Jesus Christ."* Where do we reign? We reign *in life*! Instead of Satan, spiritual death, sickness, disease, and poverty reigning over us, we reign over them!

The Amplified Bible says, "For if because of one man's trespass (lapse, offense) death reigned through that one, much more surely will those who receive [God's] overflowing grace (unmerited favor) and the free gift of righteousness [putting them into right standing with Himself] *reign as kings in life* through the one Man Jesus Christ (the Messiah, the Anointed One)." Notice the phrase, "reign as kings in life." Do you know anyone who is doing that? Well, every child of God should rule and reign.

In Bible times, the king was the ruler of a country. He ruled and reigned. He dominated a country; it was his domain.

So what is Romans 5:17 saying to us? Instead of Satan and spiritual death dominating us, we reign in life by Christ Jesus. We rule as kings. Instead of circumstances dominating us, we dominate circumstances. Instead of disease and sickness dominating us, we get into the Bible and find out what already belongs to us. We rule over disease and sickness.

Confession:

I rule and reign as a king in my domain in this life. I rule over Satan. I rule over circumstances. I rule over disease and sickness.

For if by one man's offence death reigned by one; much more they which receive abundance of grace and of the gift of righteousness shall reign in life by one, Jesus Christ.

— ROMANS 5:17

A Complete Redemption

Let's continue reading in Romans chapter 5. *"Therefore as by the offence of one judgment came upon all men to condemnation; even so by the righteousness of one the free gift came upon all men unto justification of life. For as by one man's disobedience many were made sinners, so by the obedience of one shall many be made righteous. Moreover the law entered, that the offence might abound. But where sin abounded, grace did much more abound: That as sin hath reigned unto death, even so might grace reign through righteousness unto eternal life by Jesus Christ our Lord"* (Rom. 5:18-21).

If man's redemption from spiritual death (and that's what these verses in Romans chapter 5 are talking about) is to be a complete redemption, it must be a redemption from disease as well as from sin. God has clearly shown us in His Word that He has made provision for the healing of man's body.

In Isaiah chapter 53, God lifts the curtain, so to speak, and let's us see Him dealing with sin and sickness.

Verses 4 and 5 say, *"Surely he hath borne our griefs, and carried our sorrows: yet we did esteem him stricken, smitten of God, and afflicted. But he was wounded for our transgressions, he was bruised for our iniquities: the chastisement of our peace was upon him; and with his stripes we are healed."* The words *griefs* and *sorrows* are better translated "sickness" and "disease." God's great plan of redemption not only took care of man's sin; it also took care of man's sickness and disease.

Confession:

Jesus bore my sickness and disease and purchased healing for me in His death, burial, and resurrection so that I could enjoy health and healing. Jesus consummated God's great plan of redemption so that I could be free — spirit, soul, and body.

Yet it pleased the Lord to bruise him; he hath put him to grief: when thou shalt make his soul an offering for sin . . .

— ISAIAH 53:10

Jesus Was Made Sick With Your Sickness

God not only laid our iniquities upon Jesus, but our diseases as well. Settle that in your heart. Jesus was made sick with our diseases. He was made sin for our sins. In the mind of our Father God and in the mind of Jesus, our diseases and sins were borne by the Lord Jesus Christ. And if they were borne by Him, then it's wrong for us to bear them.

I've seen this simple truth get down into the hearts of terminally ill people. The best doctors of medical science said that they would die. But after twenty-five years, they are still alive! So how did this simple truth get down into their hearts? They accepted it as truth. They meditated on it. They spoke it over and over to themselves until it registered on the inside of them.

Through the ministry of Christ upon the earth, God our Father revealed that it was His will to heal man physically. In redemption, God broke the power of disease over man and set him free by laying disease and sickness upon Christ.

Confession: ✗

Because my disease and sickness were laid upon Christ, I am healed and free. I accept as truth that Jesus bore my disease and sickness. And I confess that I am healed and made whole.

He sent his word, and healed them, and delivered them from their destructions.

— PSALM 107:20

The Word Will Change Your Circumstances

A pastor friend of mine once said to the Lord, "Lord, You know I believe in divine healing, but no one in my church is receiving. What's the matter?"

The Lord said to him, "Why don't you preach on it?"

So he started preaching on divine healing, and his whole church got healed. Before, nearly all of them were sick. But they all got healed. That's what happens when the Word of God is preached. The Word of God is what does the work.

We are affected by the words we hear — whether it's truth or untruth. You could listen to someone talk who is worried and oppressed. And when you left his presence, you'd feel oppressed yourself. Some people are so full of doubt and unbelief that the very atmosphere around them is charged with darkness. That kind of atmosphere is created by words.

Thank God for the Word of God! His Word is His will. Psalm 107:20 says, *"He sent his word, and healed them, and delivered them from their destructions."* Let's talk about the Word of God. Let's talk about healing from the standpoint of God's Word.

Confession:

I speak the Word of God. I speak faith-filled, life-filled words that change the circumstances around me. I refuse to speak doubt and unbelief.

December 19

And he said unto them, Go ye into all the world, and preach the gospel to every creature.

He that believeth and is baptized shall be saved; but he that believeth not shall be damned.

And these signs shall follow them that believe; In my name shall they cast out devils; they shall speak with new tongues;

They shall take up serpents; and if they drink any deadly thing, it shall not hurt them; they shall lay hands on the sick, and they shall recover.

— MARK 16:15-18

The Great Commission

In Mark chapter 16, Jesus gave the Great Commission to His disciples. Jesus is about to depart and be with the Father, and His disciples are going to take His place in the earth. They are going to be His representatives and continue His ministry — to do what He would do if He were there. Jesus gave the Great Commission to herald the Good News to a world for whom He died. He revealed that the twofold ministry would continue.

First, the Commission was given to meet the spiritual need of man. Jesus said, *"He that believeth and is baptized shall be saved. . . "* (Mark 16:16).

Second, Mark 16:17 says, *"And these signs shall follow them that believe. . . ."* The Greek word for "believe" in verse 17 is the same word that you'll find in verse 16. Both promises stem from the simple term "believing." The act of believing brings one into the family of God. And then, the rich cluster of miraculous promises that follow also belongs to them who believe — or, as the Greek says, to "the believing ones."

Confession:

I believe and am saved. And signs follow me because I am a believing one. I cast out devils in Jesus' Name. I speak with new tongues. I lay hands on the sick, and they shall recover.

And these signs shall follow them that believe. . . .

— MARK 16:17

December 20

Signs Will Follow You

People everywhere have clung to the first part of the Great Commission: *"And he [Jesus] said unto them, Go ye into all the world, and preach the gospel to every creature. He that believeth and is baptized shall be saved; but he that believeth not shall be damned"* (Mark 16:15,16). Why have people clung to the first part?

They knew how to use that part to believe and be saved — to receive salvation, and the remission of sin. But many people have turned away from the rest of the Great Commission because they didn't know how to use it.

Verse 17 says, *"And these signs shall follow them that believe; In my name shall they cast out devils; they shall speak with new tongues."*

One man said to me, "Now that can't be so. I'm just as saved as you are, and none of those signs follow me."

I said, "It didn't say that the signs would follow them that *don't believe*. It said that the signs would follow them that *believe*. You just finished saying that you don't believe."

He said, "I don't."

I said, "Then why would you expect any signs to follow you? You have to believe what God said first and *then* the signs will follow you."

Provision for man's healing is also found in this Great Commission. Let's continue reading. Verse 18 says, *"They shall take up serpents; and if they drink any deadly thing, it shall not hurt them; THEY SHALL LAY HANDS ON THE SICK, AND THEY SHALL RECOVER."* This is another sign that follows those who believe.

Confession:

I am a believer, not a doubter. Signs, such as speaking with tongues and laying hands on the sick and seeing them recover, follow me.

355

And they departed, and went through the towns, preaching the gospel, and healing every where.

— LUKE 9:6

Healing Is the Dinner Bell

As a young pastor, just before my twenty-fourth birthday, I remember hearing Rev. Raymond T. Richey (a man who was used mightily by God in the area of healing) say, "Divine healing is the dinner bell." I knew exactly what he meant when he said that. At that time people living out in the country had a big bell on their back porch, and when dinner was ready, someone would ring the bell to let everyone in the fields know it was time to eat.

When I heard Rev. Richey say that, I wasn't having healing services at my church on a regular basis. But I said to myself, "I'm going back home, and I'm going to start ringing the dinner bell." We had Wednesday night, Saturday night, Sunday morning, and Sunday night services. I told the congregation, "Every Saturday night is divine healing night. I'm not going to preach on anything but divine healing." So I started ringing the dinner bell.

Initially, the crowd on Saturday night became smaller, and, as far as I could ascertain, no one was getting healed. I would anoint them with oil and lay hands on them. I would have a healing line every Saturday night. Still, no one was getting healed. But I kept on ringing the dinner bell! Finally, after six months, things started happening. People started getting healed.

I didn't understand it then, but I know now that when I first began teaching on healing, I was planting seed. I had to keep watering that seed, and that takes time. I could have become discouraged and stopped holding healing services. Or I could have resigned the church and left. But when the harvest came, I wouldn't have been there to enjoy it.

Confession:

I plant the seed of God's Word in my heart. And I continue to water that seed. Eventually, I will see a harvest of health and healing.

Don't Give Up!

I remember hearing about the man who brought in the first oil well to east Texas. (At one time, east Texas had the biggest oil field in the world.) He had made a million dollars and then lost it.

This man decided to drill another well. But the people who were financing it tried to get him to shut it down, because he had used up all the money. His fortune was gone. He had borrowed everything he could from the bankers. He owed everyone! But he said, "I'm not going to quit."

He kept telling his men to keep drilling. They were just about to quit because he hadn't paid them when they hit a gusher! They tapped right into the edge of a great lake of oil. This time, instead of losing all of his money, he was wise and ended up saving his millions.

What if that man had quit? What if he had listened to what everyone was telling him? His financial advisors — men in the oil business — had been trying to get him to quit. They told him, "There's no oil there." But he just kept saying to his men, "Keep drilling. It's there. I know it's there." And he eventually tapped into it because he was persistent.

Confession:

I refuse to give up; I refuse to quit. I know that health and healing belong to me. I continue to meditate on and speak the promises of God. And I will see the manifestation in my body.

... *In my name shall they cast out devils; they shall speak with new tongues.*

— MARK 16:17

God Confirms the Word

We need to know what our rights are. We need to know what belongs to us. Healing is our Gospel right. It is our redemptive right. It is our family right, because we're in the family of God. Our right to healing, which was given to us in God's plan of redemption, has been invested in the authority of Jesus' Name. Jesus said, ". . . *IN MY NAME shall they cast out devils; they shall speak with new tongues*" (Mark 16:17).

God watches over His Word to perform it (Jer. 1:12). Mark 16:20 says, "*And they went forth, and preached every where, the Lord working with them, and CONFIRMING THE WORD with signs following. Amen.*"

As we go forth to preach and teach, is the Lord with us? Someone might say, "Yes, He's working with us to save people." Well, thank God He is. But that's not what the Bible says. It says that God works with us *confirming the Word with signs following*. What are the signs that follow? They are the signs Jesus was talking about in Mark chapter 16. They include casting out devils in His Name, speaking with new tongues, and taking up serpents (if you are accidentally bitten by a snake, it won't hurt you). There is also another meaning of "taking up serpents." We see an example of this in Luke chapter 10 where we can read that Jesus appointed seventy disciples (*see* verses 1 through 20). Devils and demons were subject to them through the Name of Jesus. And devils and demons are subject to us in that Name.

Confession:

The signs Jesus talked about in Mark 16 follow me! I can speak with new tongues. I can exercise authority over devils and demons. And I can lay hands on the sick, and they'll recover.

*My son, attend to my words; incline thine ear unto
my sayings.
Let them not depart from thine eyes; keep them in
the midst of thine heart.
For they are life unto those that find them, and
health to all their flesh.*

— PROVERBS 4:20-22

Don't Neglect the Word

When God said, "Attend to My words," He meant to put everything else
out and put His Word in. Put His Word first, above everything else!

We need to ask ourselves the question, "What does God's Word say?"
Many times we pray without asking ourselves, "What does God's Word say
on the subject?" I think we endeavor to receive just through prayer what
God's Word offers. But sometimes it doesn't come through prayer. In other
words, if we are going to neglect the Word, prayer won't work.

So find out what God's Word has to say about your situation, and it will
change your prayer life! It's amazing how many prayers you'll have to throw
away when you find out what God's Word says about your situation.

People will turn in the most outlandish prayer requests you have ever
heard in your life! That's the reason when people come to me and say,
"Brother Hagin, I want you to pray for me," I always say, "What for?" Why
do I say that? Because I've found out that many times the Bible already
answers their need without their even praying about it.

They already have their answer. They just need to accept what the Bible
says about it.

Confession:

*I attend to God's Word. I put it first place in my life. I find out what God's
Word says about my situation and I believe that. I accept what the Bible says
about my situation as truth!*

... *I* [God] *will take sickness away from the midst of thee.*

— EXODUS 23:25

Incline Your Ear

In Proverbs 4:20, we find that in addition to attending to God's words, we are supposed to incline our ear unto His sayings. It's strange, but we often incline our ears to what everyone else is saying, rather than to what God is saying.

One time I was laying hands on the sick in a healing line. I came to a woman and asked, "What did you come for?"

She said, "I *guess* I came for healing."

"What's wrong with you?" I asked.

"The doctor said I have an incurable disease," she answered.

"Well," I said, "isn't it wonderful that you and I have inside information! We have information inside the Bible. Himself took your infirmities and bare your sickness. The Lord will heal you."

She said, "Yes, but the doctor said it was incurable. I don't think I'll get anything."

You see, she was not inclining her ear to what God said. She was inclining her ear to what the doctor said. She needed to listen to *God's* sayings, and *He* said, *". . . I will take sickness away from the midst of thee."* (Exod. 23:25).

Confession:

I incline my ear to God's sayings. I listen to what He said. And He said that He would take sickness away from me.

My son, attend to my words; incline thine ear unto my sayings.
Let them not depart from thine eyes; keep them in the midst of thine heart.

— PROVERBS 4:20,21

Keep the Word Before Your Eyes

Back in September 1957, I knew an 82-year-old evangelist who had been bedfast for two years with cancer in her stomach. Doctors couldn't understand how she had lived even that long. When they opened her body up and saw several malignant growths, they just sewed her back up. They said nothing more could be done.

I felt led to read her Proverbs 4:20 through 22. I said to her, "When I was on the bed of sickness, I got hold of these verses and saw one place where I had been missing it."

I continued, "Proverbs 4:21 says not to let the Word depart from before your eyes. And this was a turning point for me. You see, I had seen myself dead. And when I got hold of this scripture and put the Word of God before my eyes, I began to see myself alive. I began to see myself doing things I'd never done before."

So I shared with that dear woman, "Every time you look at that stomach that's so huge, see it down flat. See yourself preaching again. God doesn't want you to die like this. You can die if you want to. But let God heal you first and then die. Don't die like this. He won't get any glory out of that."

Confession:

I keep the Word of God before my eyes and my ears. God's Word is true. His Word is life unto my spirit.

See Yourself Well and Whole

I shared with this dear old woman, "The doctors said I was dying. I lived and relived my death over and over in my mind. In my mind's eye, I saw the doctors turn my body over to the undertaker to prepare it for burial. I saw them take the casket and go to the church. I saw them roll the casket down the aisle and set it before the pulpit. I heard the people sing the last song and pray the last prayer. I saw them close the lid and roll the casket down the aisle. I saw the pallbearers put it into the hearse. I saw the funeral procession. I saw all of this many times in my mind. I watched as a graveside prayer was said. I saw everyone leave. I saw them put the casket into the ground. I saw the flowers on the fresh mound of dirt. I saw the flowers wither and die. I saw the hot sun of summer beat down on the grave. I saw myself dead. But I got hold of Proverbs 4:21 and began to see myself *alive*. I asked myself, 'What would I do if I were up?' I said, 'I'd preach. That's what I'd do.' So I began to make sermon notes and get ready to preach."

I said to the woman, "See yourself well. See your huge stomach shrunk down to its normal size. See yourself preaching again. See yourself traveling and holding meetings. It doesn't matter if you are eighty-two years old. God doesn't want you to die like this. God wants to heal you."

Ten months later, I went back to that church, and that woman was perfectly healed! She was traveling and preaching. Instead of looking eighty-two years old, she didn't look a day over fifty-five. She said to the pastor and me, "I'm sure glad you didn't let me die. I just came back from my first meeting since I received my healing. I'm going to preach all summer and the rest of the winter.

"I did what you said, Brother Hagin. I began to see myself well. I looked at my huge stomach and saw it flat." She had kept the Word of God before her eyes.

Confession: ✗

I see myself well. I see every symptom leaving. I see myself living a normal and healthy life.

Keep thy heart with all diligence; for out of it are the issues of life.

December 28

— PROVERBS 4:23

Guard Your Heart

Proverbs 4:21 says, *"Let them not depart from thine eyes; keep them in the midst of thine heart."* You are to keep God's Word in your heart. Then Proverbs 4:23 tells you to keep or guard your heart. How do you do that? By keeping the Word in your heart! How are you going to keep God's Word in your heart? By meditating on God's Word continually. In other words, think deeply about it until it becomes a part of your inner conscience. Don't just memorize scriptures and forget them. You can memorize scriptures and say them by rote, and they won't mean a thing in the world to you. Those verses are just in your mind. But, no, *think* on them until they get down into your heart. Feed on them. It will take a little time to do that. But, eventually, the scriptures will register on your heart.

God's words are life unto you and health, or medicine, to all your flesh. I don't know about you, but I never see myself sick. I always see myself well. If a need arises — whether it's healing or anything else — the first thing that pops into my mind is what the Bible says about it. Many people start to panic if something comes along, saying, "Oh, dear Lord, what are we going to do now? What in the world are we going to do now?" They are not guarding their heart when they do that.

I tell people all the time, "Know your Bible. If you can't find it in the Bible, don't accept it. Don't let it get into your heart. I don't want your faith to be in what I or another preacher says. I want your faith to be in what God's Word says. The Word does not fail."

Confession:

Father, I will attend to Your Word. I will put Your Word first. I will incline my ear unto Your sayings. I will not let those words depart from before my eyes. I will keep them in the midst of my heart. I will walk in health and healing. I will walk in the life of God.

363

... *Whatsoever things are of good report; if there be any virtue, and if there be any praise, think on these things.*

— PHILIPPIANS 4:8

A Testimony Inspires Faith

I remember a woman who was bedfast at the age of thirty-six. She had terminal cancer and was living with her mother so that her mother could take care of her. She was brought up in the Pentecostal church so she knew about divine healing. People all over the country were praying for her. She was on her deathbed, and doctors said she could die just any minute.

She was brought to one of my meetings. She listened to my healing testimony, and I laid hands on her.

The very next day, this woman was perfectly all right! Instead of an ambulance coming to take her body away, her husband came to her mother's and took her back home. She was able to do housework and tend to her two small children.

This is what she did. She said to her mother, "Well, that man who gave his testimony didn't lie. He's a preacher, but God is no respecter of persons. What He did for him, He will do for me. I'm healed now. I won't need any more medicine. Just throw it away."

She never had any more pain, and all of her symptoms left. She had been on pain medicine for so long that she should have had withdrawal symptoms. But she didn't; she was perfectly fine.

I would never advise anyone to throw medicine away, but my testimony inspired her faith. A good testimony inspires faith. The Word of God gives faith, but sometimes a testimony *inspires* a person to use his or her faith.

Confession:

The Word of God gives me faith, and a good testimony will inspire my faith.

But whoso looketh into the perfect law of liberty, and continueth therein, he being not a forgetful hearer, but a doer of the work, this man shall be blessed in his deed.

— JAMES 1:25

Study the Word

Many Christians are *trying* to have faith. They are *trying* to believe. They meet together in services, each one urging the other to do what he's not doing himself. They use scriptural expressions and high-sounding phrases that have no meaning to their inner consciousness.

One problem is that they are *listening* to preachers, but they're not *digesting* what they're saying. They are not doing any original thinking on their own. They are not spending time in the study of God's Word. They are what the Bible calls "hearers of the Word" and not doers. And that's the reason these people go under when the storms of life come.

Jesus said, *"Therefore whosoever heareth these sayings of mine, and doeth them, I will liken him unto a wise man, which built his house upon a rock: And the rain descended, and the floods came, and the winds blew, and beat upon that house; and it fell not: for it was founded upon a rock"* (Matt. 7:24,25). Jesus said that the man who built his house on the sand is the man who heard the Word but didn't do it. But the man who built his house on the rock is the man who heard the Word and did it.

So many people are hearers of the Word and not doers. If you're not a doer of the Word, you don't have any foundation under you. Smith Wigglesworth made a statement: "If you wait until you need faith to get it, you're too late." That's the reason you need to study the Word for yourself and find out what it says.

Confession: X

I am a doer of the Word and not a hearer only. I spend time studying God's Word. And I am blessed in every area of my life.

December 31

That at the name of Jesus every knee should bow, of things in heaven, and things in earth, and things under the earth.

— PHILIPPIANS 2:10

The Name of Jesus Belongs to You

The Name of Jesus belongs to us as believers. We have a right to use the Name of Jesus. The right to use Jesus' Name is a blessing given to the Church, to every child of God.

We have a fourfold right to use the Name. *First*, we're born into the family of God, and the Name belongs to the family. *Second*, we're baptized into the Name. And being baptized into the Name, we're baptized into Christ Himself. *Third*, the Name was conferred upon us by Jesus. He gave us the power of authority. And *fourth*, we're commissioned as ambassadors to go and herald the Name of Jesus among the nations. We're representatives of Christ.

Now I can't find in the Bible where it says we need to have any special faith to use the Name of Jesus, because the Name already belongs to us. You don't need any special faith to get in your car and use it or drive it. You wouldn't think about saying, "Brother Hagin, I want you to pray for me that I'll have enough faith to put the key in the ignition of my car and drive it home." No, you already know that you have the key in your pocket, and you know what to do with it. So you act in faith unconsciously.

You see, it takes knowing what is yours. When you come to know that the Name of Jesus is yours and that you have a right to use that Name, you'll begin to use it as unconsciously as you use the key to start your car and drive it.

Confession:

I am a child of God, and the Name of Jesus belongs to me. I use the Name of Jesus and the authority He has given me in that Name.

God has a *specific* plan for your life.

Are you ready?

RHEMA Bible Training Center

"... Giving all *diligence*, add to your faith *virtue*,
to virtue *knowledge* . . . .
For if these things are yours and *abound*,
you will be neither barren nor *unfruitful*
in the knowledge of our Lord Jesus Christ."

—2 Peter 1:5,8 (*NKJV*)

- Take your place in the Body of Christ for the last great revival.
- Learn to rightly divide God's Word and to hear His voice clearly.
- Discover how to be a willing vessel for God's glory.
- Receive practical hands-on ministry training from experienced ministers.

Qualified instructors are waiting to teach, train,
*and help **you** fulfill your destiny!*

Call today for information or application material.
1-888-28-FAITH (1-888-283-2484)—Offer #5077

www.rbtc.org

RHEMA Bible Training Center admits students of any race, color, or ethnic origin.

RHEMA

Correspondence Bible School

The RHEMA Correspondence Bible School is a home Bible study course that can help you in your everyday life!

This course of study has been designed with you in mind, providing practical teaching on prayer, faith, healing, Spirit-led living, and much more to help you live a victorious Christian life!

Flexible

Enroll any time: choose your topic of study; study at your own pace!

Affordable

Pay as you go—only $25 per lesson!

(Price subject to change without notice.)

Profitable

"Words cannot adequately describe the tremendous impact RCBS has had on my life. I have learned so much, and I am always sharing my newfound knowledge with everyone I can. I feel like a blind person who has just had his eyes opened!"

Louisiana

"RCBS has been a stepping-stone in my growing faith to serve God with the authority that He has given the Church over all the power of the enemy!"

New York